REFLECTIVE PA ....

Have you ever wondered what's going on in your child's mind? This engaging book shows how Reflective Parenting can help you understand your children, manage their behaviour and build your relationship and connection with them. It is filled with practical advice showing how recent developments in mentalization, attachment and neuroscience have transformed our understanding of the parent–child relationship and can bring meaningful change to your own family relationships.

Alistair Cooper and Sheila Redfern show you how to make a positive impact on your relationship with your child, starting from the development of the baby's first relationship with you as parents, to how you can be more reflective in relationships with toddlers, children and young people. Using everyday examples, the authors provide you with practical strategies to develop a more reflective style of parenting and demonstrate how to use this approach in everyday interactions to help your children achieve their full potential in their development – cognitively, emotionally and behaviourally.

Reflective Parenting is an informative and enriching read for parents, written to help parents form a better relationship with their children. It is also an essential resource for clinicians working with children, young people and families to support them in managing the dynamics of the child–parent relationship. This is a book that every parent needs to read.

Alistair Cooper is a clinical psychologist and site consultant within the National Implementation Service, Michael Rutter Centre, implementing and researching evidence-based parenting programmes for children in care.

Sheila Redfern is a consultant clinical psychologist at the Anna Freud Centre, helping develop interventions for children and young people, and before this she worked in NHS Child and Adolescent Mental Health Services (CAMHS) teams.

REFLECTIVE PARENTING

A guide to understanding what's going
on in your child's mind

Alistair Cooper and Sheila Redfern

Routledge
Taylor & Francis Group

LONDON AND NEW YORK

First published 2016
by Routledge
2 Park Square, Milton Park, Abingdon, Oxon OX14 4RN

and by Routledge
711 Third Avenue, New York, NY 10017

Routledge is an imprint of the Taylor & Francis Group, an informa business

© 2016 Alistair Cooper and Sheila Redfern

British Library Cataloguing-in-Publication Data
A catalogue record for this book is available from the British Library

Library of Congress Cataloging-in-Publication Data
Cooper, Alistair.
    Reflective parenting : a guide to understanding what's going on in your child's mind / Alistair Cooper and Sheila Redfern.
        pages cm
    Includes bibliographical references.
    1. Parent and child. 2. Parenting. I. Redfern, Sheila. II. Title.
    HQ755.85.C665 2016
    306.874—dc23
    2015011678

ISBN: 978-1-138-02043-6 (hbk)
ISBN: 978-1-138-02044-3 (pbk)
ISBN: 978-1-315-76410-8 (ebk)

Typeset in Sabon
by Apex CoVantage, LLC

As a new parent, I found this thoughtful and beautifully written book not just immensely interesting but bursting with practical support. *Reflective Parenting* stresses how we can benefit our children's development by focusing on what we love doing best: feeling the enjoyment of relating to and being with our children! This guide is not just the perfect gift for all new parents, but a useful tool for those with older children who want to think about how to make lasting changes in their connection with their children and tackle difficult behaviour without having to resort to shouting and/or punishments.

– **Rosie Nixon, Editor, *HELLO!***

Reflective Parenting is turning out to be a key to mental health. This book really helps us understand what it involves in practice.

– **Sue Gerhardt, author of *Why Love Matters* and *The Selfish Society***

If you want your kids to mentally flourish and be able to have a great life in a world that's gone insane, then this book will tell you everything you need to know. It's the ultimate guide on how to be the parents you wished you had.

– **Ruby Wax**

While this book is aimed at parents, it is just as important for professionals working with parents to read. The authors offer sound advice throughout, and do so in an entertaining and perhaps even gripping style. There is a 'page-turner' quality to the book, which comes from the application of a key principle of reflective parenting: they arouse curiosity in the reader. You read and you want to find out what happens next. The curiosity is hopefully infectious – in the sense that curiosity about what is going on in a child's mind is what reflective parenting is all about.

– **Peter Fonagy, from the Foreword**

This exciting book is a welcome addition to other approaches to parenting, and it takes a new methodology to the task of bringing up children successfully. It proposes that a major aspect of the parenting task is explicitly to connect with what the child is thinking and feeling. The authors argue that this will not only make children feel understood, but crucially, will also help them understand their own feelings and therefore manage them better. The joy of such an approach is that it can easily be combined with other proven approaches to parenting such as sensitive responding to the child's needs, spending positive times together, and calmly setting limits when necessary.

    – Stephen Scott CBE, Professor of Child Health and Behaviour at the Institute of Psychiatry, Psychology and Neuroscience, Kings College London; Director of the National Academy for Parenting Research.

In short, the authors have not given a cookbook for behavioral management for parents to use with their children. Rather, they have provided parents with a guide for developing their own self-awareness as well as their awareness of their children's thoughts, feelings, and motives. They have shown us the central importance of reflection in becoming the sensitive, responsive, and authoritative parents that our children need us to be.

    – Daniel Hughes, author of *Attachment-Focused Family Therapy Workbook* (2011), *Attachment-Focused Parenting* (2009) and many other books and articles. His office is in Annville, PA, USA and he presents and travels internationally regarding his model of treatment and care.

CONTENTS

CONTENTS

 Summary pages at the end of the chapters are available for download at https://www.routledge.com/products/ 9781138020443

FOREWORD

It doesn't happen to me often that I feel worthwhile. Most days I do what I feel I have to do, and if I have done 50 per cent of what I needed to, I feel good. The outcome I aim for is just to have coped. In reading Sheila Redfern and Ali Cooper's book, I briefly stepped into a different world. Here was the application of ideas and research findings from two decades of work suddenly being turned into something worthwhile. For this I am immensely grateful.

The conceptual framework and empirical findings concerning reflective function or mentalizing have been influential in research and have found their way into some aspects of social work practice. What I did not realise could happen is for these findings to have the power to influence the way parents bring up their children. Of course, this was exactly what we had in mind originally when thinking about the transmission of secure attachment patterns across the generations and how this could be mediated by the extent to which parents are able to think about the thoughts, feelings, beliefs, wishes and desires in their child's mind as they responded to the child's actions. But few of us dared to hope that the translation from theory to practice could *actually* be achieved. In the real world, ideas are easy: we can all have them. The tougher task is to make something real out of abstract concepts. The authors are generous in their attribution to those whose research initiated the work they have undertaken; yet truly it is in their application of these ideas to working with parents where the real creativity lies.

This book is one of the best I have read in terms of providing a coherent and eminently practical framework within which the quality of the social environment that the family creates for the child can be genuinely improved. The book is not just practical in the sense of being easy to implement while providing firm direction as to what needs to be implemented; as the time-honoured quip goes, 'there is nothing as practical as a good theory'. In using ideas on reflective function to create a guide to Reflective

Parenting, Sheila and Ali also implicitly develop the theory they work with. They integrate parenting with the notion of emotion regulation; they bring in a number of behavioural and cognitive-behavioural principles in line with the mentalizing model; and most intriguingly, they extend the model to cover systemic theorising. What is extraordinary is that they achieve all this high-level integration while remaining 100 per cent in touch with the people they are working with – children and their parents.

While this book is aimed at parents, it is just as important for professionals working with parents to read. The authors offer sound advice throughout, and do so in an entertaining and perhaps even gripping style. There is a 'page-turner' quality to the book, which comes from the application of a key principle of Reflective Parenting: they arouse curiosity in the reader. You read and you want to find out what happens next. The curiosity is hopefully infectious – in the sense that curiosity about what is going on in a child's mind is what Reflective Parenting is all about. It is this natural wish to find out that is so often lost among the competing priorities of modern living, where it is so much easier to take a shortcut, even if this entails making massive assumptions about another person's thoughts and feelings. Yet, at least as far as our children are concerned, we so rarely bother to find out if we were right or wrong. The curiosity also works in another way: the parent's curiosity about what is on the child's mind should – and in my experience, does – create curiosity in the child's psyche about his or her parents. There is nothing like feeling that someone is interested in you to make you curious about what might be going on in that person's mind. This is perhaps the single most important reason why reflectiveness generates a secure bond and a good child–parent relationship.

Quality of parenting remains an important predictor of most outcomes we value in our children. One particular finding I am fond of sharing concerns the likelihood of persistent aggression and violence across childhood. We know that children are at their most violent at around 2 years of age. They do not have sufficient verbal skills to be persuasive, so physical aggression has an adaptive, if slightly asocial, role. Not all children are like this, of course; temperament plays an important part. But most children, thankfully, desist from this violent behaviour during the ensuing few years. Sadly, 5–10 per cent do not, and these can develop serious conduct problems. It will not surprise anyone to find out that those children who desist are twice as likely to have positive interactions with their parents, to receive consistent parenting and to have parents who appear less hostile and more effective. These findings come from a Canadian study which looked at over 10,000 children (Cote et al., 2006). The reason I am mentioning this is because of the striking power of these observations. The likelihood that these observations were due to chance is less than one in a billion billion!

The parents have an important role to play, and that role has become increasingly important as family size decreased from ancient times, when it was genuinely a village who raised a child, to modern times, when the task falls on just one or two adults. The pressure sometimes can be almost unbearable. Humans did not evolve to be sole carers of their children; our genes dictate that there should be grandparents, aunts and uncles, cousins – an extended family network. The increased mobility linked originally to the industrial revolution has made parenting harder, and the time that reflection requires more precious than ever. What we know about child development suggests that children require quality rather than quantity: that is to say, the occasional experience of the true presence of a parent is more important than his or her constant physical, but unreflective, presence. By 'true presence' I mean being there for the child, having the child's mind in mind, thinking about the child's thoughts, feeling the child's feelings. It is this capacity that engenders the capacity to think and feel in the young human. It is this capacity that is the foundation for our humanity. It is this capacity that this book attempts and succeeds in making just that little bit more accessible to all of us. I wish I had had this book when I was bringing up my children!

by Peter Fonagy FMedSci FBA OBE
Professor and Head, Research Department of Clinical,
Educational and Health Psychology, University College London;
Chief Executive, Anna Freud Centre, London.

ACKNOWLEDGEMENTS

We are both indebted to the friends, colleagues and family who have shown continued interest and curiosity and provided their invaluable insights as both professionals and parents. Thank you Hayley Cook, Emily Cooper, Antonia Godber, Daniel Hughes, Darron Kokutt, Norka Malberg, Katherine Mautner, Anna Motz and Richard Sharp for reading chapters and making helpful comments. We are grateful to Claire Cross for her editorial input and reflective comments on the content and structure of this book. We are indebted to the wonderful researchers, academics and clinicians whose work has inspired and underpins this book: without them this book would not have been possible.

We appreciate the help of the Routledge editorial team, especially Joanne Forshaw and the anonymous readers who commented on the original proposal.

Alistair would like to thank the people who have inspired the inception of this book: Deborah Page, for starting this journey through her wisdom and kindness, and Daniel Hughes, with his commitment to his work, generosity and compassion for others. A special mention to the children and young people with whom Alistair has been incredibly fortunate to work with and learn so much from, especially about resilience and courage in the face of adversity. Finally, a very large mention to Emily, Sam and Izzie, for their understanding and continued interest, without whom I would have been unable to do this.

Sheila would like to thank Peter Fonagy and Judy Dunn for providing the inspiration for this work, and for their original work in so many fields, and for making it make sense. The real inspiration for continuing to develop this research in clinical practice comes from the parents, children and young people who have shown such determination to improve their relationships. The biggest thanks go to my family: Richard, Gabriel, Joseph and William – the people who have taught me the most about what it means to hold another person's mind in mind.

ACKNOWLEDGMENTS

PROLOGUE

The following fictitious families are described throughout the book. Some of their everyday struggles and family scenarios we hope will be familiar to you.

Family One

Jon (38) and Lisa (36) have two children, Charlie (6) and Ella (4). Jon works in local government and gets very stressed by his work. He has a group of friends outside of work that he likes to meet up with regularly to take his mind off work, and to have time out from his family. Lisa also works part time for a travel company. She likes to be organised and get things done on time, but finds the commitment of a job and two young children makes it hard to always be as organised as she would like. Lisa does the majority of the childcare and at times this can cause tension. Jon sometimes takes over the care of the children when Lisa has work commitments, and enjoys this, but finds it also conflicts with the demands of his stressful job. Jon has both his parents who can help with childcare from time to time. Lisa's parents are no longer alive. Charlie is a boisterous 6-year-old and likes to be active and physical as much as possible. He and his younger sister Ella can play well together, but often get into battles, vying for their mum and dad's attention. Charlie likes the fact that he is the eldest child.

Family Two

Karen (41) and Tom (44) have three children, Maddy (12), Sam (10) and Molly (2). Tom works for a finance company and has a critical boss. He would like to change jobs to something he enjoys more, but the family depends on his income to support them, and so he feels stuck. He is a keen cyclist and will sometimes go away for long cycling trips on his own or with a group of friends. Karen supports his interest but wishes she had something similar so that she could have more of a break from the children. Karen also works part time as a receptionist in a health clinic. Her job is poorly paid for the hours she works, but is very busy. Karen's parents are divorced and she had a difficult childhood with her parents arguing much of the time. Her mother is involved with the children and offered childcare when the children were little, but as her mother gets older, Karen is finding she needs to care for both her mother and her three children, which puts a strain on her and the family. Her relationship with her mother is quite tense. Tom's parents are both still alive, but live overseas and so are much less involved with the children.

Family Three

Rachel (32) and Matt (31) have three children, twins Grace and Lilly (7) and 9-month-old baby Jack. When Jack was 3 months old, Rachel and Matt, who were not married, separated and are now living apart. Matt sees the children on alternate weekends, but because Jack is still a baby, he does not have them to stay overnight at his house yet. He finds it hard being separated from the children and enjoys taking them out when it is his weekend to spend time with them. Matt works as a furniture maker and has his own small business, which means he does not always have work. Rachel is unable to work because it is too expensive for childcare for the baby and after-school care for the twins. She has mixed feelings about being a stay-at-home mum. She enjoys the one-to-one time with Jack, but finds the responsibility of three children on her own much of the time very difficult. Rachel has a wide circle of friends on whom she depends. Her parents are both alive and help out whenever she asks, although Rachel finds it hard to ask for help sometimes and would like to show that she can manage on her own. Matt's parents live locally to him and are involved with the children. They would like Matt to try to resolve his relationship with Rachel.

Throughout the book, when referring to a child, we have used the masculine 'him' for consistency. The principles of Reflective Parenting, however, apply to children of both genders and of all ages and developmental stages.

INTRODUCTION

It is early on a Monday morning after a stressful family breakfast. A family is busy preparing for the start of the week. Lisa, the mum, is getting the children ready for school, but Charlie, her 6-year-old son, is being oppositional, saying 'No' to just about everything and running around the front room refusing to put on his uniform. Both parents are running late for work, and consequently tempers are running high. Threats of sanctions seem to be inflaming the situation and bribing with treats offers no resolution. Both parents subsequently try ignoring Charlie's difficult behaviour, then Lisa changes tack and tries to find a way to praise Charlie, but, with little success, after having tried all week during half term to get Charlie to follow her routines, gives up and pretends that she has to get something important from upstairs for work.

Suddenly Jon, the dad, takes a moment to step back and reflect on Charlie's behaviour. He takes Charlie to one side and asks in a kind voice 'What's going on today? Why do things seem so difficult this morning? Are you anxious about going back to school after such a long time off?' Charlie's body instantly relaxes; his head turns to the floor as he confirms with a nod that he is worried. After a brief discussion about his worries about being away from home again and what might help (in this instance taking a toy in his book bag to remind him of home) they trot off to school, leaving Lisa in a curious state wondering what had just happened and how a simple question could have such a powerful effect.

Being a parent offers some of the most joyous and fulfilling experiences of your life – but it can also lead to conflict, confusion and some of the most stressful, even life-changing encounters. Almost every day parents can become overwhelmed with intense emotions that are related to their children, many of these emotions positive and fulfilling, but others more

1

negative. Within these often contradicting and confusing experiences, parents frequently wonder whether what they are doing with their children is the right thing – whether the ways in which they interact with, discipline and motivate their children are really working. For example, Lisa, as she drives to work, wonders just what was making her son so worried about going to school and why and how this had affected his behaviour.

Have you ever wondered what's going on inside your child's mind?

Have you ever wondered what's going on inside your child's mind?

Have you wondered what the inside story behind his behaviour might be? What kind of parent would you like to be and how would you like your child to behave? We are guessing that you picked up this book because you have asked yourself these kinds of questions and are motivated to think about your parenting and what will help your child develop. You may also have turned to this book because you have tried other approaches, but find that you are still trying to get on top of difficult behaviours and situations that leave you feeling less than satisfied with your relationship with your child. In this book, unlike a more traditional parenting book, we do not promise to offer you solutions to specific behaviours or give you a set strategy that we claim will work in a specific situation with any child. What we do promise is to offer you a different way of thinking about you (as a parent) and your child, which will benefit both of you enormously. In our work, we often draw on specific theories we find helpful, such as mentalization-based treatments, the concept of mind-mindedness and attachment theory. If you want to understand a bit more about these theories, we have given you a summary at the end of this chapter.

When we started writing this book, we thought about how we could get the ideas that we use in our professional interventions with children, young people and their parents and carers across to parents reading this book, so that they could use these theories to help them in their everyday parenting. First, though, let's look back at the scenario, which is likely to strike a chord with many parents:

> *Looking back on the situation a day or two later, it became obvious to Lisa that Charlie was anxious, but at the time she had no space in her mind to think about anything other than that her son was being difficult and making her late for work. A build up of stress over half term, with its relentless chores and Charlie's non-compliant behaviour, meant that she found it hard to reflect on what might be going on inside his mind in that moment. She had no clear sense of Charlie's thoughts or feelings in that moment. Instead she was simply absorbed in her own experience, overwhelmed by feeling helpless, irritated and distracted by her own thoughts about work and what she had on that day, and was exasperated with getting nowhere in her attempts to manage his behaviour.*

What just happened in this situation and what helped? Jon's effectiveness was not solely down to the fact that he took charge of the situation, or because Charlie realised his dad had the authority; it had very much to do with *how* Jon approached the situation, and how Charlie experienced him. First, he did not approach the situation as a problem, but simply as a normal, everyday interaction. Second, and importantly, he did not focus on the behaviour itself, but was more interested in why the behaviour was there: he focused on the meaning of Charlie's behaviour and *his* experience. And finally, he did not become overly frustrated and managed to keep his emotions in check throughout the interaction. Here lie the effective ingredients in managing these everyday challenging interactions, and they relate to a style of parenting we refer to as Reflective Parenting. The final two ingredients, which relate to theories we will be drawing on throughout the book, are especially important: how sensitive a parent is to the mind of their child, and how sensitive the parent is to their own mind, both of which we will discuss in detail in the following chapters.

So, how were we drawn to Reflective Parenting, and what makes us so convinced that this is the way forward if you really want to improve your relationship with your child? Both as clinical psychologists working with struggling families and as busy parents ourselves, often peddling hard to keep everything running smoothly, we know something of how hard it is to manage family dynamics plus our own emotional and work lives. After training in clinical psychology, we were both immediately drawn to working with children and young people (Ali with children who were in care and leaving care, and Sheila with children and young people who were referred into Child and Adolescent Mental Health services (CAMHS)). In our separate services, we became increasingly interested in the impact and influence of early attachment relationships – the relationship children have with their parents in the first weeks and months of life – on how children develop socially and cope with emotional challenges later on in their childhood and into adolescence. So it never felt sufficient to look simply at the problematic behaviour that children were referred to us with. Instead, helping parents to improve their relationship with their child, and to think about what is going on inside his mind, often led to the most positive changes in his behaviour and a more harmonious relationship. The theories underpinning this book are also concerned with helping parents promote a feeling of security and build resilience in their children. Resilience and security are essential for children's overall development and how they make their way in the world. Children who have been parented in a reflective way are better able to navigate their way through the joys and difficulties encountered in life and relationships. How you interact with your child will determine, to a great degree, how he will grow up and interact with other people. With this in mind, there are two central questions:

1. What exactly is Reflective Parenting?
2. How can parents become more reflective in their parenting?

The core purpose of this book is to answer these two questions. We will make the ideas behind the psychological research on this area accessible to parents who want to understand what is at the heart of this style of parenting, and how it helps children develop emotionally and reach their potential.

The term 'reflective parent' links closely to an established concept within the field of research on parent–child relationships, known as reflective functioning (see section on theory at the end of the chapter). The construct of reflective functioning was introduced by Peter Fonagy, Miriam Steele, Howard Steele and Mary Target just under 15 years ago (1–3). Through his research, clinical psychologist and psychoanalyst Peter Fonagy found that parents who have high 'reflective functioning', that is who are able to consider what is going on in their child's mind as well as being aware of their own thoughts and feelings, bring clear benefits to their children, including promoting secure attachment, good social skills and the ability to 'read' others, and an ability to manage, or regulate, their own emotions, sometimes in difficult and challenging situations or interactions. So when we use the term 'Reflective Parenting', we mean a style of relating and responding to your child that has characteristics that are associated with parents who have high reflective functioning. We believe it is important that all parents are able to benefit from the research on Reflective Parenting, and it is this belief that motivated us to write this book.

Reflective parents do not focus solely on the external behaviour of their child, but also keep a focus on their child as an individual with his own mind. The expression 'he has a mind of his own' is often used in a slightly derogatory way to describe a wilful and oppositional child. However, reflective parents more often than not would see that their child does indeed have their own mind that is a rich tapestry of interwoven thoughts, ideas and motivations, and they wish to understand the workings of this mind. At the same time, they realise their child's experience can be very different from their own – that is that their interpretation of an event could be quite different from their child's experience of it. Reflective parents can frequently see that their child often does things for reasons that are linked to how he is thinking or feeling – that there is an inside story. Parents can then respond to that inside story of thoughts and feelings, rather than just reacting to the behaviour. Reflective parents are also more likely to be in touch with their own thoughts and feelings when interacting with their child, and to have some understanding of how their own emotions might affect interactions and the actual outcome of situations.

Karen was at the local supermarket with her 12-year-old daughter, Maddy. As she walked round the aisles she asked Maddy to look for certain items, but Maddy's face looked troubled and she stared at her mobile phone, ignoring her mum. Karen snapped at her daughter, 'Can't you take your eyes off that phone for a minute and help me here?' Maddy stormed off to the area near the tills, refusing to help her mum.

Let's have a think about what's going on. Maddy might be failing to help her mum out with the shopping for a variety of reasons that are particular to her at that specific time. Perhaps Maddy is refusing to help her mum because she simply finds supermarket shopping boring. Or maybe she feels it's unfair that she's had to come and do the shopping with her mum whilst her younger brothers get to stay at home. If Karen is able to respond to Maddy in a way that helps her feeling dissipate this is likely to change the way that Maddy acts. For example, if she notices that she has seen a message on her phone, she might stop, ask her about it and reflect that something has happened that has really upset Maddy. In fact, Maddy just received a text from a friend to say a group are all going ice skating but that she hasn't been included. Karen might ask about the message and tell Maddy that she must feel really upset to be left out. This is likely to help Maddy to feel closer to her mum and more willing to help her out with the shopping. However, if Karen is tired and frustrated, she might react to the situation differently and, for example perceive that Maddy is behaving unreasonably. Karen may then respond, unknowingly, in a way that increases the negative feelings Maddy is experiencing, which in turn makes the difficult behaviour increase. For example, Karen might say 'I don't get this kind of problem with your brothers when they come with me. Why can't you be more helpful and stop being so moody?'

Throughout the book, we promote the idea that children's behaviour has meaning and intention – it is rarely random. We will look at how Reflective Parenting helps you to think about your child's inside story and also your own. Recognising this and taking an interested stance towards why your child does what he does is at the heart of Reflective Parenting. Some parents, a lot of the time, seem to guess intuitively why their child is behaving in a particular way. Often, though, parents can find it hard to focus on the *why* – the feelings and thoughts underlying behaviour. And we are all capable of making snap judgements about why our children are behaving in a certain way, which often are based more on what's going on in our own minds than what's going on in our child's.

In reality, all parents fluctuate on a scale in their ability to relate to their child in a reflective way, depending on internal and external influences.

We will show you how to develop skills that will enhance your relationship with your child and increase his confidence and self-esteem, as well as help you to feel more successful in your parenting. Essentially, we will invite you to observe yourself more from the outside, to imagine how you might come across to your child, and we will encourage you to see your child more

Being preoccupied can make it hard to even notice your child.

from the inside, to consider what their experiences, thoughts and feelings (their mental states) might be within certain situations – both extremely important concepts. To help you achieve these aims, we start by helping you, as parents, to think first about your own feelings, as the ability to do this is vital before you can start to think about your child.

Of course, it would be virtually impossible to be able to do this all of the time in your relationships, but the chapters will share a common focus: to develop and enhance your awareness of and ability to practice Reflective Parenting. You may or may not want to read about the theory underpinning this book, which we make reference to from time to time throughout, but either way we hope you will use this book principally as a guide to help you through the difficult parenting experiences that we all face, almost daily. We hope that, within your relationship with your child, there will be fewer mis-understandings and greater harmony, and that behavioural problems will be resolved more easily.

A theoretical background to Reflective Parenting

A number of respected theories inform the idea of Reflective Parenting, and provide the backbone for the straightforward, practical parenting strategies throughout this book. Importantly, these practices aren't exclusive to any one group of parents – families from all cultural and socio-economic backgrounds can benefit from trying out these parenting approaches, helping them to build a better connection with their children along the way. Even if your own childhood wasn't ideal, you can choose to do things differently with your own children. Often, trying out a new parenting approach can provide a real sense of excitement, as you anticipate the opportunity to try something new, to embark on this new adventure; as you do so you can feel reassured that the well-researched, tried-and-tested theories discussed here back you up and are there to lean on when things get really tough.

Attachment theory

Attachment theory was first discussed by John Bowlby (4) and his work has had an incredibly powerful impact on how we understand parent–infant relationships. Bowlby proposed that all infants have an innate motivational and behavioural system that drives them to seek proximity with their primary caregiver – usually the mother. In an evolutionary context, this desire to stay close to the mother would have ensured protection when a child was in danger or threatened by danger. The most important aspect of attachment theory in relation to understanding parent–child relationships is that every infant needs to develop a relationship with one important primary caregiver for their social and emotional development, and more specifically for learning how to regulate, or control, their feelings. In other words, when an infant enjoys a good attachment early in life, this relationship gives them the security to explore their world, and works as a template for future successful relationships. Mary Ainsworth (5), who joined Bowlby at the Tavistock Clinic in London researching the effects of maternal separation on child development and worked extensively in the area of parent–child development, devised a famous experiment where she established four classifications of attachment. She found that most people had experienced 'secure' attachment as a baby, having enjoyed a responsive and close attachment to a parent. The experiment found that when children in this group are separated from their primary caregivers, they experience distress, but are quickly comforted upon reunion. The classification of attachment is made on the basis of the relationship between an infant and his main, primary caregiver. In most cases this is the mother, but obviously not in all, and not across all cultures. The 'secure' infant uses their primary caregiver as a safe base from which to explore the world. Parents who consistently (or at least most of the time) respond sensitively to their infant's needs will have children who are securely attached. These children will learn that when they are distressed, their parents will comfort and soothe them, and so they grow up with the expectation that other people are also available to help and support them. Importantly, these children develop a complementary model of themselves as worthy and deserving of that love and comfort. Secure attachment underpins the development of good 'mentalization' (see following subsection). You can think of attachment theory as the fertile soil that the following theories all grow out of – that are, in essence, all part of the same family. While there are subtle, and important, differences between the following constructs, at the same time they are extremely closely related to one another.

Mentalization

The term mentalization, first used by Peter Fonagy in 1989 (6), describes the ability to reflect on the mental states, that is the thoughts and feelings, of others. The ability to understand another person's mental state is strongly linked to whether an individual was securely attached to their primary caregiver as an infant. One important study (in the theory of attachment) looked at how a pregnant woman's own attachment as an infant could predict whether her own baby would be securely attached and found that the most significant predictive factor was whether the mother was able to mentalize her relationship with her own parents, that is whether she was able to think about and reflect on her parents' behaviour, emotions and states of mind. The parents who could do this were said to be high in reflective functioning (see following subsection).

When we 'mentalize' this means that not only do we recognise that others have emotions, but we also understand and respond to these emotions. The ability to mentalize is thought to be rooted in our early relationships and whether our primary caregivers were able to reflect accurately on our own thoughts and feelings, and, crucially, was able to show by their corresponding actions and words that they understood and could interpret our mental states. When parents are able to reflect on the mental states (internal thoughts and feelings) of their child, the child in turn becomes better able to control their own emotions. This process occurs because when parents 'mirror' back to the child (through the way they speak to, look at and behave with the child) how the child is feeling, the child begins to understand, and eventually to control, their own emotions. Without a parent who can reflect back, infants don't know how to make sense of what they are feeling. The parent becomes a trainer to the infant in learning to understand himself and his feelings.

Reflective functioning (RF)

Reflective functioning, a term also coined by Peter Fonagy and his colleagues, is what this concept actually looks like in action. RF is the capacity to understand or describe both one's own and another person's behaviour in terms of underlying mental states and intentions. As described earlier, a mental state describes how someone is thinking or feeling. So a person's reflective functioning would be evident in how they talk about their own and others' underlying mental states and feelings. For example, a child might say, 'My Mum was really cross when she saw I hadn't done my homework, because she was worried I was going to get in trouble with my teacher, and thought I was being a bit lazy.' Or a parent might say, 'He used to cry all the time as a baby, and it used to make me feel so inadequate when I couldn't comfort him, but I think he was just very frustrated.' When parents show that they are able to think about their child's mind in this way and respond sensitively, they are showing a good level of reflective functioning. (This has also been called *maternal mind-mindedness*, see following subsection.) RF is also linked to secure attachment.

Mind-Minded

Elizabeth Meins (7) researched the importance of the *way* that mothers and carers speak to children, and the use of language generally in the family. She found that this way of talking to and about children was more important than secure attachment itself in predicting a child's eventual ability to understand another person's perspective. The concept of *mind-mindedness* can be seen in action in families when parents (particularly mothers were studied) talk to their children about what they think might be going on in their children's minds. Meins showed that when mothers talked naturally to their children about the children's thoughts and feelings – their mental states – this was a good predictor of the children's later understanding of other people's thoughts, feelings, wishes and desires. Importantly, it was the *accuracy* of this description of what they thought was going on in their children's minds that predicted how able the children were at understanding themselves and others.

Theory of Mind (ToM)

In 1978, two eminent US psychologists, David Premack and Guy Woodruff (8), developed the concept known as Theory of Mind. Having a 'theory of mind' enables a person to recognise that others have thoughts, desires and intentions that may be different from their own, and that these mental states can predict or explain another person's actions. This ToM ability enables us to understand that mental states can be the cause of how other people behave, so it allows us to understand other people, and their motivations, much better. Normally developing children are thought to develop a ToM around the age of 3.5–4 years of age. However, there are signs much earlier on, from very early infancy, that babies can recognise that other people have intentional minds separate from their own. Many of the studies on ToM have focused on autistic children and their failure to develop this skill, which seriously impacts on their relationships with others as it means they are not able to understand how things look from another person's perspective, which is an important part of friendships and relating to others in general. When ToM is studied in children it is found to be related to children's social competence. Studies show that ToM skills in children relate to their level of social competence, empathy and perspective-taking skills, the last two of which are key components in children's social relationships. ToM skills are also related to how securely attached a child is (9).

In addition to these theories and research, we have also drawn on a therapeutic intervention, largely built on the foundations of attachment theory, but with a set of principles all of its own, which we have found useful to the thinking behind the book.

Video Interaction Guidance (VIG)

Originally developed by Harrie Biemans (10) (1990) in the Netherlands and then brought to Scotland by Colwyn Trevarthan and developed by Hilary Kennedy, VIG is an evidence-based method that uses recorded interactions to enhance what is known as the 'attunement' between parent and child. The practice was developed originally from Video Home Training (VHT) in the Netherlands, and from Trevarthan's work on what he termed 'moments of vitality' between parents and their infants. Trevarthan (11) observed a 'communicative dance' happening between a parent and infant; he noticed the way that the parent followed the child, the child the parent, in a sort of rhythmic dance, in which the parent and the child in this partnership both developed 'space in their mind' for the other. By this, he meant that the child and the parent start to view themselves in relation to each other. When a child makes what is called an initiative – which may be something as simple as smiling at the parent or holding a toy up for the parent to see – and the parent 'receives' it – which may involve smiling back or commenting to the child that they have a fun looking toy in their hand – this sets up what is called a 'yes cycle' whereby parent and child connect with each other and which involves sharing positive feelings. This has a very powerful effect on the child and on the relationship with the parent. For example, where the parent notices the child's pleasure in showing them the toy, and expresses an interest in the child showing it to them, the parent shows their child that they are paying attention to the child, and to the child's thoughts and feelings. This increases the feeling of being attuned and has a powerful effect of bringing closer connection between parent and child, and where there might have been tension previously, de-escalates this tension quickly through the attunement. Where the parent misses the child's 'initiative' and the child misses the parent's turn (i.e. where the parent fails to pick up on an invitation from the child to interact) a 'no-cycle' starts, which happens often, and quickly, in families where there is stress. VIG encourages parents to pay attention to interactions and, through watching video clips of positive moments they have shared with their child, teaches them how to interact better. Once parents start to give the child greater attention, they can then build up to more attuned interactions – whereby the parent and child manage to listen well, respond positively and take turns. This can have a profound impact on the relationship as the parents learn to de-escalate difficult interactions. Parents are encouraged to see how a certain set of behaviours can lay the foundations for attunement with their child. This set of behaviours includes when they look interested in their child, for example by turning towards their child; giving their child time and space (e.g. not rushing in to intervene or tell the child what to do); wondering aloud what their child is doing, thinking and feeling; looking for initiatives; naming positively what they see, hear, think and feel about their child and so on. Using the principles of VIG together with mentalization theories can be really helpful in forming an active plan for how you can approach your relationship with your child from the stance of looking at what is going on inside.

Our aim in this book is to draw on all of these theories and bring to you a method of parenting that you can try for yourselves with your children. The test of whether we have done a good job of translating these theories into action will be in any changes that you start to notice and feel in your relationship with your child and in your child's behaviour, and in whether you feel that you are beginning to understand your child's inside story by being more reflective in your parenting.

1

THE ORIGINS OF REFLECTIVE PARENTING

In this chapter we take a closer look at the main ideas behind Reflective Parenting, and how important these are in helping you and your baby or child to enjoy a positive and harmonious relationship. We explain briefly the research behind the ideas we are bringing to you in this book to help you understand the foundation for this approach. Reflective Parenting has many benefits for children. With its roots in secure attachment, Reflective Parenting leads to happier, confident, successful and resilient children, who are also more able to understand the thoughts and feelings of other people (1).

The rest of the book will take you step by step through the techniques you need for becoming a more reflective parent, increasing the skills you require to achieve this, as well as looking at problem areas where it can feel especially hard to see things from your child's point of view. We will give you some tools and strategies, and introduce you to the concept of the 'Parent APP', a guide to the essential qualities needed for truly Reflective Parenting, explained in Chapter Four, which you can refer to when you find yourself stuck for ways to manage your relationship with your child, or where you feel you have tried absolutely everything to manage a difficult behaviour and you need a new approach. First, though, let's look at where the ideas on Reflective Parenting come from, and what it is about this approach that will be so helpful to both your baby or young child's development and your relationship with him.

The research on babies and children shows that we are motivated to understand what the actions of other people mean, and it seems that this motivation is present almost as soon as we are born. From the minute babies are born they have an instinct to relate to their main carer; they are hard-wired, if you like, to interact. More importantly, babies are supersensitive to adults who show them attention and act in ways that match their own emotional states – who seek to engage with them in a way that mirrors how they are feeling and what they are doing. When you respond to your baby in this sensitive way, your baby is very capable of holding his attention so that he can interact with you. He can take part in an ongoing 'conversation' over the course of his early childhood, which, if all goes well, continues as he grows up. In this way, your baby's mind begins to form, be built and moulded as he purposefully interacts with you.

Your baby is totally dependent on you from the minute he is born . . . to feed him, change him, keep him warm, protect him, touch him and make him feel safe. His relationship with you is incredibly important, as it is through this relationship and the way in which you respond to him that you can help him develop the skills he will need to bounce back from adversity throughout his childhood, adolescence and into adulthood. Think of the relationship your child has with you as a training opportunity. With you, he can practice and experience what it's like to be in a relationship, and this training prepares him for interacting with the world of people beyond his family. Teaching him about how other people work, through your everyday interactions with him, will be one of the most important lessons of his life. Within your relationship with your baby and child you can help him to develop emotionally by taking a particular interest in how he thinks, how he feels and why he does things. And by talking about all of these things with him, you will help him learn about himself and how people interact with him. The more you can learn to think about your relationship with your child and to help him understand his emotions as well as how you are feeling, the happier your relationship will be.

Let's start by setting the scene for how babies learn to interact with the world around them, and centrally their parents. For your baby, this 'training programme' for relationships throughout his life, with you, his parents, starts early – in fact, as soon as he is born.

When your baby comes into the world, the way that he looks, acts, interacts, etc. will already have been influenced by his genetic history and temperament. There is a large body of important research around these areas. We want to acknowledge these influences, and briefly explain them, but our focus is going to be much more on your relationship from the moment your baby is born and what you can each bring to this relationship.

There are many factors that influence the unique emotional makeup that babies are born with. Every baby has an innate temperament which then interacts with the experiences the baby has with the important people and events in his world. This might include being cuddled, feeling criticised, receiving attention or being ignored. Think of temperament as tension in a tennis racket. The tighter the tension, the more reactive the racket might be to an approaching tennis ball. In this way, some babies react more to experiences in their environment, whatever they might be.

Maternal hormones influence the baby's development in the womb, and the emotions a woman feels during pregnancy can affect her hormones, so this in turn can have a big impact on the baby's development, particularly on brain development. The most compelling link is between maternal stress and a baby's development in the womb. The hormone cortisol, released during stressful situations, is particularly influential, and studies show that where mothers are very highly stressed, babies tend to be more fussy and irritable when born. It's believed that this is due to the negative impact of an 'overdose' of cortisol during pregnancy, which affects the baby's developing brain. On the flip side, the impact of affection and love when the baby is born has far-reaching positive effects (2) including helping babies to develop what is known in the research as a 'social brain' (3) (4). We now know from neuroscience research that the baby's developing brain is designed to be moulded by the environment it encounters (5). In this way, a brain can begin to understand the thoughts, feelings and intentions of other people. This ability, known as 'mentalizing' (6), is going to be a word we refer to quite a bit throughout the book. Essentially, what it means is the ability to make sense of one's own actions, and also the actions of other people, with reference to beliefs, desires and feelings. When things are going well, your baby needs to experience a relationship with a sensitive parent. We will help you throughout this book to understand why this skill of mentalizing is not only important, but quite simple to start doing in your everyday interactions. And you are probably doing a lot of it already, without even knowing it.

There may also be developmental factors that can make it more difficult to interact in a reflective and sensitive way with some babies. Babies born blind or on the autistic spectrum, for example, will send out a different set of signals to their parents than babies without these developmental issues, and so as a parent you may have a baby who needs a different level of sensitivity, or different cues from you, in order to maximise the closeness and security he feels in his relationship with you.

Reflective Parenting helps to buffer children from the negative effects of some of these early influences. Growing evidence demonstrates that where babies have reflective parents, these children grow up to develop the means of being able to understand and be more in control of their feelings (self-regulation) and develop the skills they need for establishing and maintaining relationships.

The origins of children learning to manage feelings

The origins of how your baby learns how to manage feelings, and to be able to regulate them, lie in the first few weeks and months of his interactions with you. Your baby's brain makes him respond to things that happen before he has any understanding of what these feelings and experiences

mean. He can be easily overwhelmed by unfamiliar things in his environment, such as smells, noises and separations from a parent. For example,
baby Jack is lying in his cot, squirming around and grizzling. He gets more
uncomfortable and starts to cry. Inside his mind and body his brain and
nervous system are trying to manage this unpleasant feeling. Before his mum
Rachel comes to him, he lacks any reference point from this inside feeling to
what happens on the outside. It is as if his feelings inside just happen almost
randomly without any anchor of an outside event to hang it on. So what
would help Jack to manage this feeling? Fortunately, Jack can rely heavily
on an external manager of his feelings, which is his mum.

Your baby's emotional development is a complex process and almost
entirely dependent on you, his parents, and others close to him. Luckily,
much of the time you will be naturally supporting this process without necessarily even realising. You need first to notice and then to understand your
baby's emotional states (what's inside his mind) and then to link these emotions in your mind to a triggering event or action (what's outside his mind),
such as in Jack's case an uncomfortable sensation from a wet nappy. In practical terms, this could be as mundane as a mind-minded comment from his
mum when Jack cries that helps him connect his feeling of discomfort and
distress with his wet nappy, such as 'Ah, does Mummy need to change your
wet nappy? It's not very comfy is it?' In this simple statement, Jack's mum is
telling him that she understands that he has a mind that contains thoughts
and feelings, which are not only separate from her own, but that she can
tell him about. Each time you link what your baby is feeling to the physical world, your baby begins to understand how things connect and work
together. When you state out loud what you feel is going on inside your
baby's mind, you are really helping him to understand himself, you and the
outside world. And all of this can be done in typical everyday interactions.

> Have you noticed times when you do this? Try asking yourself the
> question: 'What might be going on in my child's mind right now?'

These kinds of mind-minded statements can be made directly *to* your child
or *about* your child to a partner or family member. Research has shown that
'tuning in' to what your baby is thinking and feeling – in other words, being
more mind-minded – means that your child is more likely to be securely
attached, have better language and play abilities at age 2, and have better
understanding of other people's thoughts and feelings when he starts school
(7). Being mind-minded when your child is a baby also means that your

child will be less likely to have behaviour problems in the preschool years. Using mind-minded statements beyond this age is enormously helpful for helping your child to understand other people, manage his own emotions and help him stay connected to you.

When you are making these mind-minded comments, your attunement with your baby's feeling will naturally change your facial expression to match his feelings. This is known as marked-mirroring. Your baby would see his feelings reflected back at him in your facial expressions or tone of voice.

Marked-mirroring.

When your baby sees your facial expressions in response to his own feelings, he can start to link and connect emotions, and your response begins to make sense. In essence, the way you look tells your baby how he feels inside. This is the beginning of your child learning about *how* he feels, and crucially this is the start of him learning to manage his feelings so that they don't overwhelm him. The way that you can do this is basically to respond to his emotions in a way that shows him that you can both understand how he is feeling and do something about it. For example, Jack's mum might say, 'Let me change that wet nappy for you into a nice warm dry one', whilst her facial expression would be warm and comforting. Jack sees his mum as the regulator of how he is feeling. In other words, the supportive and in-tune presence of his mother is what helps him to manage his feeling of distress, which over time as he grows, teaches him that feelings can be managed. As he gets older he will be able to increasingly do this for himself, as if this ability gets passed from his mum to him. If something has upset you, connected with your own life, and your baby cries out in distress, it might take extra effort to match your tone and expression to how your baby feels, and so you might bring your own (quite separate) state of mind into the interaction. This is perfectly understandable and normal, but it does usually mean that it takes longer for the baby to regulate how he is feeling, as he needs your help to do this. In this situation, it would be best to take a few moments yourself to manage your own feelings, and then you will be in a better frame of mind to be reflective with how your baby feels.

As your baby grows into a determined, busy toddler to an increasingly independent child, continuing to be alert to what he is thinking or feeling is still incredibly valid and helpful. Reflective Parenting – developing a greater awareness of your own emotions and then thinking about what is going on inside your child's mind – has been shown to be a key influence on children's emotional development. The more often you can be reflective in your interactions with your child, the more you will be helping him to understand his own feelings. Children don't just grow out of difficult behaviour of their own accord; they need you to show them how to grapple with emotions, which then impacts on misbehaviour. You might find that over the course of his childhood he will need your help more as his feelings about events in his life become more powerful. This kind of challenging behaviour is a natural part of childhood, just like growing physically. If children don't get this kind of help from you, then these emotions can become more exaggerated as they make greater efforts to get a response from you.

Do babies have relationship skills?

When Rachel's ex-partner Matt was at a play zone with his 9-month-old son Jack, and talked to two other dads about their views of the first year of their children's lives, there was disagreement about how much, if anything of interest, happened when their children were babies. One parent thought that being a father with a young baby was a little boring as they did not seem to do much, but then after about a year things improved markedly. Another found the first year fascinating, if a little daunting. The experiences of having a baby for mothers and fathers can differ enormously and as we are writing this together as a male and a female psychologist, a father and a mother, we hope to be able to bring you these different experiences throughout the book. So, whether you are a father or mother, is there more to babies and how we relate to them that could make this experience a great deal more interesting, both for the parent and the baby?

What did you feel like when your baby was born? When you looked at him, what did you imagine was going on inside his head? Did you even think about that? And what was going on inside yours? What did you imagine he was capable of doing? And did you think you had any direct influence on this? Maybe you remember your own son or daughter, newly born, staring in wonder at the chaos of light, noise and smell, and then looking at you? Your baby had a preference for you, his parent, and preferred the smell of you, the sight of you and the sound of your voice to anything or anyone else – he was born with an innate desire to interact with you. You might have found yourself so focused on keeping this little person alive, you gave little or no thought to what was actually going on inside him.

What must it be like to be a newborn baby, a little person who knows nothing about the world? It is easy to assume that a baby is unable to understand anything either inside his mind or in the outside world: that babies come into the world a completely blank slate. Indeed, until the start of the twentieth century, many researchers believed just this: that babies had no awareness of either themselves or other people around them. If you think back to those first few days and weeks of your baby's life, what was your main focus? Wondering what was going on inside him, what kind of person he was going to be? Or making sure that you had his temperature just right at night time, and that he wasn't getting a nappy rash and was feeding well?

Sometimes it seems though that this view of a baby's limited abilities is still around today, with some parenting books focusing only on programmes for managing feeding, sleeping and toileting routines, instead of on your relationship with each other. While these are all important and essential to your baby's survival, we believe it is also helpful, and indeed vitally important, to start thinking at an early stage about what else might be going on in your baby's mind. It can be hard to make this your focus, as understandably you are taken up with thoughts about how to keep this new life fed and warm, and most importantly alive. However, by doing this, you will be better able to manage difficult behaviour later on, and to iron out difficulties in your relationship with your child. The research tells us that starting to think about what's going on inside your baby, and importantly, showing him this through your interactions with him, is a great way of helping your baby to both think about and manage how he feels.

The tide of thinking started to change in the 1970s when developmental psychologists such as Trevarthen (8) spent a lot of time observing infants and their parents. By watching babies, he found that when they were feeling calm and comfortable they seemed to move in purposeful ways, as if a baby has an idea of what he wants to do before he does it. The research showed that babies were not always randomly kicking and moving or making sounds with no awareness of their parents, but often moved and made noises in interaction with them. Research on newborn babies (9) showed that, just hours after birth, newborn babies could move their fingers when they saw other people moving their fingers. Babies also got better at copying over time, showing their potential for learning and improving the coordination of their actions. What all of this tells us is that from the minute they are born, babies already have a strong inclination to think about and interact with an 'other'. And the most important other is most certainly you.

Babies are immediately skilled at communicating with others, and make a great effort to do so. And as a baby gets older, he becomes really interested in experiencing how other people see him. Think of a 9-month-old baby, holding up a toy for others to see. For a young baby, it is fun discovering new things, but it becomes much more fun when you find out that you can share these things with other people who can take delight in joining in your fun. For your baby, even objects become intrinsically more interesting when he sees that another person is interested in them. This is worth remembering for later on, as you will see that in your play with your baby, and later in childhood, showing your own interest in something that he has focused on will make it immediately more appealing and interesting for him. This can be a very useful tool that you might not have realised you even had. Or imagine when you find yourself standing at the checkout in the supermarket and a baby in the buggy in front of you looks at you with wide eyes and grins, your instinct is most likely going to be to widen your eyes and grin back. Babies automatically seek out and respond back to positive, expressive communication from other people. Also babies can draw interested attentive adults into a pattern of interacting and conversing that grows over the weeks and months in an almost ritualistic fashion. Think about how expressive a baby's face is. When you notice and take delight in your baby's expressions and movements, such as frowns, pouts, grimacing or furrowing of his brow, or turning his head or kicking his feet, you motivate him to repeat these actions. Your baby learns that by using expressions and actions, he triggers a response from the adults around him, and so when you react in this way, you are helping your baby to engage in communication. Babies begin to anticipate their parents' responses and take enjoyment from them, and crucially learn that they can have an effect on other people.

Have you ever said to a friend or relative who is interacting with your baby, 'He is so interested in you' or 'He likes you doing that'? If so, you had accurately guessed that your baby has a mind of his own and had already begun working out what he likes and does not like. You would have also noticed that he is interested in interacting with other people. A baby is not just someone who needs his physical needs met and to have consistency and routines. He also needs you to interact with him and to enter into a relationship with him. This may sound obvious, but it's striking how many of us can get so wrapped up in the daily care of our baby's physical needs that we forget to find the time to turn our attention to what's actually going on inside our babies' heads.

Babies have a preference for whom they interact with

Even though a baby is interested in people generally, he is much more interested in interacting with people who reciprocate this interest. Babies naturally respond better to people who are sensitive to them. They like it when people make good eye contact, raise their eyebrows at them in an expressive way, take turns and wait for a response, and can match how they are feeling through their tone of voice and facial expressions. Babies love people who show these verbal and non-verbal signs of interest; expressive, interested faces are definitely more appealing and immediately engaging for a baby than blank or hostile faces. This makes sense for us adults too. A sales person has a much better chance of selling us something if they make an effort to engage with us and understand what we want. However, the sales pitch cannot be over the top – it needs to be matched to our feelings and intentions at that moment; an overeager salesperson is almost as bad as a disinterested one. Researchers (10) showed that babies at 14 months old are much more likely to pick up an object that the researcher has shown an interest in and give it to the researcher if that person had spent time engaging with them first. Babies seemed to be more motivated to connect with one object over another if the adult they are interacting with authentically connected with them and shared a dialogue. When babies get a sense that 'you have noticed and understood what it is like to be me' they are more able to learn about the world and explore. They feel listened to, which builds trust.

Am I boring you? Having a mind that is interested in yours

If babies have a set of skills to bring to their relationship with you, what do you think you bring to the relationship? In an ideal world, when we interact with our children it would be similar to an improvisation between two musicians. The improvisation would be based on what was going on in the moment, like musicians responding to each other unhindered by old musical scores or patterns. Over time, hopefully a nice tune would start to emerge and the musicians would be in synch with each other. In our parenting, we would bounce off our children's ideas and they would bounce off ours, unhindered by other influences. This would allow us to be fully attentive to what our children are doing or saying and we would be able to follow their lead. This is certainly an aspect of Reflective Parenting. This doesn't always happen though in our interactions with others.

Have you ever been with someone where you feel you aren't being interesting enough for them? You're chatting away about something that happened to you, telling the person what you thought was a funny story about a friend, and you notice that they seem distracted, checking their watch for the time, and then perhaps even starting to text someone on their mobile. What's that feeling like? Does it make you want to try harder to hold their attention? Tell a funny story? Even perform a bit more? Or do you withdraw? Start to feel a bit inadequate and go quiet, resolving that next time you might not bother coming out for the evening, as you're better off being on your own if that's the kind of disinterested reaction you get? You start to wonder if maybe you're just a bit boring. Now imagine yourself as a young baby or child, feeling that you aren't interesting to your mum or dad. You might engage in any one, or in turn all, of the attention-seeking strategies described earlier – or you might simply withdraw.

Rewind to the evening out with your friend, and this time you sense that the person you're with is interested in what you have to say, and how you feel about it all, and is giving you their full attention, both in their facial expression and the way they ask questions and listen to you. Immediately, you feel not only closer to them, but in some way better about yourself, and the conversation flows. This is the same for children, because when the person they are closest to listens to what they are saying and feeling, and then responds to them in a way that supports what they are feeling, they feel interesting and of value. And when your baby or child feels that you are there just for him, and interested in his thoughts and feelings, he makes himself wide open to learning about not just his own mind, but yours as well. Just as you experience a more enjoyable evening with your friends if they are paying attention to you and showing interest, so it is that a baby experiences a feeling of being valued if you show that you see something of value in him.

The important thing here is the difference between someone not only noticing your mind, but being able to respond to it, in a way that fits with how you are feeling, and moreover being curious about how your mind works. Compared with being with someone who not only doesn't appear interested in what's going on in your mind, but maybe hasn't even noticed its very existence.

Now imagine Rachel waiting at a bus stop in the rain with baby Jack. There are several ways of dealing with this everyday mundane situation, but the subtle differences between how Rachel might handle it can make a big difference to how both she and Jack might feel by the time they get home. If Rachel is able to interact with Jack in a way that draws him in, by being both interested in him and showing him the world around him, there will almost certainly be a different experience for both baby and parent. For example, imagine if Rachel pulls funny faces or starts to show an interest in the raindrops, smiling as the rain hits her hand and showing her wet hand to Jack to pass the time. Jack can engage with this, particularly if he sees his mother's expressive face showing her own interest, and he is likely to respond with interest and excitement himself. However, if Rachel feels a bit bored, is a little preoccupied with worries about money and her ex-husband, and only shows irritation at waiting at a bus stop in the rain, then interacting with Jack may not even come into her mind. Rachel feels impatient about the bus not arriving and ignores Jack; Jack begins to get bored and frustrated at the lack of interaction and attention, and starts to cry. Parent and baby get on the bus feeling irritable and less willing to interact with each other, and, in a worst-case scenario, the journey home involves a screaming baby on a full bus and a very irritable or angry mother. It is important to note that acting otherwise can sometimes feel impossible, and it is something you have to make a conscious effort to do at first. What this example shows us is how the behaviour and emotional states of the parent affect the behaviour and emotional states of the child and vice versa.

What do you bring to the relationship?

In your everyday interactions with your child, we would imagine that there are many times when you haven't acted exactly how you had thought you should have, with hindsight. Maybe later you felt a sense of shame or disappointment in how you acted? It could be you felt drawn into an interaction and gave a response that seemed over the top or overly negative? For example, a simple question from your child has you snapping back and feeling extremely irritated. Have you ever wondered why this happens? There are many factors that interfere with how we respond and react to our children, but there are two factors in particular that influence us and make it extremely difficult to enjoy a free, unhindered improvisation with our children a lot of the time. These factors are the impact of the parenting you received as a child and being influenced by strong emotions when you are relating to your child.

The influence of how you were parented

Everyone sees situations differently. We might react to certain situations more than others, whereas some things we might not even notice. For example, Karen walked into a shop to buy something and heard the shop assistant sigh after she had asked him a question. She reacted in an extreme way to this, perceiving his sigh as a personal slight and thinking that the shop assistant was showing her a lack of respect, and shouted as she walked out of the shop. In the same situation, some people may not have noticed the sigh, while others may have assumed that the sigh was probably due to the shop assistant having had a long tough day at work and nothing to do with them. However, if we found out more about Karen and learned that she had a history of critical and rejecting parenting, it would be easier to understand why she was so hypersensitive to perceived rejection. Past experiences can have a really strong influence on the present. This is quite an extreme example, but you may be able to think of examples from your own life where you have found yourself, for example, sensitive to criticism and feeling extremely hurt; perhaps at work, or in the local Parent Teacher Association meeting, you didn't feel your ideas were listened to, and this may connect back to feeling undervalued or unheard when you were much younger. It is helpful to be aware of these influences, and to know that we all look at the world and our relationships through a different lens, depending on our past influences.

The same is true of how we notice and interpret our children's behaviour – we all do this differently. How we see and interact with our children is influenced by our experiences of our own parents when we were young. Your parents and the home environment were all you knew during your most vulnerable and impressionable stages in life. Whether this was when you cried when you were a baby or were a child anxious about going to school, your parents reacted in particular ways to everything you did. The way you were raised as a child has an impact on the rest of your life. Even if you are not aware of it, the imprint of your own parents' responses remains inside your head, influencing your parenting. And how you deal with this influence could be much more important to how you handle your relationship with your own child than you might already realise. Your early experiences form your view of the world and can impact on how you parent your children. An interesting study (11) found that when pregnant mothers were interviewed about their own childhood experiences of being parented, it was possible to predict from these histories the type of relationship they would have with their future child. For example, a secure parent went on to have a secure attachment with her own child. Notably, the important factor in linking the past with future parenting styles was not what the parent had experienced in her early childhood so much as how she talked about it and reflected on it, telling a coherent story. This is important to how we understand and think about how you can become reflective in your current approach to parenting. The next two chapters will particularly focus on this.

If in your own childhood a parent, or caregiver, was able to recognise and comment on what was going on in your mind as a baby, then it is highly likely that you will have felt secure in this relationship and experienced being understood. Achieving this level of understanding with your child may sound difficult, but it's actually quite easy as most of this commentary takes place during the most mundane of everyday interactions, such as during a nappy change, a feed or a bedtime routine. This would look something like this: as you lean over to change your baby's nappy you might say, 'ooh, poor baby, are you feeling a bit wet and cold? Shall mummy change you into a nice clean snuggly nappy?' And as you do this, your expression would reflect both the baby's current discomfort, and then your expression would change to offer comfort and soothing. So, being reflective promotes security, but what can you do if your own childhood didn't have this type of attachment, but you want to try to achieve this now with your own baby? Can it be done? Even if you had a really difficult experience in your childhood, we will take you through ways in which you can take on a reflective stance and develop a more secure relationship with your baby.

It's important to realise then that all interactions with your child are impressionistic, that is you are interpreting and making sense of situations rather than responding to them in a factual way that is totally correct. We all do this in different ways, and they are real for us. What is important is to start to think about how you can separate your own experience from what you feel now with your child.

For example, when Karen's 2-year-old daughter Molly said 'No!' to her mother's request to go to bed, Karen experienced strong feelings of rejection, based on her own history of being rejected frequently by her own parents. In this present interaction, her reaction was based on a strong sense that her own daughter was also rejecting her and she felt compelled to withdraw from Molly as she did her own parents. Obviously, if this continued over time the worry would be that Karen's negative reaction to her 2-year-old's behaviour would result in Molly feeling rejected and unsafe, possibly leading to further rejection of her mother in a negative cycle of rejection.

So one of the important steps towards learning to become a more reflective parent with your own child is recognising the part that your own history plays in this relationship. If Karen in this example was able to begin to separate her own past childhood experiences from this present scenario, she would be more able to reflect on her child's behaviour with curiosity and interest. She might also be able to see Molly's reaction as a developmental stage, or realise that the response related to her daughter feeling upset that her mum missed out on her bath time. Karen's understanding would promote a feeling of security in her child, and would enable a more positive interaction to evolve, as her daughter would start to experience her mum as someone who was able to comment on what was going on in her mind. This is another example of mind-mindedness: the ability of parents to talk about what they think is going on in their child's mind. It's interesting to note that where parents are able to comment accurately on what they think is going on in their child's mind, these children then go on to be able to understand other people better. An example of how this would look would be for Karen to say, 'I think you're a bit fed up that I didn't get home in time to spend enough time playing with you before bed time tonight. It doesn't feel fair, does it?'

The influence of strong emotions when relating to your child

You can be influenced by strong emotions that arise from situations both outside of and within your relationship with your child. Try to think back to a recent difficult moment with your child, and ask yourself whether the level of your emotional reaction fitted the situation. Was your reaction disproportionate, and what do you think may have contributed to you reacting in this way? How might a friend have experienced you in this situation, what would they have seen? Can you link your reaction in this situation to previous situations?

Here's an example:

> Lisa returned home, stressed from other events from earlier in the day. Although she wasn't aware of how she was feeling, too many demands and having to meet other people's needs had led to her feeling irritated and resentful. Consequently, when her daughter Ella asked for ketchup, a drink and complained that her brother Charlie had more chips than her at the table before she had even sat down, she overreacted and responded angrily, throwing her plate hard on the table and storming off into the kitchen, muttering expletives to herself.

These kinds of moments can happen in every family and it can be helpful to check back to what happened before these incidents, to rewind and reflect, so you can be more aware of the impact of events leading up to difficult moments. Being aware of strong emotions experienced within the parent-child relationship is important. For example, feeling stressed out is likely to influence how you respond to a scream from an overtired baby. It may change your interpretation from a need for comfort or food to an intention to torment you when you feel the need to be left alone. Take this example from a bedtime routine with Lisa and her 4-year-old daughter Ella.

> The routine starts well, with Lisa taking Ella up the stairs. A fun bath-time is followed by two stories in bed and a kiss goodnight, after which mum starts to make her way downstairs. She is feeling close to her little girl and happy that they have enjoyed a lovely shared moment of intimacy, where both felt loved and secure.

Suddenly as she's halfway down the stairs she shouts out, 'I'm still hungry. I need a snack.' Lisa calls back, 'It's too late for snacks now, you've had your dinner. Just go to sleep my love.' Ella calls back, 'I don't like it in my bedroom. Can I have a little lie on your bed please Mummy?' Lisa calls back, a little snappier now, 'Time for sleep now, Mummy's very tired.' This conversation goes back and forth until Lisa gets angry and starts muttering to herself, 'I've had a really long day myself, when do I get to sit down and have a minute's peace myself?' Ella becomes distressed and before long both are upset and close to tears.

So how has this relationship switched from feeling intimate to antagonistic so quickly? Lisa has clearly reached the point where she lost the capacity to think about another person. The impact on her child was to feel upset and not thought about, and both lost the ability to feel concerned and close to each other. So how can you handle this sort of situation in a way that doesn't lead to a tantrum of your own?

Being misunderstood is highly aversive, and so when both parent and child are feeling this at the same time, it's a toxic dynamic that both parties will feel keen to get away from. Lisa was feeling misunderstood by her 4-year-old. The sort of question running through her mind at this point was 'Why can't she understand that I've had a really tiring day, and can't give any more to anyone else right now?' On the other hand, the thoughts running through her 4-year-old's mind might have been something like, 'I haven't seen my Mummy all day while she's been at work. I want a bit more time of just me and her and another story.' In this example it is difficult for the mother to respond to her child's needs because of the strength of her emotions in the relationship at that moment. This strong emotion then dictates how she reacts to and interprets her daughter's behaviour. When we misunderstand a situation, we tend to act on a false assumption. So in this example, Lisa may begin to feel that Ella is 'getting at her' or even intentionally provoking her. Ella may feel abandoned, neglected, maybe even unloved or unvalued.

What Reflective Parenting feels like for children

When your 1-year-old grins at you, wide-eyed with excitement at her first birthday party as she eats a piece of chocolate cake really too big for her own mouth, imagine the impact on her of the following three reactions from you:

A. You grin back at her, your own eyes widening, and say 'Wow! That chocolate cake is absolutely yummy isn't it? It's bigger than your mouth, but you can still just about get it in!' Then you laugh.

B. You scowl at her, eyes narrowing and say, 'You're making a big mess with that all over your face. If you try to eat a piece that big you'll probably be sick, and I'll be the one who has to clear it all up!'
C. You look at her momentarily, but your face is blank, not smiling or scowling. You're trying to remember if you ever had a cake on your birthday, and are suddenly struck by an image of your parents arguing; you can't remember how old you were at the time.

These three different reactions have the following different effects on your 1-year-old, not consciously thought of course, but experienced in a very real way:

A. Mum can see that I love my cake and I'm feeling happy at my party. She's happy that I'm happy and she is really interested in me feeling this way.
B. This cake tastes good, but I'm not sure I'm enjoying myself. Mum looks angry, I feel a bit bad inside, and I'm not sure why. Maybe it's not really very nice eating cake.
C. I don't know what I feel right now. I don't know if I even have a mind / who or what I am.

The experience for the 1-year-old in example A is one of feeling that the parent has really joined her in her experience of her delicious chocolate cake. What the mother does in this example is open up her mind totally to the experience of her young child, in a way that is receptive to the child's state of mind. Her mum's reflections on the 'yummy-ness' of the cake and statement that 'It's bigger than your mouth, but you can still just about get it in!' says 'I know what you are feeling and thinking about that cake and this whole experience.' Her laughter afterwards is a moment of shared pleasure in the experience. The mother is of course smiling at her own enjoyment at seeing her 1-year-old having such a great time, but the smile is also her reflection of her young child's state of mind. This moment of sharing the same feelings with each other is a moment of simple, but intense, shared enjoyment for both mother and child.

Experiencing great pleasure in something, and seeing this reflected back at you in the face and voice of your parent, is about as good as it gets for a baby. The feeling that not only does this feel good for me, but it also looks like you are enjoying showing me how good it feels for both me and you, mum, makes that experience of eating the chocolate birthday cake like a black-and-white photo going into bright technicolour for your baby. Nothing feels quite as good.

Conclusion

When you reflect back at your baby what is going on in his mind, he learns that he has a mind that is separate from his mother's, and one that is interpretable and makes sense. Reflective Parenting is driven by an accurate mirroring of what the parent infers is going on in her baby's mind. In reflecting back your own thoughts and feelings, you are also helping your baby to understand that other people have their own thoughts and intentions. When you start to talk to your baby and child about what you think is going on in his mind, you are doing what we refer to as mentalizing, that is helping to show him that you understand he has thoughts, feelings and wishes that are separate and different from your own, as well as that you can understand these and reflect them back to him. Even more importantly, your baby can't learn this without you teaching him. The good news is that teaching your child about thoughts and emotions is actually pretty simple, and you're undoubtedly doing a lot of this already without even knowing it, in the everyday exchanges you have between you and your child. With some help, you can start to notice when you are doing this well (when you are mentalizing) and when you are finding it more difficult. We all have times when we are mentalizing well (only about 30 per cent of the time), and many more times when we are doing it less well. Reflective Parenting is all about helping you to start reflecting back to your child what is going on in his mind a bit more of the time. And with this increased mentalizing, you will start to see an impact on how he behaves and how you connect.

2

THE PARENT MAP

In this chapter we aim to show you the importance of thinking about your-self – having self-reflection – in relation to your child. We will ask you to consider a number of things, including what might be influencing you to feel in particular ways, how you react and any patterns you can discern from your reactions, and what you think during situations. This may lead you to consider your strengths and weaknesses as a parent – we all have them. You may find that specific areas and roles associated with parenting might come quite naturally, whereas other aspects might be more challenging.

> *If we could get into your child's mind, and be able to see how he sees you as a parent, what would you want him to see? What would he say about you, what are your strengths? What qualities would you really want him to highlight?*

Being a parent takes a great many skills, and you often need to adopt very different roles in relation to your child depending on the situation. A parent is someone who at times teaches and supports, provides love and comfort, maintains firm boundaries and discipline in spite of upset or anger, instils routines and also strives to understand their child's perspective. How comfortable are you with these varied roles? Does one come more naturally to you than the others? One way of thinking about these questions is to think about your emotional reactions during situations, as they can help you to identify those areas of parenting that you might be finding more problematic. To help with this process of self-reflection and thinking about what makes you the kind of parent you are, we have developed the idea of the Parent Map.

We feel that becoming a parent is like going on an expedition into uncharted territories; you do not know what the destination is, how to get there or how the journey will affect you. A pre-prepared map would be very helpful, to show you a way to think, feel and act as a parent and help you through. However, there are none available as everyone's experiences and expeditions are unique and are influenced by different things. Instead, you can draft your own personal Parent Map. This means building up a picture of how you are as a parent and is a process that will probably continue to be pieced together throughout your child's childhood and often far beyond this point. The process of thinking about, and working at, your Parent Map is more important than actually completing a finished picture. A Parent's Map constantly changes, mainly because your child changes what he thinks and feels as he develops and interacts with his world. Also, aspects of your own life are probably always changing, so Maps need to change, too. Our aim in this chapter is to start the process of constructing your Map, your own inside story put together through self-reflection, and thereby help you get to know yourself in a different way. Then, in Chapter Three, we provide you with strategies for both noticing and managing strong feelings.

Constructing a Parent Map: being aware of your own mind

Constructing your Parent Map, by becoming more aware of the influences on how you come across and interact with your child, is important to Reflective

Parenting. Creating coherence in your Map is a lifelong adventure. Once you start to reflect more on your Map you will be in a better position to think about your child, and how you approach your interactions with him. This can lead to some positive and long-lasting changes in behaviours that you might have previously struggled with.

Let us guide you a little with constructing your Map, and suggest three important features that will help you increase your self-awareness. These reference points, when you become more attentive to them, will help you establish and define yourself as a parent.

Reference point one: current state of mind

The first important step of creating your own Parent Map is to be aware of *yourself* and be curious about your own state of mind. Try asking yourself the questions: 'How do I feel right now? What has made me feel this way?' and 'What am I thinking?' Start to observe your thoughts and feelings from the outside. Of course, this is work in progress for all of us because we are never constantly aware of ourselves. We often act without fully knowing why, and react without thinking. While this is fine a lot of the time, by increasing your awareness of how you are feeling, and focusing on what's going on inside *you*, you will discover how you can enjoy a better quality of interaction with your child. The reason this is important is that your own feelings have a powerful impact on how your child both feels and behaves and how you handle your interactions.

Why do we have to feel?

A big part of being aware of what is going on in your mind is being able to understand your emotions and feelings. But why do we have to have feelings? What function or use are they in our lives? We often don't have any choice over whether or not to have an emotional life – our feelings are just there. Over the centuries, our brains have evolved and changed, but the parts of our brain that have remained constant are those areas responsible for our emotions. This means our ability to experience emotions came first, and other functions such as reasoning and rational thought developed much later, suggesting emotions are essential to our survival in some way.

Because of the architecture of our brains, the emotional centres have greater power over the rest of the brain, including power over our thoughts. This means the emotional brain can take over the rational brain quite easily. We can be hijacked by intense feelings and have explosive outbursts, not always knowing why this happens or understanding what came over us. In terms of how we act then, our feelings are often more in charge than our thoughts.

Consider the following scenario. Imagine you are travelling home by train during a busy rush-hour commute and a man standing nearby becomes increasingly agitated as he is jostled around by the other passengers. He suddenly gets extremely angry about the fact that, as he perceives it, someone is intentionally trying to prevent him from sitting down in a vacant seat. A sudden rush of fury, driven by adrenaline, overwhelms the man being pushed around and he starts shouting at the man who pushed him (even though this was probably unintentional) and an actual fight ensues. In this example, an intense feeling takes precedence over any rational thoughts about what to do in the situation, or about what might have been the other person's actual intentions or thoughts.

Emotions are perhaps best thought of as impulses to act, providing instant plans for handling life that we may or may not be aware of. The tendency to act is there without us knowing it or consciously controlling it. So why do we have feelings if they have the capacity to affect our behaviour and relationships so negatively, as in the previous example?

Compared with other animals, we humans have a far more complex and varied range of emotional responses to situations. Our social lives are equally complex and our emotions can help us to manage socially. From the moment we are born, we are hardwired not only to seek out the warmth, food and comfort of our mothers (our physical instincts), but we are also driven to connect with and relate to other people (our emotional instincts). Through these emotional connections we learn not only about others but also ourselves. To underline just how important emotions are, when the emotional centres within the brain are removed during brain surgery, patients lose all interest in people; they report having no feelings and fail to recognise feelings in others. They are able to converse with those around them, but they seem to prefer to spend time on their own. So emotions can act as *signals* within relationships and help us connect to others. Although we are not conscious of the process happening, when we feel an emotion it tells us something about the external world and how we have reacted to it.

The reason we want to draw out the importance of becoming more aware of how you feel is because when we know how we feel, and even understand *why* we feel a certain way, we can use our feelings to make good decisions in life and learn to control our impulses. If we find ourselves snapping at our child, we might be able to make more sense of whether this was really about something that we felt about ourselves or our own lives. By making sense of the feelings we are experiencing, instead of just reacting, we can start to moderate our emotions and become better able to express them appropriately.

Think back to the busy train commute. If the man near to you had been more aware of how he was feeling and thinking and how these thoughts and feelings were causing him to become increasingly agitated, he might not have reacted so impulsively or aggressively. Being aware of how you are feeling offers the opportunity to analyse whether or not to react, and how.

How this part of the Map applies to Reflective Parenting

So we know feelings are essential for relationships and our communication with others in the social world around us, and it follows that an awareness of our feelings can help us to be more reflective about what's happening with our child. How does noticing this reference point on your Map apply to Reflective Parenting and help you become more self-aware, and how does this help your developing relationship with your child? Let's think through an example of how thinking about your feelings can be helpful.

> It is a cold and wet Saturday afternoon. Jon is indoors looking after the children. He was meant to be seeing friends in the evening, but his friends had cancelled. His wife Lisa has gone out with her friends instead. Meanwhile, the children are either being clingy or misbehaving and being oppositional and this is really getting on Jon's nerves. His 4-year-old daughter Ella looks up at him with tears in her eyes and says, 'You don't want to play with me today daddy.' Jon feels ashamed that he has made his daughter feel so upset and begins to wonder why he hasn't been playing with his kids. Jon notices that he has been feeling bored and irritated. He begins to understand that he is annoyed that he is not going out with his friends and feels resentful about being in with the children when he was looking forward to going out. By becoming more aware of his feelings, especially his frustration towards the children's behaviour, he has a greater awareness of how he might be behaving towards his children. In other words, Jon's awareness of his state of mind and how this might be impacting on him increases his awareness of how he might be impacting on his children. A sense of guilt enters his mind. He is asking them to entertain themselves and getting frustrated at them when they won't. By becoming curious as to why this might be, and by thinking about himself, he can start to think about altering his behaviour.

In the example above, the last sentence is really the most important one to consider first. Jon starts to become curious about why the children might be misbehaving, and starts to make the connection with his own feelings about being frustrated and let down. This important first step, of being curious, is interestingly one that often gets missed, or lost, in our everyday interactions as we often just react. However, being curious about how you feel is crucial to Reflective Parenting as it allows you to understand how your own emotional state is impacting on your children, and it also allows you to reflect further and to link together your emotional states to what might be going on in your world. What matters most is the message that our children receive, and not the one that we think we're giving (1). So, understanding the difference between how we *intend* to come across and how we actually come across is really very important to understanding how our children perceive us. Being able to develop a curiosity and understanding of what makes you feel negative feelings will help you in future interactions with your child.

> *Have you ever snapped at your child, and then later realised that you were really angry because of something that had happened to you, and not because of anything that he had done?*

Curiosity involves first being interested in your own emotions and then observing the emotional 'tone' of your child's communication. And once you become curious about your child's world, you start to develop the ability to think differently about the reasons your child is behaving in a particular way – you start not just to notice, but also to interpret, your child's behaviour. If you can become more aware of your emotional states, you are less likely to react impulsively to your child's behaviour, which can only be a good thing. Let us return to the example:

> *Jon realised he was initially interpreting his children's behaviour as being whiny, clingy and oppositional. After Ella's tearful reaction he realised they were misbehaving because they were feeling ignored. He then started to think that perhaps they were feeling unwanted when they saw his lack of interest in them, and that maybe the acting up and misbehaving was a way to get noticed and get him to play with them. By making sense of his state of mind, Jon was better equipped to see that his mood was affecting his children and that his children wanted to spend time with him. This allowed him to connect with his children, tuning in to them and finding a way to spend a more positive time together.*

This guide then, to trying to understand what might be going on inside your child's mind, begins with trying to understand what's going on inside your own. It will be harder sometimes to get his inside story when you lose the thread of yours. Reflective Parenting, then, encourages you to create an awareness, or space, in your mind for thinking about how you feel, and what's going on in your mind. In other words, being reflective helps you to see the importance of shifting your attention to yourself and how you are currently thinking and feeling so that you can then create space in your mind for thinking about what might be going on in your child's mind. The real benefit to doing this is that you then start to interact with your child in a different, more understanding way. When you start to interact differently, you begin to see real and significant changes not only in how your child behaves, but also in how you and your child actually feel about each other. Adapting your thinking in this way isn't easy, and takes some practice, so don't feel too worried if it doesn't come naturally at first. However, doing this often enough builds continuity and helps build a story of how you react to your child.

Reference point two: past experiences and relationships

It's in our common language to refer back to what our parents did, sometimes blaming them for things that we feel and do now, and sometimes paying tribute. Phrases like, 'He's just like his father', however innocuous

Constructing your Map means reflecting on how you were parented.

they may sound, are evidence of our tendency to think of the influence of the generations that went before us. Clearly these early relationships have a major impact on our sense of security, and on our personality and development. In the world of academic psychology, whole books have been devoted to the subject of the influence of early childhood experiences on our current emotions and our ability to deal with our emotions and enjoy healthy relationships, and we can't possibly do this topic justice here. All we are asking you to do, in terms of being aware of yourself and your own emotions, is to reflect on the influence of your past experiences on how you might be feeling right now, or on your everyday interactions with your child. Hearing voices from our past relationships might make us stop in our tracks and do something completely opposed to how our parents would act, or conversely, may make us smile at the recollection of something helpful and familiar. Whatever your own reaction as a parent, the imprint of your own parents, or those who looked after you when you were growing up, will remain inside your head and be more or less accessible depending on the nature of the experience. What we mean by this is that some of us can feel very preoccupied by early experiences, while others may be more detached from their past; what's certain is that how you deal with your past influences could be much more important to how you handle your relationship with your own child than you might realise. Being aware of this influence, and not ignoring the importance of it on your current emotional state, will be a big help in your interactions with your child.

There are times when we might catch ourselves doing or saying something where we can hear the echo of our mother's or father's voice. We may have inherited small mannerisms: for one mum, rummaging through her handbag full of papers, lipstick, phone and so on, for a set of keys, immediately took her back to a memory of her own mum rummaging in her purse in a shop while she stood by somewhat awkwardly, feeling embarrassed by her mother's forgetfulness. A totally benign memory as it happens, but the mother experienced a very strong sense of herself doing something that she had somehow unconsciously 'inherited'. However, it was only when her own child nudged her out of this memory by saying 'Mum, hurry up! You are so embarrassing' that she became aware of how she might be impacting on her child in the present.

Fortunately, most of us have had a sufficiently good experience in early life, which means we are able to transfer a sense of security to our relationship with our own child. Crucially, what all babies need is a parent who is emotionally available to them and present – that is aware of their baby's needs (2). We can't emphasise enough how babies need their parents to notice what is going on inside their minds and to be able to respond to this in a way that is in tune with how they are feeling, and to a certain extent with what they are thinking.

How this part of the Map applies to Reflective Parenting

Our experiences with our own parents can sometimes lead us into patterns of behaviour that may feel way beyond our control. So when you become a parent, you may find that you are carrying around the belongings from your own childhood experiences – a bit like setting off on a journey, carrying a backpack that's got a lot of someone else's gear in it, and not much of anything that looks or feels like your own. At the very bottom of the backpack, you may find something that's useful, or it may feel as though you are carrying a really heavy bag on your back that seems to be dragging you down each time you embark on a new day and the responsibilities of looking after your child. One of the steps towards learning to become a more reflective parent with your own child is about tuning in to the part that your own history plays in this relationship, and this may not always be a totally comfortable experience. Let's look at an example.

Karen's parents argued for as long as she could remember. Meal times with family friends could be fraught affairs as they frequently became battlegrounds between her mother and father. Karen used to wish that any contentious topics were avoided as she learnt that disagreements could easily escalate into conflict. When Karen and her husband Tom became parents, they found themselves frequently disagreeing about how much they should intervene in the siblings' disagreements, and Karen often felt a strong wish to pacify and defuse tensions quickly, whereas her husband thought that their children should learn how to do this for themselves.

In the above example, Karen might start to reflect on what her need to intervene in disagreements is about, and what it is linked to. Understanding the link between her childhood experiences and how she manages situations in the present would be very helpful for her and Tom to understand and be aware of, not because she is necessarily wrong to intervene, but because her urge to act in the present is driven by strong emotions that belong more in the past. Karen might then be more able to separate out her own feelings of anxiety and worry from her interactions with her children.

However, while past experiences can clearly influence current emotions, it's also incredibly important to be aware that your history is not necessarily your destiny. When you became a parent, you may have resolved that you were 'not going to do things the way my parents did them'. You may even be actively working hard to forge a different kind of bond and relationship with your own baby. But for some people this is not so easy. So how do you turn your mind to your own baby, with all his demands for food, comfort, attention, love, and interaction, when your own early experience was less than ideal? Or what if your young baby's demands feel just too much for you, and you can't quite bring yourself to give him everything he needs because there are many things you feel in need of too? By increasing your self-reflection and constructing your Parent Map this will help you to work on preventing these negative experiences from your past impacting strongly on your current relationship with your child. It may sound strange or somehow unbelievable, but it is the active process of thinking about yourself and finding this meaningful that makes a difference. Over time, linking together your reactions and feelings, the influence of memories and past relationships, and considering how these influence patterns of behaving and interacting, starts to prevent past negative experiences impacting strongly on how you interact with your child. Being aware is the most crucial step. We will all find ourselves at times slipping into patterns of behaviour that we aren't happy with, and which are part of our past experiences – be assured that this is normal.

Reference point three: current influences

Just as past relationships can affect your state of mind, current relationships, beliefs and circumstances can also have a significant impact. We all have our own individual needs, independent of our children. We have a need to feel validated, empathised with and listened to, and if we can get this from our current relationships (e.g. a partner and friends), it can really help you in your interactions with your child. This does not necessarily have to come from the other parent of your child; it may come from a close friend who is also a parent. For example, a supportive relationship with a partner, friend or relative in which your needs are taken into account, and in which you have a strong sense that how you feel is both thought about by others, empathised with, and validated, is likely to have a calming, containing and generally positive impact on your current state of mind. You need to look after yourself first in order to help others. It is like being on a plane during an emergency and the oxygen masks come down – the advice is to put your mask on first, because then you are more able to help your child put his on. I wonder how many parents would do this in a real-life scenario, but the message is clear. Get your current relationships right and you will be more able to help your child.

On the other hand, a relationship characterised by criticism will leave you feeling more intense feelings of worthlessness, anger and helplessness. It may not be that this criticism comes from your partner, or the other parent to your child; it may come from your friend, work colleague or your extended family. The reference point on the Map is really the emotions brought up by the current relationships you find yourself in, and their influence on you. These strong, negative emotions can be intense and make it hard to think clearly, both about yourself and about others, and when you do find you are able to think, they can have a major impact on the type of thoughts and feelings you have.

Your current relationships may not be the most important reference point for you to consider when putting together your Parent Map. For many of you, your religious and cultural beliefs may be the predominant guiding influence on how you want to parent your child. The important point is to understand yourself well enough to bring into your awareness the influences that are around you right now that go into making up your identity as a parent. For many parents, society's expectations and cultural norms have a huge influence. For example, in Western cultures there has been a shift away from mothers as the sole carers of children, to fathers taking a more active role in day-to-day child-rearing, including childcare and feeding regimes. This type of societal expectation may or may not fit with how you want to parent your own children, and so it's important to reflect on these expectations, along with your other current influences.

How this part of the Map applies to Reflective Parenting

When you are with someone who seems to be in tune with how you are feeling, this is likely to bring your own feelings into greater awareness. Being in a relationship with someone who allows you time and space to reflect, or having time and space to yourself to reflect, helps raise awareness of what you are feeling and thinking. On the other hand, being in the presence of one or more people who are bringing their own intense feelings to a situation, or simply making demands, makes it hard even to bring into your vague awareness your current thoughts and feelings. Equally, being aware of the influences on your current life, including any religious beliefs you might have and what you think that society expects from parents today, and being aware of the social and cultural environment you and your children live in, will help you to decide if these are a strong enough influence to consider in putting together your own Parent Map, based on the coherent story you have built up inside yourself. Becoming more attentive of this reference point can help you increase your awareness of your parenting.

The Process

We have shown you the reference points, the features of your emotional life, to notice and pay attention to, but how do you fit them together? You will see that the process of thinking about yourself involves both emotions and thoughts, and perhaps a slowing down of situations in your mind, in order to get more of a sense of yourself.

First, try to work out your triggers for experiencing certain strong emotions. Triggers can come in many forms and may include the following:

1. A particular situation or interaction
2. A tone of voice your child uses sometimes
3. A comment someone makes
4. A thought you have
5. A strong belief system

These triggers can often elicit a strong emotional reaction in everyday situations with your child. When parents think about what might have triggered their emotions, they are often able to link a number of other similar experiences and discover repeating patterns. A helpful strategy for identifying triggers is to think back to situations where strong feelings caused you to overreact to a situation and work out what happened to create the emotion. For example, if we go back to the example of Jon earlier in the chapter, he noticed that when he felt he hadn't had any time to go out with friends for a long time and have time away from the family, he was snappier with his children and less likely to feel willing to meet their demands. He could feel frustrated, and only see his children as being deliberately demanding and irritating. In this situation, Jon's trigger was having his plans cancelled by his friends, which resulted in him having no time away from his family.

It was helpful when Jon noticed this so that he could step out of the cycle and get new understanding and meaning. He was able to begin a new inner dialogue – 'when I feel isolated from my friends I can feel frustrated easily at home, so when my children ask for things I often feel they are being unreasonable'. The next time this happened Jon could see that it wasn't his children's behaviour that was so troubling, but rather his own feelings were having a strong influence on how he was dealing with their behaviour. Jon was able to keep this in his mind in future interactions and interpret that what his children's behaviour really means in these moments is 'Daddy we need you to pay attention to us.' It is highly unlikely that Jon would be able to change his reaction straight away, as he might continue to feel let down by his friends, but over time once he has identified these triggers, it will get easier to anticipate how he might feel in certain situations and at certain times. At some point he might think during these emotional times, 'Oh no, here I go again, taking my disappointment out on my kids', and this might be enough to shift him into a more helpful state of mind before it affects his children. This trigger becomes part of Jon's Parent Map, part of his profile, and something that would be very helpful to keep in mind for future times with his children.

When you have identified a strong feeling, ask yourself, 'What is this feeling about?'

Once you are able to reflect on your feelings during a situation the better able you will be to think ahead. So, asking yourself questions such as, 'what situations are likely to bring up these difficult feelings?' will be helpful to you. Reflecting on times where you feel less able to cope can be very informative. Let's look at one mum's account and think through how it might help.

Lisa said that she had become really angry at her 6-year-old son Charlie last week when he was refusing to put his shoes on, and shouted at him harshly. She felt that this was out of character, and because she felt so guilty and bad about the incident, she decided to think about what had triggered her to act in this way. She focused both on the circumstances of the event and her feelings and thoughts leading up to the event, as well as thinking about what Charlie's motivations might have been for being uncooperative.

Lisa remembered that she was running uncharacteristically late while getting Charlie ready for school, and had felt very rushed and flustered. When Charlie seemed oblivious to her need to get ready and out of the door on time, Lisa believed Charlie was deliberately stalling to irritate her.

When thinking about your triggers, it is important to try to think about your own reactions and the meaning behind them. For example, what are your beliefs around particular situations and why are these situations important to you? In this example, the trigger for Lisa would be a strong belief system; Lisa always liked to be on time for everything, and so really didn't want to be late for school, so she could identify a general anxiety around lateness.

For Lisa, her feelings around lateness were a reference point that was important to her Map. Holding this in mind helped her to plan ahead to try to reduce the chance of similar situations happening. The most obvious thing she could think of was to start getting ready earlier, for example to turn off the television 25 minutes before leaving the house and to structure the time in the morning more effectively. She also thought about explaining the situation to Charlie and then helping him make some choices around getting ready, as well as providing incentives for him, such as explicit praise for getting ready on time and spending five minutes in the school playground playing together.

Some emotions are pretty straightforward, but in our relationships with others, however, emotions can become more complex, and a whole host of factors can govern how we are feeling at any particular moment in time, and in relation to another person, or even to several others. Take the following scenario, where feelings are influenced by both past and present experiences, and linked to more than one person, and it's easy to see how complex emotions can be:

> *Karen is preparing a Sunday lunch for her family. Her mum has come to stay for the weekend and while Karen cooks, the children are in and out of the room asking for snacks, and if they can play on Mum's tablet. At the same time, Karen's mum is asking what time they will be eating lunch, and is it beef that Karen's cooking as she doesn't like beef.*
>
> *The next time her son, Sam, comes into the kitchen, he asks if he can have a biscuit as he's starving. Karen suddenly shouts at him, and everyone jumps, startled by the aggression in her tone. Her mother comments 'Calm down Karen, it's only a biscuit!'*

What are the triggers for these feelings? Our first reaction might be that it's obvious that Karen is busy and trying to meet many needs at once, and she's being criticised by her mother. However, it's likely that a combination of past and present experiences is interacting here at a level that's outside of Karen's immediate awareness. The actual triggers for Karen experiencing these feelings are the comments made by her mum that she doesn't like the beef that Karen is cooking. If Karen reflects on her feelings about her relationship with her mum, she might recognise that she has felt in her past that she has to take care of her mum more than she would like, and that there has been some criticism in the relationship that often has left Karen feeling that she doesn't quite meet her mum's needs, and even that she can be a disappointment to her mum. Furthermore, Karen becomes aware of a feeling that she has never been allowed *not* to take into consideration her mum's feelings, so that they have somehow got in the way of her own thoughts and feelings. Combined with a current feeling of being the person with sole responsibility for meeting the needs of others, the question from her son about the biscuit becomes the final straw that leads her to snap. What kind of steps could Karen have taken to help her to deal with this situation differently? And how can she take the first step of becoming more aware of her own mind?

First, stepping back and realising that this interaction is important to the process of learning about herself and developing her Map. It will be helpful for Karen to recognise a pattern of behaviour as well as her state of mind. Is it the case for example that whenever her mum makes a criticism of her, she 'lashes out' at others? Noticing this tendency in herself could start to help her to be able to think more about what's going on for her son at this particular moment, or just to respond to him in a calm way. Karen might also become more aware that the comments from her mum that imply criticism or demands easily trigger her to feel an emotion that is extremely strong, and that she needs to take control of. She is likely in this type of situation to sometimes overreact to any small demand from her children, and so being aware of this can help Karen to separate out her feelings and thoughts about her mum from her thoughts and feelings about her children. When Sam asks for the biscuit then, the answer might still be 'no, you can't have another biscuit before dinner' but the more measured delivery will ensure that the situation doesn't escalate unnecessarily.

Here is another scenario involving Rachel and her children.

Rachel has been feeling isolated from her friends and struggling to find any space in her mind for anything other than the children, worries about her finances and her difficult separation from Matt. She has been looking forward to her friend Stella coming over to see her. Rachel feels this is a good time to leave the children to their own devices, and as they are usually good at entertaining themselves and playing happily and harmoniously together, she feels happy to spend some much needed time talking to her friend. Stella, a relatively new friend, was telling Rachel how she wished she could be as relaxed as Rachel with her kids and Rachel was saying how getting stressed about the small stuff really wasn't worth it. Just then, Lilly, age 7, came into the room blowing her recorder in a way that Rachel found really annoying as she was trying to talk to Stella. Lilly had been doing this for a while, and Rachel found she couldn't listen to Stella properly, and she suddenly lost it with Lilly, telling her she was making her feel she was losing her mind. She yanked the recorder off Lilly and tossed it up above the oven where she couldn't reach it. Rachel left the room for a minute and quick as lightening, Lilly climbed up on to the worktops to retrieve it, knocking all of Rachel's glass jars full of pasta and chutneys all over the floor, as well as her brand new, very expensive food processor (including the glass jug part). Everything was smashed

*to smithereens and baby Jack and Stella's baby Joe were left sitting
in a sea of broken glass. There was silence and then Rachel started
shouting at Lilly, who was not at all remorseful. After Rachel and
Stella spent nearly an hour sweeping up the glass and cleaning the
floor, Rachel finally calmed down enough to speak to Lilly and
explain why she was so cross. She explained she was angry because
these were her special things and it was like Lilly having broken all
her favourite toys. Lilly was very sorry and wrote her mum a sorry
note. Afterwards, Rachel reflected that she had reacted so strongly
because she felt that her much needed and longed for time with her
friend had been taken away from her, and she found herself reacting more strongly than she normally would have done to something
that was essentially an accident.*

For Rachel, her triggers were her strong feelings about her current circumstances – including her stress about her feelings of being stuck at home
with three young children to care for on her own, her stressful separation
from Matt and her worry about money. She felt a strong need to talk to a
friend, and her reaction to the accident with the glass jars, which was probably a result of her children feeling that they were not getting the attention
they wanted for themselves, resulted in an outburst that took time to repair
and left both Rachel and the children feeling bad. In constructing her Parent Map, Rachel could try to identify that these current stressors are making her more impatient than she would normally be with her children, and
hypersensitive to their demands. She might want to ask a friend if they could
have the twins for an hour, or meet her friend during school hours with baby
Jack, so that she could have some uninterrupted time talking to her friend
and feel free to concentrate on her own needs.

*Matt was reflecting on an extremely challenging Sunday looking
after Grace and Lilly, who had just left to go back to their mother's.
Matt had repeatedly become irritated and rejecting of Lilly, who he
perceived had been clingy and overly needy and demanding. Rachel
had called Matt and expressed upset and anger that Lilly had a
temperature and seemed ill.*

*Upon hearing that Lilly had in fact been ill, Matt became tearful
and had a strong feeling of shame and guilt for not realizing this
and being more understanding of her need for his comfort and nurture. His mind turned to his own childhood memories with his parents, and specifically to a time when he was 10 years of age and had
returned home from school. He had tearfully told his father that he
had been bullied at school and his father had responded with anger*

and criticism and told him to 'stop being a baby'. This was the first time that Matt had looked at that memory from a different perspective – he realised that he needed comfort and love from his father, as did Lilly earlier in the day, that just like Lilly he deserved comfort but that his own father struggled to give this to him. He was able to begin to see that this role of parenting was difficult for him, because of the impact of how he was parented himself, but resolved himself to try and keep this in mind in an effort to give his own children a different, more caring experience of a father than he had.

What makes constructing and applying your Parent Map difficult?

If you have reached this far in the book and started to think about some of the reference points you would like to put on your Parent Map then you are already starting to become more reflective in your parenting. Taking time to think about all the things that influence you in your approach to parenting your child is an enormously helpful step towards creating a better connection with your child. This will probably take you some time and effort though, and there are obstacles that can get in the way, both to constructing your Parent Map in the first place, and then in applying it in your relationship with your child.

Tiredness

We all have times of the day when we feel at our sharpest. For some this might be 6.30 a.m., while others might be at their best at 10.30 p.m. But for all of us, tiredness usually has an impact on our level of self-awareness. Waking up in the middle of the night with a newborn baby, two, three, or maybe more, times, is not only physically exhausting, but mentally too – the 'baby brain' that mothers often refer to is quite an accurate description of a brain that at times is literally unable to think. Being aware that how tired you are has a major impact on how aware you are of your state of mind is important as this self-awareness is an essential part of becoming reflective, helping you to recognize your limits and have empathy with yourself at these difficult times. You are not likely to be your most acutely self-aware, and therefore able to be reflective, when you are sleep deprived. Wait until you are more rested, and then it will be a great deal easier to think about your own feelings clearly. If you are a new parent who has been sleep deprived for months, try and find a pocket of time in the day when you can have some time to yourself to reflect on your feelings. And before you do this, if you can, try to get in a time to have a nap whilst your baby is sleeping, so that you are more rested and able to reflect. Equally, you may have an older child who has an erratic sleep pattern, and it may feel harder to get the empathy of other parents who have passed through this stage with their babies, but it is still important to reflect on the influence of tiredness in your relationship with your child, and in other close relationships. You may need to voice aloud to your child sometimes that your mood, or tone of voice, are due to the fact that you are tired, and not a reflection of the degree of warmth you feel towards your child.

Drugs and alcohol

Excessive use of drugs and alcohol dims levels of self-awareness, but even mild use of alcohol and drugs can impair your ability to be aware of your state of mind. Understanding that if you drink or abuse drugs this will impact significantly on both your level of self-awareness, and capacity to think about how you are feeling, is an important part of thinking about how and when you can best be aware of your own mind. Times when people drink alcohol or take drugs are often coupled with tiredness, and the combination of the two is a recipe for an almost total absence of a reflective self.

Physical health

Your state of mind might feel quite separate from what's going on in your body. But take a moment to think about how you feel emotionally when you have a really bad dose of flu. It's hard to think positive, happy thoughts when your body is wracked with aches and pains. In fact it can be hard to think of anything much more than that you feel unwell – and it is especially hard to think about other people and their needs. Where someone experiences more extreme pain or has a chronic illness, it can be hard to think about emotional states at all. Again, bring this awareness of your body into your mind, and understand that it is an important part of your own inside story and strongly influences your sense of vitality and the degree of energy you bring into your relationship with your child.

Mental health

It is clear that an acute mental health disorder such as psychosis or schizophrenia will have a major impact on a person's state of mind, causing confusion about themselves and the world around them. But even other mental health problems, such as anxiety and depression, will shape your state of mind, causing you to see the world and the people in it through a very particular lens. If you are feeling anxious or depressed, recognising that these feelings will affect your viewpoint will help you to validate how you feel and allow you to reflect on your current state of mind as normal and understandable. Even everyday low moods, rather than an ongoing feeling of depression, will have an impact on your ability to reflect on your own feelings and state of mind. Of course, when you are feeling robust, it will be much easier to reflect on your state of mind in a clear and open way. If the problems you are experiencing feel more severe, it is important to seek professional help for these if possible. Going back to the oxygen mask analogy, it is only when you feel robust enough in yourself that you are able to really focus in on what's going on inside your child. So addressing any mental health issues you might have will be in the interests of both you and your child.

Life events

Significant life events such as bereavement, a birth, divorce and separation, moving house, or losing a job, living with financial hardship, or being below the poverty line and having inadequate housing, all interfere significantly with our emotional well-being, and have a major influence on our state of mind. Parenting undoubtedly becomes more of a challenge when you are experiencing these life events, and it's important to acknowledge this and accept that you are under additional strain. Major life events can lead to depressive feelings that can endure and therefore need to be acknowledged (3). It is important to reflect on the impact they have had, or are still having, on you, as it is to accept that they have changed how you feel and think. It is equally important to reflect on these within your relationship with your child. For example, if you have experienced the loss of a parent, you will undoubtedly show feelings of sadness and loss around your children. This is perfectly normal, and it will help your children to understand that the relationship was an important one to you if they know that you are sad because you have experienced a loss. This will be far less confusing for them, and actually helpful to their own emotional development, to know that you can show these feelings and come to terms with them, rather than showing an emotion which doesn't seem to fit with the experience of loss.

REFLECTIVE PARENTING SUMMARY

THE PARENT MAP

What it is . . .

The Parent Map is a way of reflecting about yourself and how you parent your child. It encourages you to map out and think about what influences your parenting, such as current feelings, your past experiences and wider influences, such as beliefs and relationships.

It helps you by . . .

The Parent Map helps you become more aware of yourself and how you relate to your child. It also helps you to be more aware of the difference and separateness of your emotions from your child's. It helps you identify times when you are more likely to have strong feelings, which can be unhelpful in some situations.

It helps your child by . . .

The Parent Map helps your child because the more reflective and aware of yourself you are, the more stable your relationship can be. Your child will experience you in a more regulated and considered way.

It helps your relationship by . . .

The Parent Map makes links between past and present, which helps prevent past negative experiences impacting strongly on how you interact with your child. Your relationship benefits by being more stable and less reactive.

Keep in mind . . .

1. Think about the need to be aware of yourself.
2. Think about what influences your parenting, include your thoughts and feelings, the influence of past experiences.

3. Use strong feelings to trigger self-reflection and make a connection with how this influences your parenting.
4. Identify times when you think there might be a link between current and past experiences.
5. Build a story of how you got to feel and think the way you do now:

   a. Did your level of emotional reaction fit the situation?
   b. What do you think may have contributed to you reacting in this way?
   c. How might a friend have experienced you in this situation, what would they have seen?
   d. Can you link your reaction in this situation to previous situations?

6. Use your awareness of your 'triggers' to help guide you during future interactions; imagine, predict and reflect on where and how similar feelings and thoughts may arise.

3

MANAGING YOUR FEELINGS

Rachel was sitting on her sofa, lost in her own thoughts and texting a friend. She was vaguely aware of her 7-year-old twin girls, squabbling together, and half-heartedly called over to her daughter Grace, 'Stop annoying your sister!' Grace cried out in distress and ran up the stairs in tears, feeling blamed and picked on when really it was her sister who had hit her on the head with a toy, which Rachel had missed.

Grace came back downstairs and continued to niggle her sister as Rachel watched with increased irritation. Her irritation grew until she suddenly got up, snatched the toy they were arguing over out of Grace's hand and said 'I'm going to throw this toy away. If you can't play nicely you won't play at all!'

You are now hopefully more aware of the reference points on your Parent Map and the types of emotions that arise for you in the midst of your parenting. Noticing what triggers you to feel certain feelings, and act a particular way is hugely important. Next, we would like to help you to think more about how being more aware of what you're feeling can help you to *manage* your emotions when you are interacting with and responding to your child. In the example above, Rachel could start to think about all the things that are making her irritable and unable to think about what is going on really with her children, but she also needs to start to think about how she can manage this irritation if she is going to make any changes in these tiresome interactions.

The emotional thermometer

There's an expression, 'strike when the iron is hot' – to act decisively and take your opportunities as they arise, however, when it comes to our emotions, this isn't always the best advice. Often it is better to wait until our feelings have cooled a little, especially when it comes to responding to our children – and to strike when the iron is *warm* rather than hot. One of the first ways to manage how you are feeling, then, is to use this thermometer as a gauge of when it's best to act, and when it might be better to wait. Most of us are inclined to leap in when our emotional thermometer is near to boiling. Let's think about how you could use this thermometer more helpfully so that situations between you and your children don't escalate beyond your control.

Imagine that you have a thermometer with a red or silver line in the middle that moves up and down as it responds to the temperature. However, instead of measuring temperature, this thermometer measures your emotional arousal: how intensely you are experiencing a feeling. On the thermometer there is an 'ideal' range, where you are able to use your emotions in a constructive and informative way when interacting with your children. If the thermometer is too cold, indicating that there is little or no emotional intensity, this makes it difficult for you to identify how you feel, to connect with your mind and be aware of what you are experiencing. With little awareness of your own emotions, it then becomes hard to connect with your child in a meaningful way. When the emotional thermometer gets too hot, indicating high emotional arousal, it means you are vulnerable to becoming overwhelmed by your feelings and more likely to act impulsively, as we can see in the example of Rachel.

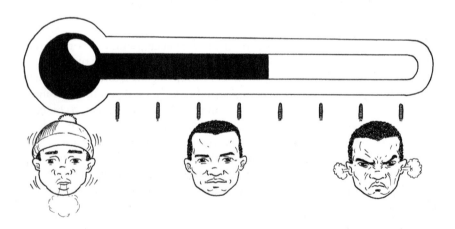

Being in a 'warm' emotional range is ideal as it means you are likely to be more aware of what is going on in your mind, which then makes you more receptive to your child. But how can you keep in this range? In this chapter, we look at strategies that can alter the level on your emotional thermometer, bringing it into a range that makes your interactions with your child go more smoothly and leads to better understanding between you and your child. We are going to help you to bring your temperature into a range where you are able to be more reflective. Try out the following strategies as you interact with your child:

1. Recognising and labelling feelings – where are you on the thermometer?

Let's start with the obvious, what are you feeling? Most of us remain unaware of the emotions we are experiencing much of the time. In fact, when everything is going well we can get by without really having that much awareness of exactly what we are thinking and feeling. However, if you want to make some changes in your parenting style, then it is important to take a step back and start to consciously think about how you are feeling so that you can bring this awareness into your new style of Reflective Parenting. You won't need to be doing this all of the time – that would feel odd and a little stilted – but it is a helpful first step, and also helps you to separate out what is going on in your own mind from the things that are going on in the mind of your child. In the example at the beginning of the chapter, Rachel would start to become aware of her general level of irritation, which may be related to a text message she was getting from her friend, or a leftover mood from a previous event in the day. Recognising the feeling and owning it as hers is an important first step.

> 'What am I feeling right now?' Imagine you are asking yourself this question whilst you look at yourself from the outside.

So, although we may be largely unaware of how we are feeling from moment to moment, there are other times when we can be jolted into thinking about our thoughts and feelings, when something happens that shifts our attention on to ourselves. Let's look at the following example:

Karen was driving to work one day and listening to some music on the car radio, not really thinking about anything much at all, when suddenly a dog without a lead ran across the road, right in front of her car. Without looking in the rear-view mirror she braked suddenly, and then noticed that the people who were queuing at the bus stop were all looking in her direction, probably alerted by both

It's so important to reflect on what goes on in your mind.

the sound of the car tyres and the dog on the loose (which she had managed to avoid). Her heart was pounding, and Karen felt pretty furious, not only at the dog and the missing owner who had let him run off, but at the thought that she might have caused a crash, injured someone else and possibly injured herself. The feelings were strong, but also relatively short-lived, but notably, she couldn't fail to notice them. In the heat of the moment, though, Karen certainly wasn't able to do much thinking (not reflectively at least) about the consequences of what she was doing, or of what else might have been going on around her. We could say that in this moment, due to *being highly emotionally aroused, Karen had a lapse in being able to think about others.*

Sometimes then, when we are forced into feeling a strong emotion, such as the example of Karen, we become compromised in our ability to think about what might be going on in the mind of our child. If you imagine in the above scenario that Karen had had her three children with her in the car, with Sam telling her that he had too much homework again and was feeling fed up, and Maddy complaining that Molly gets away with behaving badly in the car, understandably Karen would have found it difficult to turn her mind to what they were thinking and feeling. Using an emotional thermometer at this time, to become more aware of the impact that being in this boiling range has on her ability to think about other people's minds, would be helpful in preventing a possible conflict between Karen and her children as she struggles to take notice of their thoughts and feelings.

Once we start to think about noticing our thoughts and emotions, we can then develop our ability to be a more reflective parent by noticing those times when it is more or less difficult to identify these thoughts and emotions, as this will inevitably vary from day to day and circumstance to circumstance. In the previous example we can see that there are times when you can't help but notice how you feel because you are jolted into this awareness by something so arousing that it's impossible *not* to acknowledge your feelings. The rest of the time, though, when we aren't in a state of high emotion, our awareness of how we are feeling varies.

This means you might not know where a growing feeling comes from or how a feeling might be influencing you in a situation. The more you are able to name what you feel, the more you can bring the feeling into your awareness and moderate it if necessary. Sometimes just this action can lower the intensity of a feeling. Take this example of Lisa picking up her daughter from nursery after work:

Lisa rushed out of work to her car, increasingly preoccupied with whether she would miss the terrible rush-hour traffic on the main road out of town and be in time to collect her daughter Ella. As she swerved out of her parking space, she narrowly avoided hitting a colleague in the car park. A beep from a car behind jolted Lisa into thinking about what was going on. She managed to think to herself 'I am stressed, I am not calm.' She then was able to start saying other things to herself that helped her feel less stressed. 'There is nothing I can do to get to the nursery any quicker. I don't want to have an accident.'

Becoming more aware of how she felt in the moment meant that Lisa was more able to rationalise her feelings and then lower her emotional temperature. Once Lisa understood what she was feeling, she was better placed to understand what she needed to do, which was to calm down and realise that she could not do anything about the traffic. The other advantage of being aware of how she was feeling is that Lisa was able to separate out her own feelings from other people and things going on around her. On another day though, Lisa might have really struggled to do this, as, like the rest of us, it is not always easy to reflect on our emotions in the moment. Awareness of your own feelings then, will help you to separate out your mind from other people's, and this is a great step towards becoming more reflective and being able to mentalize about other people.

Being aware of our emotions helps us to notice what else is going on around us, so it's good to accept and embrace our feelings. And just as being aware can help us to moderate our emotions, being unaware can have the opposite effect. In the previous example, Lisa said that when she was unaware of what she was feeling, she acted like a robot fuelled by strong emotion. Very strong feelings still make us act and interact, but in autopilot, and often in ways that are unhelpful. For Lisa, the jolt of a car horn helped her to switch off from autopilot and made her think about her feelings, bringing them back into her awareness. You might think back to the last time you had an argument with someone and recall that your strong emotions made you say or do things that you later regretted, and perhaps later on when you were able to think back you could start to think about the reasons you felt annoyed in the first place and perhaps think that the strength of your reaction and feelings might have been out of proportion with what you said in the heat of the argument.

It can be difficult to acknowledge some of the feelings that are related to parenting – perhaps you feel guilty about negative emotions and think that you shouldn't have them. But it is normal for parents sometimes to feel bored, angry, hopeless and depressed in relation to parenting, and this is not surprising when you consider what a life-changing experience having children is. However hard it might seem to be aware of your thoughts and feelings, it is important to try not to deny them, or to increase negative emotions by feeling guilty for having these feelings. It is also important to acknowledge that for some people it can take a long time to adjust to becoming a parent.

When Matt and Rachel lived together, and Grace and Lilly were little, the twins cried a lot. Matt used to detach himself from their crying and imagine himself in another place. He would start to think about his past travelling experiences and feel far away in his mind. He said that it took him a couple of years before he could really start to understand what the crying was about, and how he could do something to respond to it and make it better. By connecting with his feelings of wanting to remove himself when his twin daughters wouldn't seem to stop crying, Matt was able to reflect on the difficulties of parenting, and also on his need to manage this feeling and try to help his daughters to settle with his help.

For others, this response comes much more naturally and quickly, but everyone will learn these things at a different pace and the first step is to just acknowledge these feelings and think about what they mean.

2. Watch, listen and step back

Another way to start managing the emotions that are brought into your awareness when you are interacting with your child is to take a step back from the feelings. Recognizing and labelling how you are feeling makes that feeling 'visible': a feeling that is seen, felt and thought about. Once you learn to name feelings in this way, you can try the following technique.

Once a feeling comes into your awareness, wait before you do anything else. Step slightly away from the feeling, which can sometimes stop you reacting immediately. Once you've stepped back from the situation, watch and listen, maybe only for ten seconds, and then see what happens and what you notice.

When Tom walked through the door on his return from work, he was immediately bombarded by his children's demands. He had been aware in the car that he was feeling stressed from his day at work; there were some difficult meetings and conversations that had really irritated him. The fact that he had identified how he was feeling meant he was able to check himself before responding to his children. He stopped and closed his eyes for five seconds and consciously told himself he was stressed by the difficult day. When Tom opened his eyes, he paused and just watched the scene unfolding in front of him – like an observer removed from a scene. This helped Tom to name what was happening around him without judgement. What he saw was that he was home, away from work. He saw Maddy, Sam and Molly eager to interact with him after missing him all day. He also recognized that the fact that he was not at work meant that he was away from his main stress. His stress was about something that had happened earlier, not about anything that was happening now. He saw his children's excitement at seeing him home. He immediately felt pleased about this and put down his coat and gave them all a hug, and started to enter into their world, leaving his own day behind.

In this example Tom was able to access his feelings and in doing so he learnt that his feelings were really to do with events that had happened before he arrived home. He also had an increased awareness of his children's excitement at seeing him, which he might otherwise have missed if he had remained preoccupied by the day's events at work.

What could you learn from a situation if you listened to your feelings? The next time you experience a negative feeling, try to let it into your awareness more fully, pause and watch. What do you see? By watching and stepping back, and waiting for the thermometer to be warm, it is more likely that the interaction between you and your children will be a positive one.

On a note of caution, this technique can be extremely difficult if the scale on your emotional thermometer is too high. Watching, waiting and wondering is almost impossible when you are experiencing very strong feelings in the heat of the moment. If you think back again to the last time you were involved in an argument with someone close to you, it was probably impossible to wonder about what you were feeling – you were too caught up in it. In arguments, we are classically unable to mentalize well – to think about the thoughts and feelings of other people – so later on when the emotional temperature has come down is a good time to go back to thinking about what might have been going on in the mind of the person you were arguing with.

In this case we would recommend that you walk away from the situation if you cannot think clearly about how you think and feel. You can then reflect on what happened when your ability to observe your feelings returns, and your emotional temperature has gone down. If you imagine that you are driving your car with your children in the back, and suddenly a cyclist, who has been in your blind spot, shouts loudly that you were about to run right into him, you are unlikely in that moment to be able to observe your own feelings and step back from them. You would probably just feel shocked, maybe even angry. However, you might be able to do this later, when your emotional thermometer has cooled down.

You can even share this image of a thermometer with your child and tell them that you are a bit too overheated to think clearly right in that moment. You can also check in with your child about where they are on the emotional thermometer as young children can become so consumed with feelings to the point that thinking and even talking rationally becomes impossible. Asking your child whether they are hot, warm or cold may be easier for them to connect with than asking them what they are feeling and why. For example, think back to the last time your child had a full blown tantrum, or when your older child was much younger. Were they able to articulate how they felt, or were they writhing on the floor, or stamping their feet, red-faced with fury or screaming? Letting your child know that we all have moments where our thermometer becomes too hot to be able to explain to each other clearly what is going on in our minds can be really helpful, and allowing them to cool down and explain later is often a better way to resolve a tantrum than trying to get to the bottom of it in the heat of the moment.

It might be quite difficult to think that a feeling is temporary and may pass if it is a particularly strong one, but it is important to realise that feelings pass, no matter how strong or difficult they are. This technique of watching, listening and stepping back, helps you to deal with negative emotions, unless they are extremely intense. It encourages you to accept a feeling in the moment that you are feeling it, to put up with it for a short while. That's it, nothing more. It will pass. Whatever the strength of the emotion, all feelings are transitory. We find that parents and young people alike can become quite anxious when they experience an intense, particularly negative, emotion as the accompanying thought is often 'I'm always going to feel like this', so knowing that all feelings are temporary is really helpful.

3. How am I coming across? Looking at yourself from the outside

Another strategy that will help you to manage the emotions that arise during the course of parenting is one that can help both in the heat of the moment with your child, or after an event, when you are thinking about what happened.

We are often unaware of how we're coming across to others, unless we are acutely self-conscious. However, we can learn to be aware of our body language and tone of voice, which are responsible for a significant proportion of our communication. Being conscious of how you're coming across to others when you are experiencing negative emotions is really important. Children are very receptive to subtle communication cues and are sensitive to the whole range of emotions. So, without you being aware of it, a negative feeling in you will be communicated rapidly and automatically to your child, and will impact on him. The main point is not that your negative feelings will necessarily damage or traumatize your child, but that they can affect his emotional state and lead to an increase in disruptive behaviour. His behaviour will then impact on how you feel, creating a cycle of escalating emotions.

Lisa came downstairs early in the morning, following Charlie who had got up again at 5.45 a.m. Charlie was sitting happily on the sofa, but Lisa was irritated and frustrated at being woken so early and her face was communicating this in a scowl. Charlie saw this and immediately felt upset and sulky. 'Is it my fault you feel so grumpy mum?' The impact of Lisa's face on Charlie was to make him experience a strong emotion, and he may have felt blamed or experienced shame – these are hard feelings for children to manage and can be easily avoided with a simple change in the parent's expression.

In the above example we are not criticising Lisa or judging her to be wrong, and indeed situations like this probably happen in most households each day. However, what we are highlighting is the importance for Lisa to be *aware* of how she looks to her child. If Lisa could have imagined what she looked like to Charlie – if she could have seen herself through his eyes – she might have been able to change her expression and so influence the communication with her son. These are small details that can have a large impact on your relationship. Importantly, Lisa might have managed to create an interaction where she could talk to Charlie about why she was feeling frustrated. Or she might simply have checked his expression, realising that the situation wasn't important enough to make him feel bad about it. The main point is that in failing to take note of how her emotions were coming across to Charlie, she actually made an already tricky interaction between them even more difficult and upsetting for both of them.

Imagine being able to make a movie of your life. You could record yourself, perhaps playing with your child, or sitting around the dining table together at mealtimes. You could press a pause button and notice the moments when things were going really well, the moments when you felt very in tune with your child, and you could see what you did to help that happen. In our work, we use a technique with parents called Video Interaction Guidance (1) (see Introduction), which gives us the advantage of being able actually to do this. By filming a parent and child in an everyday interaction, we can then show back clips to the parents, highlighting times when they were managing to interact and relate in ways that were positive and helpful for their child's development. Of course, none of us has the luxury of this in our everyday lives, where it can often feel more like a fast-forward button has been pressed rather than the pause button, especially at hectic times, such as getting everyone ready in the mornings. However, when you start to notice your own feelings, you can then reflect on how you are coming across – try imagining you are on video and thinking about how your actions might look from the outside – which is a very important step towards being able to notice, and ultimately change, the impact that you are having on your child. Video Interaction Guidance is really great for showing parents what happens when they change their body language towards their child. For example, parents can actually see how looking interested, maintaining eye contact and having a friendly voice and posture encourages children to interact. Video work is particularly helpful for parents who have a negative perception about their relationship because it helps to highlight how, when they are positive in their interactions, and aware of how they feel, this has a magical effect on their children and how they interact. And although as parents we generally don't get to see ourselves in action with our children, we can use the principle of imagining an audience to check our responses and think about how our children experience us.

We've all got footage of our children, family and friends on our smart phones or tablets, but more often than not, we don't feature in these clips. We're the cameraman and camerawoman, the observer of others. But imagine if you were in the film yourself, alongside these other important people in your life. How do you look? As well as thinking about yourself in a snapshot of time like this, you can take a look at your life over a longer period of time and see how your decisions and patterns of behaviour are affecting your relationships. Take the following example:

When Ella was born, Lisa gave up a full-time job to look after both her and Charlie, and she found herself setting a series of goals to achieve, in order to feel that she was being a good parent. She developed a whole checklist, including making sure they had a healthy meal each day, an outdoor activity, spent only an allotted amount of time on any screens, visited friends, had playdates . . . the list got bigger as Lisa set out what she felt was her job of being a part-time stay-at-home mum with two young children.

When Lisa reflected on what she might have looked like relentlessly working her way through this list each day, mentally checking that she had achieved all her goals, she saw that often she didn't enjoy spending time with her children and that frequently they seemed unhappy. She saw that trips to the park were sometimes greeted with screams and complaints about being too tired, and reflected that this might be the result of her setting such a full schedule in a bid to meet her daily targets. She saw that she was stressed around the children, preoccupied with this list of things to achieve, and ultimately felt unrewarded by her children, who seemed not to appreciate this huge effort she felt she was making. Looking at herself from the outside at this 'ideal' mother she had created, Lisa saw a stressed-out, slightly anxious woman rushing around trying to pack everything in, out of synch with her children. The pace of the day looked exhausting, even to her, when she examined it from the outside looking in.

Lisa made a decision to change the focus from her own goals to her children's needs and interests. Following the children's lead, she first noticed that the pace of the day was a lot, lot slower. A morning that had previously been filled with a baking session, a trip to the park, preparing a healthy meal, and a visit from a friend with similar-aged children, shifted to something altogether different. As she watched this new 'film' of herself, it was as if someone had hit the slow-play button. Following the children's lead, everything seemed to take much longer, and yet the interactions between Lisa, Charlie and Ella looked much more enjoyable, for everyone involved.

4. Remembering your child is just a child

Rachel was getting increasingly annoyed with Grace, who was whining that she didn't want her mum to keep stopping on the journey back from school, chatting to other mums on the way. She started to play up and looked sulky and Rachel snapped at her to 'grow up and act your age'. Grace hung her head in shame, feeling upset at being embarrassed by her mum in front of others and feeling unable to manage how she was feeling in that moment.

Being a reflective parent means you are able to accept that there may be different perspectives to take on why your child has behaved in a particular way. It follows therefore that having fixed assumptions about the motivations behind your child's behaviour can be a large barrier to being able to adopt a fresh perspective. In the example above, Rachel was expecting Grace to act like an adult and to be patient and interested even in the conversations she was having with her friends on the way home. She had perhaps forgotten that a 7-year-old at the end of the school day is tired, wants some time with her mum and is susceptible to being easily embarrassed if attention is drawn to her (particularly negative attention) in front of other people. Her instruction to her daughter to 'grow up' means that Grace isn't allowed to act her age and express the kind of emotions that go along with being a 7-year-old child. This causes a great deal of confusion for children as they are experiencing a set of emotions that are real and intense, whilst simultaneously being told they shouldn't feel this way, but should instead be behaving a certain way and experiencing a different set of feelings that are perhaps more appropriate for an adult.

Often, though, we are unaware that we are carrying around underlying assumptions, which makes it tricky to identify and challenge them. Moreover, we have found that many parents have assumptions about their children's abilities that, developmentally, are just not possible. A helpful statement to hold in your mind is 'My child is just that – a child', he has a child's view of the world and childlike abilities that will develop only as he grows older. Remembering this can really help you to reduce negative emotions either during a difficult interaction or when reflecting on one afterwards. For example, if you, like many parents, assume your child is knowingly manipulating you into getting something he wants, or crying because he wants to upset you, then this can be infuriating. However, are young children really capable of deliberate manipulation in the way that it can feel to parents? Do children understand other people in such a sophisticated way? By assuming that a child is doing something so knowingly and deliberately, the parent is attributing grown-up, adult characteristics to the child. Often parents feel manipulated, or feel upset, and think therefore this must be the case – that their child has set out to do something to upset them. Remember, our strong feelings can affect our understanding of other people, so we think 'because I feel manipulated that means I am being manipulated'. However, it is important to have more realistic assumptions about what your child is capable of. Children are constantly learning to understand other people, and this process continues. Although children are extremely sensitive to how their parents feel, and react to how they act, in terms of truly and accurately understanding their parents, they are a long way off. Remembering that your child is just being a child – with limited emotional capabilities – can help you not to react strongly to them.

5. Recruiting supports

Another important way to help you manage your emotions is to think more deeply about how you can get help from other people. Underpinning the model of Reflective Parenting is the principle that we influence and are influenced by other people, and that something good can come out of relating to others in a thoughtful way. It follows then that when you are struggling with parenting issues, support and understanding from friends and family is really beneficial and actually helps you to become a more reflective parent. Drawing on other people's experience or just talking things through and feeling understood all support a more reflective stance.

You can start to seek support early on, even in pregnancy, by talking to others, especially other parents or prospective parents, about your thoughts and experiences, which will also help you to think about the baby growing inside you. And once in the world, seeing the adults around him enjoy supportive and understanding relationships will show your child the benefits of relating to other people.

It's worth mentally compiling a network of supportive adults who are interested in you and how you see things. It's also worth looking into parenting groups such as antenatal groups, parenting groups or local parent support groups, and finding drop-in cafes where parents can meet and talk. If you find this hard, or are feeling especially isolated, online chat groups and forums can be good places to start to feel more connected to other parents. Finding a place where you can talk honestly and openly about yourself and your struggles as a parent is really important, and we would advocate that finding relationships where you can talk about your own feelings and not just what your baby or child is doing is vital.

6. Forgiving your child's behaviour and self-acceptance

As parents we can all easily feel filled with self-criticism and self-doubt about the way we acted and felt in a particular moment with our children. At the same time, in the midst of difficult interactions, we can feel critical towards our children and find it difficult to let feelings go. There's no doubt that parenting is a really difficult job for almost everyone at least some of the time. So it can be very helpful to remember that we all act on strong feelings at times; sometimes it is really hard not to act, and not to do and say things we regret. This applies to you and your actions as a parent, and also to how your child acts. So this strategy is about being able to accept that you have strong feelings and sometimes act in ways you are not happy with, and having the same acceptance of your child, too. Children find strong emotions extremely difficult to cope with, and intense feelings often manifest in their actions, influencing what they do.

Parents who have a history of trauma, or even just difficult experiences, can be overwhelmed by thoughts and feelings, making it even harder to think about what is happening in another person's mind. We have shown how understanding your own history, including your own experience of being parented, is important to your ability to think about other people's feelings and states of mind. These early experiences also govern how comfortable you feel with closeness. If you had an early experience of feeling insecure with your parents, you will probably find it harder to see your child's actions, and those of others, for what they really are. None of us can change our early history, but we can't emphasise enough that history does not need to be destiny, that is that patterns from the past do not need to be repeated in the present or future, and an awareness of our feelings, however complicated and troubling they might seem, is part of the path towards developing a different, hopefully secure, relationship with your own child. Equally, developing a more rounded, or flexible, view of your own early history is important, as even childhoods that had traumatic or insecure aspects to them could also have featured love, pleasure and intimacy. Accepting then that you had these experiences in your childhood, and that they have shaped who you are and how you feel, is an important strategy when trying to bring your temperature into the right range in your interactions with your child. An understanding of your own inside story, and the history of relationships that helped to form this story, will help you to bring the temperature on your emotional thermometer into a range where you can think more clearly about your child and what's going on in his mind.

Being able to forgive yourself and accept your feelings is an important step in managing your emotions and moving towards Reflective Parenting. Acceptance and forgiveness of yourself for experiencing a certain emotion or state of mind is all part of thinking in a more flexible and reflective way. In other words, it is a good thing generally to be aware of your feelings, even when these are difficult or unpleasant. Conversely, if you are frequently judgemental about your own and others thoughts and feelings, this will have a major impact on your general emotional state, which in turn will impact on how you handle important relationships.

In Chapter Four we will introduce you to our tool to help you apply Reflective Parenting – a concept known as the Parent APP, an approach to parenting that highlights three important elements that we think are crucial to becoming truly reflective in your parenting. Armed with some ideas of the things you want to plot on your Parent Map which you know have influenced your feelings and parenting, and with some tools for managing your emotions better, the Parent APP is the next step. We will show you how to use this in your everyday interactions with your child. We hope that it will really help both you and your child to feel better connected.

REFLECTIVE PARENTING
SUMMARY
THE EMOTIONAL THERMOMETER

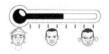

What it is . . .

The Emotional Thermometer is a way of keeping in mind how strong your feelings are at any given moment. Use this thermometer as a gauge of when it's best to act, and when it might be better to wait.

It helps you by . . .

The Emotional Thermometer helps you become more aware of what you are feeling and how intensely you are experiencing the feeling. This awareness will allow you to find ways to reduce the impact of your feeling and bring you into a calmer state of mind.

It helps your child by . . .

The Emotional Thermometer helps your child because the more regulated you are feeling when you interact with him, the less likely you are of over-reacting. Your child will see that you take responsibility for your feelings.

It helps your relationship by . . .

Keeping in mind your emotional thermometer makes it less likely situations will escalate beyond control and will help you to understand your child's feelings and bring you closer together.

Keep in mind . . .

1. Use the concept of the emotional thermometer as a gauge of when it's best to act, and when it might be better to wait.
2. Notice your thoughts and emotions to develop your ability to be a more reflective parent.
3. When you start to notice your own feelings, you can then reflect on how you are coming across.
4. Use friends and networks to help you.
5. Be accepting of how you feel and how your child feels.
6. Remember your child is just a child, with a separate and totally different set of thoughts and feelings from you, which represent both his age and the things going on in his life.

© 2016 Alistair Cooper and Sheila Redfern.

4

THE 'PARENT APP'

Have you ever wondered what goes on inside your child's head?

Maddy (aged 12) came to the dinner table after the third time of her mum calling her to come to eat. She brought her mobile phone with her and carried on texting her friends as her mum Karen tried to engage her in a conversation about her day.

Karen: 'How did the end-of-year tests go today Maddy?'

Maddy shifted uncomfortably in her chair, and picking at her food, hung her head down whilst she carried on texting her friend.

Karen: 'Maddy! Can you get off your phone please, I'm asking you a question.'
Maddy: 'Er, what? What did you say?'
Karen: 'I was asking how your tests went?'
Maddy: 'Er, can't remember.' *She carried on texting.*

Maddy's dad, Tom, who has been watching this interaction, suddenly explodes, 'Maddy, come OFF your phone, eat your dinner, and show some respect to your mum.'

Maddy pushes her plate away, gets up from the table and yells, 'I'm going to my room, nobody around here has a clue what's going on in my life.'

Karen: 'What was all that about? How am I supposed to know what goes on inside her head?'

By now you will be familiar with a few of the fundamental principles to becoming more reflective in your parenting, the central aim of which is to raise a happy, secure and resilient child. The focus in the previous chapters has been on how to start to notice your own emotions, where these have come from, and how, through developing a greater self-awareness, you can begin to bring your emotions a little more under control during interactions with your child. Now that you are following these principles, it will be easier to turn your mind to the mind of your child.

We have developed a stance called the Parent APP, which helps you see what is inside your child's mind and to connect you with what you think is in there. It will help you to attune to your child's experience by appreciating what is going on *inside* your child's mind, rather than simply responding to the behaviour he displays on the *outside*. This will give a whole new insight and meaning to your child's behaviour and can produce noticeable and tangible changes to your relationship. It will help you to avoid difficult interactions that we illustrated with Maddy and her mum (earlier) and show you that through starting to be curious about your child on the inside, you will both feel a greater connection. We have called this the Parent APP as it stands for three main elements. The elements of the Parent APP are:

Attention
Perspective Taking
Providing Empathy

Attention

The first element in your reflective attitude towards your child is attention. To understand your child, and the cues and messages underlying his behaviour, it is important to pay attention to him. This might seem obvious, but we mean paying attention in a special way, which includes being interested in him, watching him, turning towards him, and having a friendly posture while you watch and interact with him. This type of interaction will both appear and feel very different to your child from you simply looking at him. This is because when you pay attention in this meaningful way, you are more likely to let your child know that you are interested in him. Through our video work with parents (using Video Interaction Guidance), where the work is about becoming more attuned to your child, the first step is to help parents notice the positive impact of paying attention. Parents often are surprised and delighted to see how paying attention in this way encourages more fun and positive interactions.

Paying attention by definition involves being curious. When observing what your child is doing, there is always more going on than just what you can see. Being curious is the quality that helps us to be interested in seeing our child more from the inside – *why* he is behaving in a certain way, rather than paying attention only to what's happening on the outside – *what* he is actually doing. You can see from the example at the start of this chapter that this doesn't necessarily mean firing questions at your child about what they have been doing when they are not in the right frame of mind to talk, but it is more about showing a general curiosity for their state of mind. For example, it might be more helpful to ask yourself 'What is he feeling right now that is making this difficult to talk about?' In many ways, being attentive and curious are the most important qualities of Reflective Parenting as you are being actively interested about your child's thoughts and feelings. In the moments when you are able to be a reflective parent, you are being willing to be open to discovery about your child's actions and behaviours: you are interested in how your child experiences his world. This interest can start at day one of a child's life, and continue throughout childhood.

An ambulance whizzes past a window and 9-month-old baby Jack turns his head in that direction. His mum Rachel looks at her son then towards the window and back again, 'Oooh what was that sound? You seem to like that noise.'

Rachel is thinking about her baby: 'You are an interesting person who sees things in his own way and I'm interested in what you think about things.' She notices what her little boy notices, is curious in how Jack is experiencing her world and tries to understand his view on events that happen around him.

When you think about how to pay attention to your child, it's helpful to imagine how you will appear to him. Imagine if you are standing in a queue at the supermarket checkout and a baby in a buggy in front of you smiles. Your automatic response is likely to be to smile, raise your eyebrows, perhaps open your mouth in an exaggerated way and soften, or even use a sing-songy voice to say 'hello' back. This is the kind of attention we mean, having an animated facial expression, making sustained eye contact, taking an interested friendly posture, actively listening and encouraging and softening the tone of your voice – all these things will increase the impact of your paying attention from your child's point of view. Luckily, these factors will also make each interaction with your child a more interesting and enjoyable experience for you. You may become self-conscious about your behaviour and feel a little inhibited. Yet it's worth trying to overcome this feeling as we know how important a parent's responses are when we see the dramatic effect it has on a child when parents make positive changes to the way they communicate.

Imagine a parent notices their 2-year-old about to pull herself up onto the table with sticky hands and says, 'What are you doing?' This is said with an accompanying smile and outstretched arms, about to lift the child down from the table, and with a soft voice. In this way, by being aware of the impact of her own state of mind on her toddler's, and by adopting an open and friendly face, the parent can pay attention to what her child is doing, but manage her child's behaviour without the situation escalating into conflict and tantrums. For example, imagine if this scenario was dealt with in a different way. The parent comes into the room with an angry expression, shouts 'What ARE you doing?' and grabs her child down from the table. This may well get the child down quicker, but the resulting tantrum and upset in the child becomes the next problem for the parent to deal with. Often the resulting behaviour when taking this kind of authoritarian approach can be even worse than the original behaviour itself.

The same can be said for the type of questions that we parents often ask of our older children. How was your day at school? Who did you spend time with? What did you have for lunch? Whilst these types of questions are perfectly normal, they don't necessarily help you to connect in an emotional way with your child, in a way that makes them feel understood emotionally, or you feel close to them. Instead, your interest in what is going on inside your children might lead you to notice that they need to relax for a while before they are asked about their day.

The impact of paying attention

Stepping back and observing allows you to begin to wonder about what your child is doing, and what you notice can be the first steps in looking at an inside story that will enable you to understand his behaviour. Often parents feel they need to engage their children actively all the time, either feeling they have to take the lead in interacting with them or making sure they are always occupied with something. It might feel like a novel idea at first: just to stop and watch what your child is doing. However, a lot can be said for just enjoying watching your child, following their lead and wondering about what he is doing and thinking and what his motivations might be. One parent, observing her own behaviour, said:

> 'I used to overwhelm him a lot of the time. I thought I had to enter-
> tain and do something with my son all of the time and felt under
> pressure to show I was doing something. I had to learn that just
> watching and showing him I was interested in what he was doing
> was actually doing something. I guess I was following him.'

The impact of being attentive to what your baby or child is doing, thinking and feeling cannot be overestimated. Attention is one of the most powerful parenting tools you have, and both giving your attention to and withdrawing attention from your child has a very significant impact on how he thinks, feels and behaves. We often hear the phrase 'attention-seeking behaviour' used as a criticism of children, and sometimes adults. However, maybe the times when your child seems to act up to gain your attention are the cues to step back and be more attentive to him. Once you start to think about what seeking attention is for, then you can increase your understanding of what's going on inside your child's mind, and this in turn can lead to a fairly immediate shift in the interaction between the two of you. For your child, the experience of being paid attention to, experiencing your interest and curiosity, can feel great. This will be easier to do if you are both aware of and in control of your own emotional state first.

> Rachel was trying to feed 9-month-old Jack, who was fussing
> around and refusing to be fed. Rachel wanted Jack to hurry up
> as they were late in meeting some friends for a play date. She had
> already noticed herself becoming more frustrated with her baby

son, which she knew was probably disproportionate and unhelpful. She was getting nowhere with the feeding, so she decided to try and stop worrying about being late and just watch Jack instead. Rachel put the spoon down and said to Jack, 'It doesn't matter if we are late does it! What are you doing sweetie?' She then found herself beginning to actually feel more interested in what Jack was doing, and turned her attention away from her thoughts of getting ready to go out. As well as feeling interested, Rachel actually looked interested and had a friendly face, and noticed that Jack in turn looked up at her. Jack had noticed that his mum was watching him interestedly and he appeared to relax, caught his mum's eye again and smiled. Rachel and Jack carried on noticing each other, smiling. Rachel noticed that Jack was reaching out to the spoon and so she said 'Do you want the spoon? Did you want to hold it all this time sweetie? Ok, here you go, here is the spoon.' The result was that, in his own time, and under Rachel's watchful gaze, Jack began to eat his food, albeit more slowly and in a messy way.

When Rachel paid more attention to her son, adopting a friendly posture and expression, she was able to notice that Jack was interested in holding the spoon himself. Importantly, positive effects were experienced by both Rachel (who felt less frustrated) and Jack (who felt more at ease and able to eat in a relaxed way). The end result was for both of them to feel more connected to one another. This kind of mindful approach of just staying present and calm helped to make this feeling of connection a pleasant one for both mum and baby.

Being interested and curious about the reasons underlying your child's behaviour has further benefits to your interactions with your child. Let's look at an example of how curiosity can help.

Jon is playing with his two children in the park. He picks up his 6-year-old son Charlie and playfully pretends to throw him in a stream. His 4-year-old daughter Ella becomes immediately distressed and shouts 'Don't Daddy!' She then runs over to her mother and cuddles furiously into her, looking scared. Jon starts to think about what might be going on for his daughter and why she feels so strongly. A little later, Jon comes up to his daughter, deciding to follow his curiosity about why she might have got upset and worried, and said 'Did you think Daddy was really going to throw Charlie in the stream?' Ella looks away and buries her head in her mother's arm. About ten minutes later though she walked up to her dad and said 'I got scared Daddy didn't I?' Jon said back 'Yes, I think you did, did you think I was going to do it?' She replied, 'Yes, I thought Daddy was going to throw Charlie.'

In being curious like Jon you can actively show your child that you are interested in him and what's going on inside his mind, and that he is someone to be interested in. This example shows that Jon's curiosity in Ella's reaction, and his ability to share his curiosity with her, enabled his daughter to be curious herself about why she acted in that way. This teaches your child to think about his emotions more and what they mean. Over time, this is a really good way of helping your child to learn to regulate, or manage, his feelings. As a parent, you can sow the seed of curiosity in your child in this way, and over time your child will begin to show curiosity in others and wonder why others behave in the way they do.

You might also find that by adopting a genuinely curious stance about your child's actions, you will naturally be less critical towards his behaviour.

Tom was at the park when his 2-year-old daughter Molly indicated that she wanted to get out of the pushchair. Tom unbuttoned her straps and Molly immediately ran off. Tom felt a surge of anger within him (which he luckily recognized in himself) as he called out to shout to her to stop. Tom then remembered another dad talking to him about his son who also used to run off whenever he had an opportunity. This got Tom wondering why young children would want to run off and what doing this might feel like from Molly's perspective. His curiosity about the situation reduced his anger immediately as he thought about how much fun running off might be for his child (taking her perspective), and so he decided to playfully make up some running exercises for Molly, backwards and forwards, setting markers around the park for her to run to and turn around and run back. Molly had great fun, and Tom started to enjoy their time together at the park more.

Children love it when you really notice them, and pay attention in a friendly and curious way to what they are doing. To get a sense of how this attention feels to your child, it may help you to imagine how different it feels when you have someone's full attention when you are expressing yourself, compared with when you feel that you are being ignored, particularly when you are in a state of heightened emotion. It doesn't feel great to say the least. Attention and curiosity are the building blocks to your reflective attitude towards your child. Get this first quality right and become genuinely interested in your child's mind, and the next two qualities of perspective taking and empathy will follow quite naturally.

Perspective taking

The second quality to have in your interactions with your child is perspective taking. We tend to take for granted that, as adults, it can be hard to know what's going on inside someone else's head. Why don't we apply the same rule to our children? It can be easy to assume that a child sees the world through the same lens as his parents, or as parents that we know exactly what is going on in our child's mind but this is not the case.

Most of the time we interact reasonably well with those around us, accepting that we cannot know exactly how other people think. Although at times a struggle, we take a good guess about what another person is thinking or feeling. If we saw someone walking around a city with a map, checking backwards and forwards between a street name and the map, we might conclude that she is lost. While this is a more obvious scenario than trying to figure out why your child is upset or misbehaving, remembering that your child has a different set of thoughts and feelings from you, but that you can still take a guess at what these might be, can be helpful. Being accurate in our 'perspective taking', or getting another person's point of view, is of course desirable but in a way it is the effort to understand another person's perspective that is in itself valuable. This effort is all part of being curious and paying attention. When we think about parenting, and the sometimes bizarre and confusing behaviour of children, it is both normal and highly likely that you could be wrong about what you think your child is thinking and feeling, just as you can be wrong about the thoughts and feelings of your partner, friends and family.

The same experience can look very different from different perspectives, and sometimes in the heat of the moment, when a child is mid-tantrum, it can be easy to forget this. How often have you found yourself thinking that surely your child knows they are annoying or upsetting you? This kind of assumption is predicated on the (false) belief that your child can read your mind and knows what you're thinking, and is probably driven by you feeling either annoyed or upset.

It is important to note that children are not able to see things from another person's perspective fully until they are at least 3 to 4 years old. It is worth bearing this in mind because as parents we can often believe that our children are doing something intentionally to make us feel or act in a certain way. One parent said that she felt her child was repeating the same question over and over again 'just to wind me up'. Her friend wondered whether there might be other reasons why her child felt the need to ask the same question over and over again, on reflection the parent said that she thought her daughter might be 'anxious that she's not going to get what she really wants'. In this instance, taking the child's perspective, and tuning in to the emotion behind the questions, was a helpful move away from perceiving her daughter as trying to intentionally annoy her and move towards a more attuned relationship. Being aware of this developmental framework can help us to see that our 18-month-old toddler is not lying on the floor screaming because he wants to punish us, as this would involve a cognitive skill that he hasn't yet developed. It's more helpful to try to be curious about what it is that's making him feel quite so angry. So perspective taking involves not only trying to see what your child might be thinking, but also how he might be feeling. All the time, keeping in mind that this is quite likely to be something different from how you think and feel.

> *When they first had their twins, Grace and Lilly, Matt and Rachel were going on holiday and were arguing in the front of their car about who was supposed to have brought the keys to the holiday cottage they've been driving to for nearly five hours, and Grace and Lilly were crying in the back seat. If the babies could verbalise their feelings in this moment, they would probably say a whole range of things including, 'We've been sitting here being really still and quiet for nearly five hours now, and now we're tired and want to get out, and you are making us feel a bit frightened because you're shouting at each other, and we don't know if you like each other, or if you are cross with us as well?'*

Imagine if Rachel and Matt stopped their arguing and said some of what they thought might be going on in their babies' heads right at that moment. What would this feel like for Grace and Lilly? How might thinking about each baby's experience both help the parents to look at the impact their own emotions are having on the babies, and calm everybody down? If the main aim in that car were for everyone to reach their destination harmoniously, then trying to imagine how it feels for the two young babies would certainly be a very positive move forwards. For example, if Rachel and Matt stopped halfway to their cottage and said to Grace and Lilly, *'lets have a break now and get something nice to eat, you must both be getting really bored and fed up in the back all this time?'* and had organised their journey around the young twins' needs as well as their own, things may have gone a lot smoother. What is so noticeable when we start to do this with our children is how differently we then behave, and even our tone of voice changes. For just becoming aware of how our children might be feeling, rather than making an assumption about what is going on in their minds, has an immediate impact on how we feel and then behave. It is likely in the above scenario that once Rachel and Matt thought about the experience from their babies' point of view, they felt differently about arguing with each other during a long and tiring journey for their babies.

If you think about the times when you feel particularly strongly about your child's behaviour, it is quite likely that you experience negative emotions when your child is misbehaving and when you are feeling more stressed and harried than usual. Your feelings guide your perspective-taking ability, so if you find yourself feeling particularly stressed, angry or upset, it will be harder to step back and think about your child's perspective. It's easy then to misinterpret your child's behaviour. If you remember, one of the landmarks on your Parent Map is your current strong feelings, so by becoming aware of these influences on your parenting, you can then learn how to manage your own emotions. All of which will help you to step back and think about your child's mind and their own particular experience of the world.

All too often we can let our emotions get the better of us and lead us into interactions and altercations with our children that we later regret. Understanding and accepting your child's state of mind, and noting the difference between their mind and yours, is not the same as accepting their behaviour, which you might feel quite rightly was extremely challenging and unacceptable. What is really interesting to observe is how when you do make an effort to see things from your child's point of view this can lead to a change in the very behaviour that you found challenging. This comes back to the concept of the power of being paid attention, and in addition to this, feeling understood. It's actually quite amazing to see how, following a little bit of understanding and perspective taking, children and adults alike can change both how they are feeling and how they are acting. Imagine if, in the first scenario of this chapter Karen, the mum, had said, 'I don't know if you feel like talking about the tests over dinner, or if you'd rather just forget about them for now and eat with us? I'm just happy to sit and have a meal with you.' It would be interesting to see if Maddy had then been able to open up about the school tests, feeling that her mum understood a little of her experience of being tired and fed up from the day. In the case of a younger child, watch how differently your child reacts if instead of shouting at him for not hurrying up with his tooth-brushing, you observe out loud how much of a rush it is in the morning sometimes for him, and if only there was a lot more time for brushing teeth.

Try taking this approach: next time your child is shouting, see if you can step away from your own emotional response and try to take the perspective that your child is shouting because he is having a problem managing how he is feeling. Your child may be behaving in a way that is unreasonable, but for a reason that is entirely reasonable.

Let's look at an example of this from a family with an 8-year-old child.

Karen and Tom and their three children were having a family bar-becue where their son Sam, who was eight at the time, had been bouncing on the trampoline with his cousins, who had become too boisterous. Karen asked Sam to come off the trampoline and go inside, but Sam refused. Karen tried to coax him in, but then her parents joined in and started telling her that she was 'too soft' and didn't know how to discipline her son. Feeling embarrassed and under pressure from her parents, Karen shouted at Sam to get off the trampoline and let his cousins stay on. Sam swore at his mum, and Tom laughed at this.

What might they have done differently if they had been more able to take other people's perspectives? Karen might have reflected that Sam was feeling upset about being pushed around by his cousins and then more upset that he was asked to come off the trampoline whilst they got to stay on. Karen might also reflect on her shouting and perhaps conclude that she had been feeling pressured by her family to act in a way that she didn't feel was her normal parenting style. If she had seen that this was her parent's perspective and not her own, then she would probably not have resorted to shouting. She also felt that Tom had undermined her authority by laughing at Sam's swearing, and Tom accepted that he had done this out of embarrassment. Karen and Tom could then start to think about Sam's mind, and how this differed from their own state of mind and perspective, which could help them handle the situation differently next time.

Some parents report being upset or worried that they do not understand why their children behave in specific ways. It can be reassuring as a parent to understand that it is normal to be puzzled by why a child is reacting or acting in a certain way and this does not make you a less competent parent. In fact there are times when puzzling about your child's mind is helpful. We are not mind readers so there will be plenty of times when we simply don't know what our children are thinking, and it is often helpful to say this out loud to your child, and show them that you really don't know what they are thinking – but by showing curiosity and interest, we may gain insight that will help us to influence our child's behaviour.

The impact on your child of perspective taking

There are important consequences of being good at taking another person's perspective. Not only does this help your child to understand his own mind, because you are showing that it is separate from yours, and is interesting with valuable thoughts and feelings, but also because exercising the ability to step into another's shoes is one of the most important elements of being socially skilled. This means that, not only are you working on your own relationship with your child when you think about what's going on inside his mind, but you are also helping him to become socially skilled – popular and well-liked. Research shows that there is a well-established link between perspective taking, secure attachment and popularity with friends (1). The impact of perspective taking on relationships, including siblings and friends, is explored in more detail in Chapter Seven.

Recent studies have found that having very poor perspective-taking skills is linked to social anxiety. Where children find it difficult to understand and manage social situations, this is largely due to being overwhelmed by a large group of people and different things they might be thinking and feeling. The anxiety this leads to in the child may also cause him to become hypervigilant to perceived 'threats' in his environment, and this combination of factors causes the anxiety to escalate.

Providing empathy

The final quality on the Parent APP is providing empathy, which is the part that helps you connect to what you imagine is inside your child's mind after you have used the stance of being curious and taking his perspective. When we talk about providing empathy we mean being able to understand and be sensitive to your child's feelings and points of view. The difference between perspective taking and empathy is subtle but important. While perspective taking just involves you appreciating that your child's view on events is different than your own, empathy involves an emotional response to how you think he is experiencing the event: it is being touched by how he is feeling and then letting him know that he has touched you. This is what helps make the connection between him and you. The ability to experience empathy within our relationships helps us to be more deeply attached to our family, friends, communities and even strangers. We could see someone begging for money on the street and either choose not to think about how the person might feel, or connect with what it must feel like to be homeless and hungry. Similarly, it's the experience of empathising with other people's distress that leads people to donate to charity. People feel for the victims or beneficiaries and this is further enhanced when they or loved ones have also been affected by the charity's cause, or they feel connected to a community or group. Feeling empathy makes us behave in a very different way.

Empathy is a human capacity that children themselves learn as they develop. As a parent, there are plenty of opportunities to provide empathy, for example when talking to your child about situations that happen at school, around exciting times, proud times, or particular events such as when your child brings a picture home from school. You might feel particularly empathic when your child is upset and you want to help him to get over this feeling, as empathy has incredible powers of changing emotions. It is easier to empathise with your child when they are upset but it can be much harder to empathise when he is angry. However, empathy can really help children when they feel angry. It can even help when you need to discipline your child; while you may need to tell him that an action was wrong, by also showing empathy, whether through a simple statement, a well-timed hug or a concerned look, you demonstrate in your interactions with him that you understand how he feels. Providing empathy has two important functions: connecting with your child's feelings and letting him know you get how he feels. When you feel empathy for your child you experience his experience, you imagine how he feels and walk in his shoes.

Lilly comes home from school and tells her mum Rachel about something that happened in the playground:

> *'Susan and Jade were playing a game in the playground mum and when I came out and asked to play they said I couldn't play. They walked away and played at the other end of the playground.'*
> *'Oh Lilly, I'm sorry to hear that! That sounds really hard, I bet you felt really hurt and left out!? You poor thing.'*
> *'Yes I did. I felt really sad, they didn't want to play with me.'*

In this example, Lilly's mum was imagining how Lilly must have felt in that situation by using her own feelings to guide her. By being open to her own feelings about Lilly in the situation, she was able to picture accurately how Lilly would have felt. It can be hard to really feel what your child is experiencing and so we need to work hard to try to tune in to their experience. We can't actually *feel* the same emotion that our child is experiencing, so it's important to try to imagine what that feels like and verbalise this.

For empathy to be effective, your child needs to know you get how he feels. It is not enough simply for you to get how he feels inside; you need to communicate your understanding to him in a way that is helpful. For empathy to be truly communicated to your child, spoken words need to be authentic, non-verbal communication needs to be matched with your words and the energy and vitality of your communication needs to be pitched at a level that fits with how your child is feeling.

It is a great feeling for your child when you stand alongside him, experiencing his feelings and connecting with his experience of an event. The impact of empathy on your child cannot be overestimated: it can be used positively in almost any aspect of raising children and in any situation. Combine a consequence for bad behaviour with a big dollop of empathy, rather than annoyance or anger, and see how much more effective this is. When we have suggested this to some parents we work with they sometimes ask:

'But wouldn't it weaken the effect of limits and consequences if I back off and be comforting by being empathic to my child?'

Parents can seem reluctant to recognise their children's feelings and perspective for fear that this will increase the negative behaviour they are facing. There is often an anxiety that it is somehow letting a child off the hook. However, providing empathy is not the same as comforting your child and saying 'Sorry, everything is going to be okay, let's forget about your behaviour.' Instead, for your child, it can feel comforting knowing you understand him. After all, empathy is communicating a sense that you get how your child feels. Being understood feels good and children thrive when they feel understood and acknowledged. So rather than reinforcing bad behaviour, when you provide empathy the opposite is true. Children are more likely to be cooperative when they feel their parents are trying to understand them. This is because the best and easiest way to get your child to understand your perspective is to connect with their experience first. In fact one of the most powerful tools in therapy is to communicate empathy and validation. Often only when a client feels understood and has a sense that their therapist genuinely gets and cares about their view can they hear what the therapist has to say. Having someone show them that they get how they feel helps people to hear about other points of view. The same applies to your child. Let's look at an example of this in the following conversation between a mother and her son. The mother asks:

'How come you got so angry at daddy just now?'
'Because he is so unkind and a horrible daddy.'
'Oh, what makes you say that?'
'Because he always bosses me around and tells me what to do!'
'Really, is that what you think? Wow that is really hard, that must feel so unfair to you.'
'It does, he doesn't like me!'
'Oh OK, well that's even harder having a dad you think doesn't like you! I'd really hate that if I thought my dad hated me.'
'I do hate it. It feels horrible.'
'Yes I bet it does. Yes, horrible. Well I'm sorry you feel so bad about it. You know it's probably hard for your dad as well!'
'Really, why?'
'He loves spending time with you but gets very frustrated when he asks you to do something more than three times.'

By being curious and communicating empathy, the parent here was able to help her son explore how he feels about his father. If she judged her son's perspective as being wrong and tried to correct him, he might have felt judged. Instead, she focused on his experience rather than fact. By listening and being empathic the child was able eventually to see the situation in a different way, because he first felt understood and accepted. When children feel this they are much more receptive to hearing other points of views.

The impact on your child of providing empathy

When children feel understood, they are more able to discover other people's perspectives. It is the same for adults. If you think about how you feel if a partner or friend really shows that they understands how you feel, you are much more likely to be interested in what *they* think or feel than if they show you no empathy. Providing empathy to your child, in how we have begun to suggest, will encourage his empathy for others. It is long recognised through research into the effects of ongoing traumatic events on children that the normal development of empathy in children can be significantly disrupted. When children have not been thought about and their thoughts and feelings not been cared about it makes it harder for them to think about others and care about how others feel. Lacking empathy for others can then get in the way of forming supportive relationships and being able to feel cared for.

One of the most important ways of trying to help your child manage, or regulate, how they are feeling is to validate his feelings. This is vitally important because it helps your child to be more comfortable with how he feels and to be reassured that he has a right to feel this way. In Chapter Five we look much more closely at this because conveying to your child that they are right to have the feeling they have is an important part of Reflective Parenting. Whatever the nature of the feeling, it is very real as far as your child is concerned, and to have this feeling either minimised or completely invalidated creates a great deal of confusion.

We feel it is really important to apply the Parent APP during interactions with your child, and to comment on and discuss emotional events and experiences. However, while this approach is helpful a lot of the time, it is important to keep in mind that it may not always be a good time to talk about things. Focusing on the inside all the time does not always feel comfortable for your child. Ask yourself whether it is a good time to interact with your child and see things from his perspective because as we have explored in previous chapters, your own stresses and strains at a particular moment can really get in the way of being reflective towards your child. Choosing the moment when you are emotionally calm and timing talks with your child when your child will be more receptive is important to the Parent APP's success. Don't force a discussion with your child when he can't cope with it.

REFLECTIVE PARENTING SUMMARY

THE PARENT APP

What it is . . .

The Parent APP is a stance which helps you to think about what might be going on inside your child's mind and to connect you with what you think is in there.

It helps you by . . .

The Parent APP will help you to appreciate what is going on *inside* your child's mind, rather than simply responding to the behaviour he displays on the *outside*. This changes your focus during interactions with your child and will help you have new insights and meaning to his behaviour.

It helps your child by . . .

Each time your interactions with your child follow the principles of the Parent APP you will be laying the foundations for his skills of perspective taking and empathy. It will also help develop his awareness of what he is thinking and feeling, too. This will make it more likely that he grows up relating well to others.

It helps your relationship by . . .

As the Parent APP helps you see your child from the inside, it will help you respond emotionally with how he is feeling and thinking. The result will be that you will both feel a greater emotional connection and understanding.

Keep in mind . . .

1. Start to notice and be curious about what might be going on in your child's mind.
2. Be more aware of your tone, expression and the words you use.

© 2016 Alistair Cooper and Sheila Redfern.

3. Be curious about what's going on inside your child's mind, show him you are interested in his inside story, rather than just what he does on the outside.

4. You cannot be expected to always know what his inside story is because you have separate minds. It is normal to be puzzled by why a child is reacting or acting in a certain way and this does not make you a less competent parent.

5. Taking your child's perspective will help him enormously. He doesn't see the world in the same way as you, and letting him know this will help you become more reflective, and him feel better understood by you. This leads to a better connection.

6. Show empathy to your child's feelings as when he feels understood and accepted he will be much more receptive to hearing your point of view.

7. Your child may be being unreasonable for a reasonable reason (forgive them). Understanding and accepting your child's state of mind doesn't mean you have to accept his behaviour.

8. Choose a moment when you are calm. You will find this makes the Parent APP more effective.

5

HELPING CHILDREN WITH THEIR FEELINGS

In our efforts to help our children navigate their way through life, it can be easy to make their behaviour the focus, rather than their feelings. But in many ways, helping your child to manage his feelings is the most important thing you can do as it not only impacts on his behaviour, but also on his relationship with you, and with others. All children struggle to manage their feelings, especially when they are tired and hungry, or if they really want something.

> *Lisa is in the local shop with her 6-year-old son Charlie, buying some bread and milk, when Charlie spots a magazine with a toy on it at the counter. He asks his mum if he can have the toy and Lisa says,*
>
> *'No, we've just come to get bread and milk, I'm not buying you a toy.'*
>
> *Charlie starts to whine and pulls at his mum's coat, 'I want it, why can't I have it?'*
>
> *Lisa replied, 'Because you can't have a toy every time we come into a shop. OK?'*
>
> *Charlie says, 'It's not fair. I want it.' He starts kicking his mum's ankle and cries, 'I want a toy, I want a toy.'*
>
> *He starts crying loudly and refuses to leave the shop so, with her son still crying, Lisa has to pull him by the arm out of the shop and walk home with him crying all the way. By the time they get home, both are exhausted, upset and angry.*

Have you ever been in this kind of situation? Have you wondered 'why can't my child just stop crying, accept what I'm saying and learn to move on?' How would the situation be different if Charlie's mum could help him manage his feelings? And why is this so important in the first place?

There are three main reasons why it is important to know how to support your child to help him understand and cope with his emotions:

1. To help him in his development

When your child first came into the world he was not born with the ability to understand how he was feeling and why he had feelings. For babies, feelings are diffuse, all encompassing, overwhelming experiences, because they have underdeveloped brains. He needs your help and support whilst his brain matures to deal effectively with strong feelings and this continues well into childhood and even adolescence.

2. His emotions greatly influence his behaviour

If your child becomes more practiced at understanding his feelings and managing them more successfully, he will be less likely to react strongly or behave impulsively. Keeping in mind the link between emotions and behaviour will make it easier for both you and your child to understand the inside story behind how he acts and help bring some stability to his relationships.

3. It will help you stay connected with him during conflict

If you do not see your role in helping him with his emotional experience, and instead focus solely on his behaviour, it will be harder to resolve situations. In some circumstances you might actually inflame the situation and create disconnection, and then conflict can often last much longer. This is because his brain will be overheating with emotion, which means he will be unable to think about what he is doing, let alone manage his behaviour.

With these three reasons in mind, we will now turn to some strategies to help your child manage his emotions.

Strategies for helping your child manage his emotions

As the example at the start of this chapter illustrated, when your child's emotions get the better of him, it's easy for both him and you to feel overwhelmed, and this quickly leads to a breakdown of the connection between the two of you. There are several strategies you can try to help your child to manage his feelings, and to help you stay connected to your child at the same time. In the next chapter we look in more detail at how the misunderstandings you have with your child can actually be used to build a better understanding between the two of you and to help strengthen your relationship. However, this is most effectively achieved when your child has calmed down and his emotional temperature has cooled slightly, as only then will you be able to think together about what happened.

The following is a list of strategies that you can try and keep in mind, which can work on their own or in combination, depending on the situation and the intensity and type of feelings your child is experiencing.

Empathy and validation

The main aim of being empathic and validating to your child's experience is that it will help him feel understood by you, and the impact of being understood is that it will lessen his emotional experience. Thus, expressing empathy and validation is a helpful way of trying to help your child manage how he is feeling and is important because it helps you connect with your child at the same time. It also conveys to your child that he is right to have the feeling he has, which is an important part of Reflective Parenting. The impact on a child of not feeling understood can have the opposite effect:

> *Ella was feeling very unhappy about her Grandma coming to look after her while her Mum and Dad went off to a wedding for the whole day. At first she grumbled at the talk of Grandma coming to stay for the day, and then became quite rude and angry about her. Eventually, by the time her Grandmother arrived she was crying that she didn't want to see her, and she 'didn't like' Grandma anyway. Ella's parents told her off for being rude to Grandma, and told her 'You should be happy to spend the day with your lovely Grandma. She wants to play with you.'*

In this example, Ella wasn't allowed to feel angry or upset, or even express anything negative about her Grandma. For her, the feeling was connected with not wanting her Mum and Dad to go away for the day, and her upset about this was related to feeling that she hadn't spent much time with them all week. Usually on Saturdays they all did something nice together, and now she was being left out. Ella's feelings weren't validated and she felt that she was not understood, and as a result became increasingly angry and upset. Moreover, she was told that she should be experiencing a different feeling to the one she had, and so she started to get really confused about why she didn't feel the way her Mum and Dad said she should.

As you are aware, providing empathy is part of the Parent APP, and is a quality we have encouraged you to bring to your interactions with your child in order to connect with what you imagine is going on inside his mind.

Being able to make an accurate statement about what you think is going on inside your child's mind is an excellent way of helping your child to be able to manage his emotions, and also helps him to feel better connected to you. An important part then of showing empathy and validation is to have a mind-minded approach to your child.

When your child is having an emotional outburst, you may not feel like being empathic, however, empathic statements can show your child that you understand how it feels to be him, and this can really help to calm the situation and stop it from escalating further. Empathy has a strong emotional component to it, where you show your child that you get and feel what he feels. Empathy mirrors back a feeling that matches what your child is feeling. Naming and mirroring back the feeling in your face in a marked way is important. When your expression matches how your child feels this is known as marked-mirroring. We all do this quite naturally much of the time, but when we are preoccupied with something, or overwhelmed with a strong emotion ourselves, it can be much harder to mirror in our face what is going on inside our child.

For example, using an expression that matches her upset, Ella's parents could have tried saying:

> 'I know you're really disappointed you can't spend time with us. I know you love Saturdays where we all spend time together and it doesn't feel fair right now.'

The other advantage of making an empathic statement is that it tends to also bring your own emotional temperature down because when you start to imagine what it feels like from your child's point of view this can resonate within you when you start to feel empathic. This then naturally impacts on your communication, for example lowering your voice, appearing calmer, relaxing your facial muscles, which then makes conflict less likely. So this, combined with the impact on your child of the statement itself, can really take the heat out of the situation.

Sometimes, especially if your child is angry at you, being directly empathic can make him angrier. Another way of being empathic, if you have a partner present, is to express to him in front of your child how you imagine your child is feeling and why, rather than speaking directly to your child. This can be a less intense way of helping your child feel understood and can work particularly well for a younger child. Let's go back to the example of Charlie and his mother Lisa from the start of the chapter.

> By the time Charlie had got home he was very angry at his mum, both about the way she said 'No' but moreover about his subsequent

experience of not being understood or validated. In the car Lisa had tried empathizing with her son, but Charlie just seemed to get more and more angry. When they arrived home Lisa turned to her part- ner Jon and said in a sympathetic voice:

'Poor Charlie, he is so upset and angry with Mummy. He really really wanted a magazine in the shop just now. It was very hard for him when I said "No" and Charlie got really angry at me and I think I got mad too.'

Charlie's dad cuddles him and says:

'Oh poor Charlie, that sounds hard for him. He must have really wanted that magazine!'

Getting your partner to intervene can be really helpful sometimes, either in the way shown here, where Charlie is spoken about, rather than spoken to directly; or, if your child is angry at you, encouraging your partner to step in to help resolve the situation can be more helpful than trying to battle through yourself.

Additionally, you might find that when your child is extremely upset, empathic comments during the situation might encourage him to carry on expressing more negative emotion. So, if Sam's mum became really empathic in the shop this could have magnified his feelings and not help resolve the situation. It could have encouraged Charlie to express his feelings more strongly in the hope of changing his mum's mind and might plant an idea that expressing strong feelings gets him what he wants. Instead, choosing a validating statement can be more effective.

Validation is similar to empathy as the aim is to help your child see that you get his point of view, but differs in that it does not take the child too much back into the experience of what they are feeling. It does this because the tone that you communicate your understanding can be quite differ- ent from empathy. When you make validating statements you are more likely to express your concern and interest, rather than reflecting back the same feeling. Sounding genuine but not being overemotional, combined with a brief statement, can be enough to validate what your child is feel- ing. Furthermore, these statements have a mind-minded quality – in other words they 'fit' with how your child is thinking and feeling. Take a look at a mind-minded statement from Karen towards her 2-year-old daughter Molly:

Karen is watching Molly pretend to understand a game that her 10-year-old brother is playing, and getting bit frustrated that she can't play it, and comments, 'It feels so frustrating for you that you can't do it like your brother.'

In this statement Karen is accurately guessing, and most importantly ver-balising, what she thinks is going on inside Molly's mind. In the earlier example, Charlie's mum in the shop could have said:

> 'I know you would really like it if we got a toy every time we came to the shop, and it is hard for you, but that's not going to happen. It feels really disappointing and annoying.'

A simple validating statement like this acknowledges Charlie's disap-pointment with not getting a toy and communicates that from his point of view his mum gets that it is hard, but it also holds a line. When you con-vey your understanding for your child's experience this does not necessarily mean that you like or agree with what he is doing or feeling. However, it does mean that you understand where he is coming from. The accuracy of these statements is important, but if you really don't know what your child is thinking or feeling, then being explicit about the fact that you are taking a good guess is also helpful to him.

Tips for making validating statements using the Parent APP:

a) Pay attention and actively listen – make eye contact and stay focused.
b) Be aware of how you are coming across, especially non-verbal commu-nication such as tutting, rolling your eyes.
c) Can you hear what your child is saying and communicating? Allow space in your mind to think about what is going on in the inside and try taking his perspective – what is his experience in this situation right now, what is he feeling?
d) Reflect back his feeling without judgement. The aim is to let him know that you understand his point of view: 'I understand that you are angry because . . . ', 'I can see that this really frustrates you.'
e) Show tolerance. Look for his inside story and how it all makes sense from his point of view; even if you do not approve of how he is acting, you can still try and empathise with how it might feel for him
f) Respond in a way that demonstrates that you take him seriously. For example, Charlie's mum might think with him about how he might be able to save up for a magazine with his pocket money.

Using humour

Lilly is angry at her father Matt for asking her to tidy her toys away. She turns to him and shouts 'you are a bogeyman', he dramatically hunches over and puts his finger to his lips and says, 'Shhh! You can't tell anyone that's my real name!'

Injecting some humour into difficult exchanges can be a great harmoniser, bringing you and your child closer together. Humour can be especially effective when you are trying to help your child lower his emotional temperature as it breaks the tension quickly in heightened situations. In this situation, Lilly was so amused she laughed back, 'No, you're a poopy head.'

Disciplining and making sure your child is well behaved unfortunately can feel like such a serious issue but why should it? The ability to be able to laugh at either yourself or a situation you find yourself in with your child can be extremely refreshing and a lot less stressful. It follows that once you have got to the point where you can both step back enough from a situation to be able to laugh and joke about it, then you have already managed to deescalate the situation. Having a playful relationship with your child can really make you both feel more connected. You could try using funny voices, tripping over dramatically, rephrasing angry requests like 'For the last time, put your pyjamas on now!' with a friendly voice, 'I've been standing here so long I think a spider has managed to spin a web between my shoulder and the wall! Can you check for me?'

However, using humour isn't without its risks and it can be a bit of a balancing act as you don't want your child to think you are laughing at him. If you described to a friend something that was important to you and she made a joke, you would probably feel teased, which can be irritating at best. In interactions with your child, making a joke at your own expense may be a safer bet, and more helpful. This might be telling a funny story about you when you were a child, or admitting that sometimes you must be the worst mummy or daddy in the whole world, probably the whole universe. The ability to be able to laugh at either yourself or a situation you find yourself in also has the advantage of showing your child different perspectives, and mirroring for him that you can look at yourself from the outside too. When you look at yourself from the outside in a humorous way it takes the heat out of the emotion you are feeling, so you may go from feeling intensely angry about something to mocking yourself and laughing heartedly.

Distraction

Diverting attention from one thing to another is a strategy that all of us employ, often very successfully. How often when you feel worried about an upcoming event, such as an important meeting at work, or a social event with people you don't really feel comfortable with, do you try to focus on something else to take your mind off the thing that is bothering you? Similarly, distraction can be an excellent way to deal with a child's feelings.

Distraction can take a few different forms. For younger children, it can be as simple as noticing something of interest outside the window and excitedly saying something like 'Oh wow, look at Felix the cat outside on our fence, how did he get up there?!' For older children you might have to be more elaborate. You can use an earlier conversation about something your child has been talking about and is interested in and try to steer his thinking back to this. For example:

> Grace was feeling angry at her mum Rachel lay on her bed yelling and crying. Rachel had told her she couldn't have any more biscuits before dinner and they had argued over this, with Grace getting more and more angry. Her mum, with a puzzled and curious expression on her face, says:
>
> 'Look Grace, I know you are furious at me at the moment.'
> 'Go away, you are so mean.'
> 'I know you think that. But look, I've been thinking all day about something you said earlier.'
> 'I don't care.'
> 'Listen, I know you're angry with me Grace, I understand that, but what you said earlier was really important. You wanted to know how to get more bonus fruits in that game on your tablet!'
> 'AND?'
> 'Well I think I worked it out, you need to get more bananas by getting into the bonus area.'
> 'Really, how do I do that?'

Grace and her mother spent a few minutes talking about this further until Rachel decided to revisit talking about the situation that had happened earlier.

Another way to use distraction is by talking about your own experiences to draw your child's attention away from their current concern. Instead of trying to think of something you talked about earlier in the day to reconnect with him, try to think of a time when you felt similar to how he is feeling, and talk about this. For example:

> 'I know Grace you are furious at me at the moment.'
> 'Go away, you are so mean.'
> 'I know you think I'm mean. You probably hate me at the moment as well. Do you know how much I hated granddad and grandma when I was younger?'

'I don't care.'

'No, I bet. I used to get so mad at them. Do you know, once when I was really mad, I poured away grandma's special perfume, I got in so much trouble for that! Oh no, that was bad, she got so angry!'

'Really! What did she do?'

'She didn't let me go outside for 2 years!'

'Really?'

'No, probably not 2 years, probably only for a week, but she did shout very loudly at me!'

Rachel decided that it was probably a good time to leave Grace to have a bit of space as things had settled down between them and she felt somewhat more connected. However, she resolved to come back a short while after this to think through with her what had happened and to try to understand any misunderstandings.

In both of these examples, Rachel managed to distract Grace by generating her interest in something else. However, she did not dismiss her daughter's point of view or her thoughts, she clearly connected with them, but at the same time she also confidently persisted in drawing Grace's attention to something else. When you use distraction techniques like this with your children, you can take them away from the tricky feeling they are having right in this moment by shifting their attention to a more positive, manageable experience. This also shifts their attention to a different emotion. Bear in mind, though, that while using distraction helps your child to *shift out* of a difficult feeling and think about something else, it is sometimes important to revisit the initial feeling after a short period of time, perhaps by having some sort of discussion about what happened or just commenting on it – often it's easier to think about a situation after some time has passed. In shifting Grace's attention away from her own feelings, towards the story of how her mum Rachel felt when she upset her parents, also helped to lessen the intensity of how Grace was feeling. When your child is feeling sucked into a feeling, helping him orientate to future events – to think about how he will move on from this unpleasant moment – can be really beneficial. This gives him a perspective that his current emotional state will pass, and that life changes day by day and hour by hour. He can also begin to be curious about feelings and talk about them, all the while understanding that they won't last forever.

Time Alone

Parents are familiar with the concept and practice of 'Time Out', traditionally used as a form of punishment that involves temporarily separating a child from an environment where undesirable behaviour has occurred, with the aim of reinforcing desirable behaviour. Sometimes Time Out is used as a way to communicate to children that they need to get anger and frustration 'out of their system' or for children to think about their behaviour. However, the strategy has its limitations, especially when it's used in a punitive way. 'Time Alone' is different. When children get slightly older, they may actively choose to spend some time alone if they are upset and angry at their parents. And of course, at times, trying to speak directly to your child only serves to inflame the situation, so having time apart can be really beneficial for your child. To make this a supportive strategy, it shouldn't be perceived as a punishment by your child, for example 'Go to your room for five minutes', but rather as a suggestion to help them calm down:

> *'Okay, you seem really upset and angry at me at the moment and I'm sorry I can't help. I think me being here is making you feel worse. I can go downstairs for a bit, maybe that will help.'*

As with learning all new skills, the ability to use Time Alone to calm down and move into a 'warmer' range of emotional control will not just come naturally to your child. It is important first and foremost that he does not feel you are sending him off to be alone as a punishment, but that you are teaching him a new skill. However, children do not learn new skills when they are angry and upset so it is a good idea then, with you as your child's trainer, to ask him to practice when he is calm. Remember this is practice of how to be alone in a space where he can learn to bring his emotions under his control (to self-regulate). You might even want to model this by using the time to sit quietly yourself in a different part of the house. When your child has managed to practice this skill, and you can help him devise his own name for it (one child we knew called it his 'chill out time'), you should then praise him for learning this new skill. After he has learned to do this under your guidance, he will soon be able to use Time Alone by himself to help him calm down and think about his behaviour.

Older children who have learned how to regulate their feelings a bit better can often decide that they want to take themselves off to spend time alone and calm down, and you can both encourage and facilitate this. For example:

> *Twelve-year-old Maddy came home from school after a long day and the minute she walked in the door her mum Karen started firing off questions at her about her day. Maddy started to get agitated and argumentative with Karen, to the point of shutting her out and telling her to 'back off'. Maddy's mum got upset about this and said 'I'm only taking an interest in what you did today.' Maddy shouted back, 'I'm really tired, it's been a long day, I'm going to my room.'*

Later that day, Karen thought that maybe she should ask her if it would be a good idea if every day after school Maddy had 20 minutes alone time in her room, which she could take or not, to relax after the school day, and that they could have a catch up after that. Maddy agreed to this and a pattern was set whereby most days she would come in from school, chill out in her room, and then come down to talk about her and Karen's day together. This time alone created a better connection between Maddy and her mum, and also taught Maddy a bit more about how to regulate her feelings.

Use of touch with sad and difficult feelings

Touch has calming effects on children and can act as a helpful cue, along with verbal statements, to help them start to feel better. A warm, loving touch with close body contact can release oxytocin (the bonding hormone) and so this has the almost immediate effect of making both you and your children feel calmer. This can be accompanied by words, for example putting

both your arms around your child and saying, 'You seem really frustrated with that; let me help you calm down.' Alternatively, saying nothing at all, and simply holding your child in a secure and comforting embrace when he is experiencing a strong emotion will help you both to feel better.

You know that soothing, warm, loving feeling you get inside when you hug someone close? That's oxytocin. It's a hormone released in the body and brain in response to affectionate touch, hugs, and also in young infants, breastfeeding. Oxytocin has many positive effects including promoting feelings of calm and nurturance; promoting feelings of trust, security and closeness; promoting infant bonding; lowering blood pressure and regulating sleep patterns. The type of touch you give is important too as a casual pat on the shoulder will not have any of these positive benefits, whereas a really heartfelt hug where your whole chest and tummy touches your child's, and where your breathing is slow, full and relaxed, will have the desired effect of bringing your child's emotional temperature down and bringing the two of you closer to one another.

Apologising when you get it wrong

It is highly aversive for your child to feel that he has been misunderstood and that you have 'got it wrong' when it comes to understanding the thoughts and feelings behind his behaviour. However, this experience and his associated feelings about having been misunderstood will be felt even more keenly if you are not able to tell him that you got it wrong. An important element of Reflective Parenting is being open about the fact that you don't know what is going on in other people's minds, and to make it clear to your child that you are taking your best guess at why he behaved the way he did. This curiosity should be equally matched by an attitude of self-reflection, and being able to admit that you thought you knew what your child was thinking, or why he behaved in a certain way, but that you may have got this wrong, is very helpful to your child. He will feel closer to you and your connection with him following an emotional outburst can be re-established both when you accurately guess what might have been in his mind *and* when you make an inaccurate guess, but acknowledge that you got it wrong. As parents, we all make mistakes, but acknowledging this with your child is another important aspect of being reflective.

> *After trying some of these strategies, and to make sure that you have the full story of how your child is thinking and feeling, it can be helpful to ask your child the question: 'Tell me a bit more about . . . ', leaving a space for him to tell you more of his own inside story.*

REFLECTIVE PARENTING SUMMARY

CHILDREN'S FEELINGS

What do we mean . . .

Reflective Parenting reminds us how important it is to help your child to learn to understand, and eventually manage, how he feels. Reflective Parenting encourages you to take an active stance in helping build up ability to do this for himself.

It helps you by . . .

Stepping back and seeing how you can directly help him build up his ability to cope with his feelings is a stance that is more likely to help you remain calm and empathic. Also, focusing on his emotions will help resolve situations quicker, reducing your levels of stress and increasing your confidence. When he becomes more skilled at managing his feelings he will be better behaved, bringing further benefits to you.

It helps your child by . . .

Being a reflective parent by focusing on feelings and finding ways to help your child manage them himself has a direct impact on his capacity to manage his feelings in other relationships. The consequence of this will be more stable and positive relationships with peers and other family members.

It helps your relationship by . . .

A focus on feelings, in some circumstances, can be of enormous benefit to resolving situations, and encourages connection, which is so important to security in relationships, as well as shortening conflict. When you can match your feelings and expression to your child's it will help him to both manage his own feelings and develop resilience through feeling understood by you.

Keep in mind . . .

1. Helping your child to manage his feelings is important as it impacts on his behaviour, but also on his relationship with you, and with others.

2. Keeping in mind the link between emotions and behaviour will make it easier for both you and your child to understand the inside story behind how he acts.

3. Empathy and validation are both important to helping your child manage how he is feeling and connecting with him, which reduces conflict and difficult behaviours. Validation expresses interest and concern, and empathy expresses feeling for how he feels.

4. Make statements about what you imagine is going on in your child's mind and body. Making these mind-minded comments can help him understand what he is thinking and feeling.

5. Humour can break the tension between you and your child, make you feel better connected, and show him that you can look at yourself from a different perspective.

6. Distraction comes in a few different forms and helps children with their feelings; it can take your child out of a difficult emotion.

7. Make Time Alone a supportive strategy, by turning it into a suggestion to help both you and your child calm down.

8. Be aware of your facial expression when verbalising what you think your child is feeling. Try to match your expression to your child's feelings (marked-mirroring).

6

DISCIPLINE

Understanding misunderstandings

Let us start with the obvious: all children misbehave many many times during their childhood. In fact, misbehaving is so much a part of their development that it would seem incredible and completely out of the ordinary if a child didn't misbehave. Yet 'naughty' behaviour concerns the majority of parents, and generally parents want their children to be well behaved.

Why is bad behaviour such a concern to parents? Why does this issue motivate so many parents to ask the advice of friends or to buy a parenting book to look for solutions? The answer is complex and multifaceted and slightly different for each one of us. It might be linked to any or all of the following: the powerful feelings children being challenging and pushing limits bring up in parents; pressure from other parents, or grandparents, for children to behave in a certain way; messages implicit within society regarding authority and respect; concern about where bad behaviour now might lead a child in the future; or simply that it makes life easier when children comply. Of course we understand all of these concerns and why they often motivate parents to seek advice from others. A central aim with this book is to provide ideas that will indirectly, and sometimes directly, reduce problematic behaviour. We hope this chapter can address your concerns while challenging some commonly held ideas around discipline, its purpose and how useful it can be to your child.

In this chapter we want to explore and challenge the idea that bad behaviour simply needs to be discouraged or managed. Instead, we offer you a broader view: that actually the occasions when you respond to your child misbehaving also provide excellent opportunities to support his emotional development, and to help him to understand himself and others. In fact, young children in particular are not meant to behave and be obedient all the time, and the reason for this is that their needs are frequently completely at odds with those of their parents. Think about your view for example of your need to keep your child wrapped up and warm for the walk to school versus your child's feelings about wearing a jumper under a coat while trying to ride fast on his scooter to school. Your young child isn't actually feeling at all cold and wants to have as much movement and freedom as he can possibly experience while riding on his scooter. Understanding these different perspectives is one of the key elements to understanding why it's inevitable there will be everyday conflicts. What if we told you that falling out with your child is actually helpful sometimes, but only if you spend time afterwards actively trying to repair the relationship and explore what happened? The key is to help your child to 'mentalize' their experience, which will help to reduce the incidence of difficult-to-manage behaviour in the future. If you recall from the introduction, when people are 'mentalizing' they are trying to understand the mental state (or state of mind if you like) of both themselves and others that underlines overt behaviour. So in the experience of the child refusing to wear a jumper, the parent would start to try to understand what it was the child was thinking and feeling, and ideally would be explicit about what they were thinking too (e.g. 'I'm just worried that you might get cold without noticing and then feel ill at school all day').

The first important step in this approach is to take a stance of curiosity about your child's behaviour, rather than blame. If this seems odd or counter-intuitive we would like to reassure you that the ideas in this chapter do reduce problematic behaviour, not only when these ideas are being applied in situations where your child is behaving badly, but also, importantly, in the longer term as your child develops. We are going to help you see that within conflicts there can be important developmental lessons for your child that bring benefits to him and to you, and most importantly to your relationship.

Bad behaviour, conflict and connection

It is extremely common and normal for a child to act inappropriately and for there to be some conflict that follows with the parents. The feelings that come with conflict can be difficult for most parents to manage and can lead to feelings of personal inadequacy or disappointment in their children. But it's important to remind yourself that your child's motivations are often completely at odds with yours, after all, you are two very different people, and so it is very normal for him to behave in a way you consider inappropriate.

It's reassuring to know that bad behaviour and conflict is not a sign of poor family relationships. Conflict arises normally between parents and their children. Despite having different needs, parents still have to maintain boundaries and correct behaviour that is inappropriate. It is our role to set boundaries and limits on behaviour in order to help our children learn what is expected of them, what is safe, appropriate, etc. Children on the other hand are grappling with issues of autonomy and their own emerging identity, one that is quite separate from their parents. This is one of the day-to-day aspects of parenting: balancing your children's needs with the need to help them behave within acceptable limits. The potential for conflict is great as you constantly try to judge an acceptable level of independence for your child while providing support and direction to conform to your expectations.

The potential for conflict in adolescence is even greater, and it is therefore even more important to think about creating communication patterns early on in the family that will carry on through into the teenage years, and so setting the environment for understanding misunderstandings early on is helpful. There is a growing body of evidence that suggests that the ability of parents and their older children to continue to feel connected to each other while disagreeing on critical issues is the hallmark of secure relationships (1–3). If parents and teenagers are able to state their opinions while accepting the other person's point of view they are more likely to feel secure in their relationship with each other. What is important here is not that parents and teenagers never fall out, but that they continue to feel connected during a conflict, or are able to re-establish a feeling of connection quickly after times of conflict. This is synonymous with the key concepts in this book that aim to help parents connect to the minds of their children, irrespective of the child's age.

The importance of connectedness with children around times of conflict cannot be overstated. There is growing awareness of the role, and impact of, shame during parenting practices (4–5). Shame, the sense of feeling bad and awful for doing something wrong, seems to play a very important role in shaping young children's behaviour to fit within moral and social norms. This is because the main feeling that young children feel when told off by their parents is shame. And when young children feel shame they become quiet, hide their eyes and become inhibited in their speech and movement. You can probably recall a time that you told your children off and they might have hung their heads in this way, or curled up into themselves. Within this unpleasant state children feel a sense of threat to the bond with their parents, in other words they feel they are not accepted or loved. Children then learn to anticipate what might result in the same feeling of shame and learn to behave in ways that might be more in line with their parents' preferences, especially if their parents reward positive behaviour, and as children grow, they learn to inhibit their behaviour somewhat and select other more socially acceptable behaviours. Children do not like to feel disconnected from their parents, in fact it feels threatening to them, which is why they adapt their behaviour. Parents who can acknowledge the shame in their children can easily help reconnect to their children quickly, strengthening their bond with them and helping their children learn that they are okay and the state of their relationship with their parents isn't damaged.

> *Nine-month-old Jack was crawling around his front room and became interested in a plug socket. As he fiddled around with the plug, he suddenly heard his mum Rachel shout.*
>
> *'Jack, STOP! Get away from there now!'*
>
> *Jack froze and became very quiet. He looked at the floor, stiffened and refused to respond to his mum. He felt shame. His mum picked him up, held and rocked him for a few minutes, and affirmed how much she cared about him and loved. Jack started to relax and together they went over to the plug socket and Rachel told him a bit about plugs and that he should not be around them. He felt better even if he didn't really understand why plugs are dangerous.*

If there is a lack of acknowledgement of shame and children experience this emotion too much it can create alienation and weaken the parent-child bond. Children learn to cope and defend against feelings of shame, bringing in other negative states of emotion, such as resentment and anger. Children can also learn that negative interaction cycles still bring desired attention and some sense of connection to their parents, albeit with more shame and resentment. So short experiences of mild shame, followed by repair and reconnection, are positive and strengthen your child's relationship with you, whereas prolonged experiences of moderate to severe shame, followed by little repair and further disconnection, is negative, weakening your relationship and actually increasing bad behaviour.

If you're worried about your child experiencing feelings of shame, remember that disagreements happen regularly in families, and if you were totally attuned to your child's experiences, without bringing in an understanding of how he impacts on others, your child would never learn about different perspectives, and understand that people have needs that are different from his own. Furthermore, it is from these conflicts that you can learn a lot more about each other than you might from times when you are getting on really well.

The important message is to find ways to interact positively with your child, during or after conflict. This brings security to your relationship and reduces negative behaviour cycles. So while conflict between parents and their children is to be expected, it is how the parent and child negotiate conflicts and sustain their relationship that is most important. Children who feel understood by their parents trust their parents' commitment to the relationship, even in the face of conflict and strong differences of opinion. They are more able to move forward confidently from one developmental stage to the next, learning to tolerate and resolve conflict, and feeling confident that they can trust their parents while also feeling valued in their views. When you are able to work your way through disagreements with your child, he will see and learn how to manage conflict and negotiate situations himself without resorting to aggressive behaviour or heightened emotion. Then, by noticing and praising him when he is able to resolve conflict and alter his behaviour, he learns that you like this and will want to do more of it.

We will help you to see that within these conflicts there can be an important developmental lesson for children, namely to help them explore the underlying reasons for their behaviour. Also, you can start to understand your child's world a little more, and discover what is important to him. We would also like you to consider to what extent it's important *all the time* to get your children to do what you ask of them, or to bring their behaviour under control. We know from working with parents of very young children that there can be a fear that if behaviour isn't controlled very early on, 'nipped in the bud', that their children will become out-of-control monsters. There isn't any evidence for this, and the approach we'd like to advocate here might actually lead both to an understanding of the behaviour, but also to a better mutual understanding in the relationship between the two of you – even if your child doesn't behave perfectly all of the time.

The other important point to note is that through conflict and managing negative emotions, your child sees that you, their parent, can tolerate and manage these feelings. This is an important lesson for your child in both seeing things from another person's perspective and learning that differences in opinion don't have to lead to rejection or a loss of warmth or empathy. However, your children do have to see that there are expected boundaries and limits to behaviour, and that even if they push these limits and boundaries, they will reach a point where they have to adapt what they want to do to fit your expectations for their behaviour.

> Karen had made a Sunday lunch for her husband Tom and the three children and gone to some effort to make it a bit special, as it was a miserable day outside and so everyone was stuck in the house. The eldest two children, Maddy (12) and Sam (10) sat down at the table and started to eat, but Karen's youngest, Molly (aged 2) came to the table, took one look at her dinner and said, 'Yuck, me don't like cheesy sauce. Yuck! No! Me not eating.' She didn't bother to come to the table with her brothers and parents and instead sat on the sofa, sulking and saying she wanted peanut butter on toast instead. Karen said, 'I'm not doing you separate food, I've gone to quite a bit of trouble here Molly, don't be fussy.' At this, Molly threw her toy doll at the Christmas tree, knocking some of the decorations

off and throwing a cushion after it. Karen suddenly exploded and shouted at the top of her voice, 'I've spent ages cleaning up today, don't you DARE start wrecking everything.' Older sister Sam muttered to Molly, 'Silly little baby, can't eat your dinner at the table.' At this, Molly burst into tears of upset and anger and saw that she had broken her doll's arm off in the fracas. She stormed out of the room, slamming the door. Karen shouted after her, 'Come back, and tidy up your mess.' Molly ignored her and went into the other room. The rest of the family left Molly and continued to eat, then, after a few minutes, Molly came back into the room and went to her daddy saying, 'Me don't like it when mummy shouts at me. Not tidying up. Not talking to mummy. She says sorry.' Molly's dad said, 'No, it's not nice when people shout. But maybe you need to say sorry too for wrecking the room, and the tree. And look, you've broken the toy you really loved, what a shame.' Molly hung her head, looking shamed and feeling upset, about being shouted at, the broken toy, and the feeling that she had been rejected by her mum, and furthermore made to feel like the baby by her 10-year-old sister. Her dad asked Karen to come and tell Molly that she was sorry for shouting and that she loved her. Karen, having cooled off, told Molly that she didn't like shouting either, and was sorry she had made her feel bad, but she had been looking forward to a nice family meal. 'I still love you, and I'm sorry you broke your toy. You must be very upset about that?' Molly took some time, but after around ten minutes she had calmed down, and her posture changed to sitting up straight. She looked at her dinner and started to pick at her roast potatoes as her mum gave her a cuddle. And after she had finished some food, Karen suggested that she tidy up the room, but offered to help her. Molly played happily for the rest of the afternoon.

We would like to encourage you to see that when your child either empathises or conversely fails to appreciate the impact of his behaviour on others, both these instances can be training opportunities where he can learn to understand other minds. Within a safe and secure relationship, conflicts can be resolved in a positive way, without leading to distancing in the relationship, as you can see from the example of Molly. In fact, quite the opposite: conflicts surprisingly can even lead to an increase in closeness and understanding. Naturally, it is incredibly difficult for both you the parent and your child when feeling misunderstood, and as we've highlighted from the beginning, this feeling of being misunderstood by others is one of the most aversive feelings we can experience, both as adults and children. This is where conflict provides the chance to turn a perceived misunderstanding into a deeper understanding of how the other person feels.

In healthy relationships there is conflict and children misbehave. A parent's job is both to respond to disruptive behaviour and care about the child's feelings and points of view. We don't believe that responding to his feelings and taking his point of view undermines the boundaries you have set. You can see from the example of Molly that children need limits, but these should be set in such a way that preserves the relationship and actually supports the child in learning from the circumstance as well as supporting his wider development. Karen was clear that she still needed Molly to eat her dinner and tidy up her mess, but also acknowledged how bad it feels to be shouted at, and how she had lost control in that moment because of her own feelings. She was able to name and own her feelings of upset about having been looking forward to a family meal and having spent time tidying the house. You can see that connection through bad behaviour and conflict helps his development; so falling out with your child can actually be extremely helpful to your relationship, and discipline can actually help strengthen your bond. While parents may ask themselves, 'Is it more important to correct him or to connect with him?', our approach allows you to connect with your child *while* you are correcting him. If you spend time actively trying to repair your relationship after conflict, using the principles of the Parent APP in Chapter Four, and rewinding and exploring what happened, you can help your child understand other people's points of view and his underlying intentions. We have given some examples of the types of ways you might do this, but we would like to make it even more explicit and give you a tool that you can use to help you combine these two things, correction and connection, as it can feel quite tricky to imagine how you might do both things at the same time.

The Two Hands approach

Children behave and misbehave for many different reasons. While the reasons are not always clear, it is helpful to respond to your child's difficult behaviour and to try to understand what led to the behaviour. Think about your hands; in one hand you are juggling with your child's behaviour, and in the other hand trying to come to grips with why your child misbehaved in the first place. There is a great concept used by clinical psychologist Daniel Hughes: the Two Hands approach (6). Two Hands invites you to have two important components to your interactions around discipline: one hand is for focusing on understanding what led to the behaviour, and the other hand is for dealing with the behaviour. We have developed this idea by adding our idea of the Parent APP to Hughes's useful concept.

Explaining the Two Hands approach

On the first hand is 'dealing with behaviour' – this represents what you do when you respond to your child's bad behaviour, for example the consequence you give to your child.

On the second hand is understanding the behaviour – that helps you to understand the underlying reasons and motives that led up to your child's behaviour. Using the Parent APP in this hand helps you see the reasons why your child behaved in a particular way, not just the behaviour outside.

Two Hands reminds you that it is just as important to deal with behaviour as it is to understand a child's experience that has led to the behaviour. As with most of the ideas in this book, this approach is useful both in the heat of a situation and afterwards.

> *Charlie was playing outside with his friend William while Lisa, his mum, was inside speaking to William's father. Suddenly William came running inside crying, and told his mum that Charlie had kicked him on the shin. After making sure William was okay and waiting until her own embarrassment subsided, Lisa decided to wait a further few minutes before going outside to see Charlie.*

Using the ideas of the Parent APP, Lisa guessed that Charlie might be feeling ashamed about kicking his friend, but also probably in Charlie's mind there must have been a reason for him to lash out. If she were to use the Two Hands approach, Lisa knew she would have to give Charlie a consequence for kicking (dealing with behaviour hand), but she also wanted to understand what had happened as it was very unusual (understanding the behaviour hand). Lisa sat down next to Charlie and, trying to set the tone for the conversation and to help his probable feeling of shame, gave him a quick cuddle. She then said in a friendly voice:

'What happened there Charlie? I thought you liked William? What happened just now that you didn't like?'

'I hate William Mum!'

'Really? You usually like him. He's your good mate isn't he? Something bad must have happened?'

'He said his trampoline is much bigger than mine. He said his garden is bigger and that my games are all rubbish!'

'Oh, that doesn't feel nice.'

'I don't like him. Why was he saying that?'

'I'm not sure, love. People can say things like that for a lot of different reasons. I can understand why you got so mad.'

Charlie looked up at his mum, a bit uncertain. Lisa went on.

'I can see how you feel. I don't like it either when someone says something that upsets me. But it's not okay to hit people when you feel mad. I know you know that.'

Charlie was silent and hung his head down.

'You do know that's wrong don't you Charlie?'

Charlie was silent and nodded.

'You need to say sorry to William when you go in. I'm also going to speak to your dad, too, and talk about it with him. We need to help you to find something else you can do when you feel upset; being kicked on the shins really, really hurts. You wouldn't like it if he'd kicked you.'

Children are helped enormously when they experience the Two Hands approach to discipline. Charlie felt understood by his mum, but still understood that his own response to what had happened was not acceptable. All children need limits and consequences, and as your child grows older and aspects of his brain development make it easier to understand feelings and inhibit urges, he will become more able to make choices around how to respond to a feeling or perception of an event. In turn, his behaviour will improve and more desirable behaviours will become more frequent. Helping him to become more interested in his feelings and why he acts the way he does will increase these more desirable behaviours.

At bedtime, Lisa decided to speak some more to Charlie about what happened earlier. Charlie had expressed some interest in why his friend might decide to say things to him that felt hurtful. Lisa thought exploring the reasons would be a good way in and an opportunity to look at different perspectives. After talking through different ideas as to why William might have said the things he did, Charlie decided the perspective he liked best was that William might actually be jealous of what he had. Charlie also decided that he had felt angry because he felt William was criticising his family. As a consequence for kicking someone Lisa decided that Charlie was not allowed to have his friend Ollie round to play.

How does this approach help reduce behavioural problems? First, it encourages you to approach bad behaviour and interactions during conflict with interest and curiosity, which in turn means you will be more able to approach your child with a positive mindset. Just being less irritated and angry can help the outcome of situations. In the previous example, Lisa had consciously decided that she would have to approach Charlie carefully just after he had kicked his friend. She was actually really concerned and interested to know what had happened and was able to reflect on what Charlie might have been feeling, creating a space for a helpful conversation. If she had confronted Charlie straight after the incident, while she was feeling angry and embarrassed, and demanded an apology for William there and then, this would have most likely inflamed the situation.

Secondly, adopting the Two Hands approach helps you ensure that not only is there a consequence for your child's behaviour, but also that you also consider the internal experience that led up to the behaviour. This helps foster positive self-esteem and helps your child to deal with feelings of shame by allowing them to explore with you why something happened and understand that this was wrong, but also ensuring that they feel understood by you. Again, in the previous example Lisa managed to empathise greatly with Charlie. She thought about some friends she knew who tended to brag about things, and how she could never really understand why they did this. By stating this to Charlie it helped him to experience his mum as someone who understood him, and this felt good, even though he felt ashamed that he had kicked his friend. This also links in with a concept we touched upon in Chapter One, namely that it is easier to influence others when they have had a feeling of being understood and connected with. Nowhere is this more important than when disciplining your child. The Two Hands concept helps your child see that you are trying to understand his thoughts and feelings and point of view. In the previous example, feeling understood by his mother made it easier for Charlie to accept the later consequences.

Authoritative vs authoritarian parenting

One of the many questions that friends raised when we discussed this book with them was 'Am I supposed to always see things from my child's point of view then, and never tell them that they are wrong, or have been naughty?' It was interesting to us that often people equate being empathic and 'mind-minded' with letting children get their own way and take control. This is not the case, and we hope that this chapter will assuage this myth and instead look at the powerful role that the skills we suggest in the Parent APP can play in achieving a better relationship with your child, and resolving difficult behaviour and interactions. We want to address this issue by showing you the difference between two styles of parenting: authoritative and authoritarian.

A line we often hear from parents, or find ourselves saying, is 'He doesn't respect my authority'. In a conflict situation, whether it's a major or minor fallout, the issue of who is in control and whose voice and opinion carries the greater weight can be one that generates extremely strong feelings, in both parent and child. We would like to show you how you can use the Two Hands approach and keep an authoritative stance with your child, so that you understand how he is feeling, while simultaneously managing his difficult behaviour. This is quite a complex thing to do, and most of us won't be doing this a lot of the time. However, when we do manage to take this approach, it's notable how quickly and significantly things change, both in the way your child is behaving, and how you both relate to and feel about one another.

It is generally thought that being authoritative is a good thing, and something that children both need and respond to. It's important, however, to be clear about the difference between being authoritative and authoritarian, and the benefits of one over the other.

In contrast with authoritarian parenting, which involves high levels of parental control, exerting power and strict all-or-nothing boundaries without any explanation, authoritative parenting is about achieving a balance between granting too much freedom (as is the case with permissive parenting) and being too strict.

The benefits of authoritative parenting

Contrary to how the word may sound, authoritative parenting is an approach to parental control that emphasises empathy, parent-child communication and a rational explanation of rules. The authoritative parenting style is about setting limits, reasoning with children and being responsive to their emotional needs. This approach is linked with very successful outcomes in children when it comes to managing behaviour and achieving harmony in the relationship. Managing conflicts and misunderstandings in your relationship with your child using an authoritative approach would involve being able to balance the two hands well; this would make children less likely to engage in antisocial behaviour, and be more well-behaved. This is borne out by research that suggests that having at least one authoritative parent can make a big difference to how a child behaves (7).

So what are the criteria for authoritative parenting? What will this look like if you practice it with your child?

The qualities of authoritative parenting

With an authoritative parental approach, you will be nurturing and responsive to your child, and show him respect as a rational individual, with thoughts and feelings that are separate from yours. You will start with the expectation that your child will cooperate with you and you will expect a level of maturity from him, while at the same time offering him the level of emotional support appropriate to his age. It is important to emphasise that authoritative parents don't let their children get away with bad behaviour, unlike permissive parents, who don't enforce rules and boundaries, often expressing a wish to be their child's friend rather than a parent figure. As we emphasised with the Parent APP, it is important to show empathy, to see things from your child's perspective and to be *mind-minded* in your approach to your child's behaviour. In addition to these elements, you will need to emphasise and enforce the rules for appropriate behaviour with your child, and give not only the rules, but also the reasons for these rules. Taking this 'complete' approach allows your child to see that you are being explicit about what's going on in your mind, and that your role as the parent entails responsibility for both caring for your child and managing his behaviour. The message you will be giving your child when you parent in this way is that you expect them to behave responsibly.

When you treat your child with this level of respect, during a misunderstanding or incident of bad behaviour, you will attempt to reason with him and to explain the consequences of good and bad behaviour. And, importantly, when you treat your child in this way, it is much more likely that you will get a good outcome, both in terms of his behaviour, and in your relationship with one another. We must emphasise that this is not about letting your child off the hook and condoning what is unacceptable behaviour, but it is about setting a boundary around the behaviour, and trying to show your child that you are interested in learning what lies beneath the behaviour, that is what's going on inside his head – showing him how his behaviour affects others, and how he can change it in the future.

When you adopt this type of respectful and thoughtful approach, you also avoid the negative consequences of a more authoritarian approach, such as harsh punishments that shame your child, or having to withdraw affection from your child, which is completely unnecessary, even if your child has behaved very badly in your eyes. With a more authoritative approach, you give children the space to consider the consequences of their actions and work out themselves better ways to behave.

Let's look at the following example and how the two different parenting styles would influence the management of the child's behaviour:

Rachel walks into the sitting room at home and finds her 7-year-old daughter Lilly smashing up her dolls' tea set and kitchen, throwing all the pieces around the room in a fury, and hurting her baby brother Jack with one of the tea cups. Jack starts screaming, and Lilly carries on pulling her kitchen set to pieces and chucking it around the room, so that pieces are flying into walls, the TV screen, everywhere.

Authoritative approach

The authoritative approach to dealing with this situation might look something like the following:

Rachel walks into the sitting room, her expression is serious, but also curious as to what all the noise was about. Seeing the scene, she gives all her attention in the first instance to Jack, and begins by immediately checking if Jack is hurt or injured. Having established that Jack is okay and comforted him, she then puts him into a safe place. Rachel then tells Lilly in a very firm voice to stop throwing her toys around the room immediately or she won't be allowed to have her friend Amy round to play later that day. She gets down to Lilly's level and asks her why she is so angry. Lilly is too angry and upset to be able to articulate how she feels, so Rachel hazards a guess and asks if anything happened to her kitchen and tea set to make her feel so furious. Lilly screams that Jack tried to take her best tea pot from her, and wrecked her kitchen that she'd spent hours setting up in the process. Rachel says that that must have been extremely annoying when she'd spent so long putting it all together, but it's never okay to hurt someone, and so she is taking her new tea set and kitchen away for now and wants her to apologise to Jack for hurting him. When she sees that Lilly is still really furious and too upset to be able to apologise just yet, Rachel takes her onto her knee and wipes her face telling her that she can see why she is so mad, but she underlines that it is never okay to hurt anyone. Lilly's cries start slowly to subside, and feeling that her mum knows how hurt she felt by having her brother spoil her game, she finds that she is more able to think about whether Jack is hurt or not, and goes into the other room to see if he's okay. Before she leaves the room, she checks whether Amy is still coming over to play later. Rachel says she can come as long as Lilly makes friends with Jack and says she is sorry for hurting him. She tells her, though, that she can't play with her tea and kitchen set now and must put it away. Lilly is cross about this, but Rachel insists that her playtime is over for now. Rachel adds, 'I will tell Jack that he mustn't take your toys when you're playing with them, because that's really annoying isn't it?'

We can see in this example how the Two Hands approach helps Rachel to balance showing an understanding of what might be lying beneath Lilly's behaviour with holding a line around managing her behaviour. In one hand she is using the Parent APP; showing a curiosity in why Lilly got so angry, and trying both to see Lilly's perspective and to get Lilly to see how her brother feels. She is also providing empathy to her. On the other hand, she is giving a consequence for Lilly's actions that lets her know that there is a firm boundary.

Authoritarian approach

An authoritarian approach to the above scenario might look something like this:

Rachel, hearing the noise from the sitting room, walks in with a scowl on her face and shouts at the top of her voice, 'What on earth are you doing Lilly? Did you hurt your baby brother? You naughty child.' She goes straight over to Lilly, snatches the tea set out of her hand and throws it aggressively to the floor, shouting that she is going to throw all her new toys into the bin for being so naughty. All her attention is on Lilly, and Jack is still crying. Lilly starts to cry more loudly as well now, and hangs her head down in shame. 'I'm going to tell your dad what a naughty girl you've been when he comes home Lilly, and you can forget Amy coming over to play. She's not coming, and it's too late to make friends with Jack. You've hurt him.'

If we look at what is communicated in the first, authoritative approach, we can see that Rachel gives a punishment for Lilly's behaviour (Lilly is not

111

allowed her toys anymore, and Rachel gives all her attention and empathy initially to Jack). She sets down a clear boundary around her behaviour, telling her that she isn't allowed to throw toys or to hurt her brother. She also keeps hold of the boundary that unless she can empathise with her baby brother and communicate that she is sorry for hurting him, she won't be able to play with her friend later. At the same time, she shows Lilly that she can see things from her point of view, too. While it's not okay to hurt her brother, it is understandable that she is really cross with him for messing up her game when she spent so long setting it up. The approach that Rachel takes means that the outburst is soon resolved and Lilly calms down. She takes some responsibility for her own actions, but at the same time feels understood. The key elements to Rachel's authoritative approach here are that she shows a level of warmth, while emphasising the reasons for her rules, thus teaching Lilly something important about both her own behaviour and how it affects others. Plus she gets to understand the reasons behind her mother's actions, so although this may be difficult for her to accept, it is clear and understandable, and can be taken further forward into the next time there is a misunderstanding between her and her mum, or an argument with her brother. Rachel has helpfully given Lilly some important feedback about her behaviour and about the boundary she sets around this behaviour, while still maintaining a warm and loving relationship with her. Rachel keeps Lilly's sense of shame small and helps her to resolve these feelings and stay connected with her.

In the second, authoritarian approach, Rachel gives all her immediate, negative attention to Lilly, therefore communicating straightaway that bad behaviour gets attention. She then goes on to criticise not the behaviour, but Lilly herself, labelling her naughty. This leads to feelings of deep shame and upset in Lilly, who then can't resolve or understand how she's feeling, but instead feels at the same time blamed and misunderstood. Struggling to make sense of her fury, because no one has been able to reflect this back to her, her feelings of distress escalate until she is crying uncontrollably. In this frame of mind, she is unable to empathise at all with her brother as her ability to think about other people's minds is totally lost in her own heightened emotional state. She loses the playdate with her friend and her toy at the same time.

Taking an authoritarian approach often involves exploding with anger towards your child, or punishing them by withdrawing affection. You may find yourself resorting to bribing your child in order to get him to comply. While it may feel as if some of these things work in the moment, they are generally not found to be good strategies for either changing future behaviour, or for having a harmonious relationship, and so conflicts end up unresolved, and potentially escalate very quickly, and future conflicts are likely to be even more dramatic. This type of approach also leaves children feeling insecure, both about themselves and about the relationship with you, their parent.

REFLECTIVE PARENTING SUMMARY

UNDERSTANDING MISUNDERSTANDINGS

What do we mean . . .

Taking a Reflective Parenting stance to managing your child's difficult behaviour means seeing the times when your child misbehaves as an opportunity to support his emotional development, and to help them to understand themselves and others. Bringing Two Hands to discipline means both responding to your child's inside story to his behaviour, as well as responding to the behaviour itself.

It helps you by . . .

Disciplining your child in this way will make it more likely that you understand your child and his behaviour. This different focus allows you to connect quickly with him, whilst being effective in your discipline. This combination prevents negative interaction cycles, which in turn means a reduction in problematic behaviour over time and an increase in positive behaviour. When you take a reflective, but authoritative stance, you offer your child consistency, predictability and safe boundaries within which he can express his feelings and respond to your limits.

It helps your child by . . .

The times your child misbehaves are excellent opportunities to support his emotional development, and to help him to understand himself and others. Taking time to understand and respect his point of view, and then to actively re-connect, will aid his emotional development, reduces shame and brings a feeling of security within the relationship with you.

It helps your relationship by . . .

Maintaining a Reflective Parenting stance during discipline will help your relationship by allowing you to stay connected during disagreements or reconnected quickly afterwards to understand what happened. Repairing ruptures in your relationship will help bring you both closer together. You will be a more authoritative parent, bringing consistency, calmness and mutual understanding, and giving your child a clearer understanding of the motives behind your actions.

Keep in mind . . .

1. In healthy relationships there is conflict and children misbehave. This is normal.
2. You and your child have different perspectives, after all, you are two very different people, and so conflict and bad behaviour are to be expected.
3. Find ways to stay connected with your child, during or after conflict.
4. Think about dealing with difficult behaviour with having two hands – one hand for responding to the behaviour and the other hand for understanding the reasons underlying behaviour (getting an inside story).
5. Encourage your child to talk about his feelings.
6. Respect your child's opinion and encourage him to express these opinions, even if they are different from your own.
7. Being authoritative is a good thing. You should expect your child to cooperate, but also offer him emotional support. Set a boundary and rules that you expect him to comply with. Afterwards show warmth and empathy.

7

HELPING SENSITIVE CHILDREN WORK THROUGH MISUNDERSTANDINGS

Introduction

In the previous chapter we talked about the usefulness of understanding misunderstandings within your relationship with your child. How does this work, though, if you have a child who sees relationships differently because of previous difficult experiences or developmental difficulties, both of which can make parenting more challenging? When things are not going well between these groups of children and their parents, it's all the more important to remember their particular sensitivities.

We are going to focus on two groups of children in particular here: children who have been exposed to previous trauma and who have been looked after or adopted, and children who have Asperger's Syndrome. What brings these children together is that they see and 'do' relationships differently, albeit for different reasons. By building on the ideas in previous chapters, using an enhanced version of Reflective Parenting, we want to show you how useful it is to practise being a reflective parent with these groups of children. The key thing to remember with these two groups of children is that they find it harder than others to understand and be good at relationships.

> *What do you think it feels like to have never experienced someone understand what is going on in your mind?*

Young people in care

Why have we included young people in care? On 31st March 2013 there were about 68,000 children in the care of local authorities in England. Many children are looked after away from their parents' home because of concerns about how their parents cared for them, and it's unlikely that these children would have experienced much Reflective Parenting during much of their formative early years. Although the lack of Reflective Parenting is unlikely to be the main reason that these children have been removed from their parental home, it is likely to have been a feature of their experience of being parented. For many different reasons, parents have found it difficult to keep the needs of their child at the forefront of their own minds. For example, they might have found it hard to manage their own emotions around their child or struggled repeatedly to see their child's perspective, instead becoming fixed on negative perceptions of him and why he does things, which in turn might have led to punitive parenting. Or parents may have continually overlooked their child's needs, being too preoccupied by events going on in their own lives. Essentially, what connects these scenarios is that the parents have struggled to understand and truly connect with how their actions impact on their children.

Of course, it's unrealistic to expect parents to be aware all the time of how they are impacting on their children, however, when this lack of awareness becomes chronic and extreme, children may be exposed to everyday situations that are traumatic. These experiences impact significantly on how children develop, and continue to affect their behaviour even when they live in permanent alternative care. This section of the book is for the parents of these children, whether this be their foster parents, adoptive parents, special guardians or grandparents who so often take on the care of their grandchildren.

There is a great deal of extremely helpful research that informs adoptive and foster parents on how they can help their children, and really we are just touching upon this area here. However, the ideas around Reflective Parenting discussed throughout the book are highly relevant to carers looking after children who have been mistreated. A number of studies have identified how adoptive and foster parents can help their children work through earlier traumatic experiences. Interestingly, how well children adjusted in adoptive families was found to be dependent on how sensitive their adoptive mothers were to their thoughts, feelings and perspectives (1). In other words, the more reflective an adoptive mother was, the better the child appeared to recover from earlier difficult experiences.

As a note of caution, for children who are significantly struggling to overcome past trauma there may be a clear role for specialist help and we would certainly advise an assessment by a mental health professional.

What makes these children's lives more difficult?

In many cases, children who come into care have been constantly overlooked or misread by their parents, who consistently failed to notice or think about what was going on inside their child's mind. The parents would also have been unaware of their own emotions and how they came across to others. When a child has had such flawed relationships in their past, this can lead to frequent misunderstandings between a new carer and the child, hence the need to consider this group of children particularly in this chapter.

> *Suzie was 1-year-old and had developed a painful ear infection that was especially aggravating at night. She cried often. Her mother found the noise irritating and could not stand being woken up. She felt got at, as if Suzie was fussing and annoying her on purpose. When Suzie needed comfort and nurture she instead received anger and negative messages from her mother.*

Such negative interactions can involve direct harm and maltreatment, such as neglect, abuse and abandonment, and some children witness traumatic and terrifying situations at home. And these traumatic experiences come from the very people – the parents – a child would typically depend on to get through such difficult times. Ideally, parents help children feel safe and contained. Children can then concentrate on developing an awareness of their feelings. In a safe parental relationship they can also learn about how to relate to and connect with other people. However, in harmful situations, when a parent is a confusing mix of a source of safety and fear, the child finds himself in an environment where he is unable to develop the skills necessary to enjoy healthy relationships. Children like Suzie can be instead stuck in a highly emotionally arousing and distressing environment at developmentally vulnerable times. Remember the emotional thermometer? It is as if Suzie's mother's is stuck on extremely hot, and inside, Suzie's thermometer is too. When children experience life in this way there is a complex difference in how their brain grows and the structures within it are formed. A child's development of the orbitofrontal cortex (an area in the front of the brain) is influenced by interactions with their parent and this is critical to his future capacity to manage emotions, to appraise others' emotional state, and manage stress. These traumatic family situations show how critical the role of the parent–child relationship is in developing emotional, psychological and neurobiological abilities.

How do challenging and traumatic early experiences affect children later on?

Adoptive and foster parents can often find their children's behaviour confusing, hard to deal with and persistent. If you are one of these parents, or know of a child who is in care, it is so important that you understand and recognize some of the ways your child has been impacted on by his previous experiences.

Stress and how children experience emotions

Chronic stress affects certain structures in the brain that are linked to the ability to think rationally and make good choices in stressful situations. So when a young child is exposed to the chronic stress that comes with insensitive and traumatic parenting, his mind is maturing at a time when he is feeling unsafe and is preoccupied with survival. He will have higher levels of stress hormones, even when his body is at rest. It is as if the stress from the trauma causes his brain to be 'rewired' to function as if it is a constant state of high alert, and he remains ready to protect himself from danger in an instant through aggression, withdrawal or zoning out. The important point here is that his mind will continue to work in this way even when he moves to a loving and sensitive family; he will still function in the same way, getting easily stressed and emotionally aroused, being more reactive and taking longer to calm down.

> When Suzie was 4-years-old she moved to her adoptive family. Her parents became puzzled as to why she became disruptive and hyperactive when people came to visit. Suzie would hit out and seemed constantly to seek her mother's attention. Rather than (jumping in and) dealing with the behaviour as it happened, her parents stood back from the situation and realised that Suzie became stressed when there was a change in her environment, when she would become excitable and disruptive. They decided to limit the number of times people visited until Suzie became more settled and they saw progress in other areas.

If you are an adoptive or foster parent reading this you may feel puzzled and frustrated by patchy progress in your child. One month it can seem that he has settled down only for things to regress the next month. However, thinking about these ups and downs in a child's behaviour as normal can help adoptive and foster parents to cope with difficult behaviour and not become downhearted when things aren't going well. Specific spikes in your child's difficulties can often be traced back to stressful events, such as transitions to school, holiday, birthday, peer difficulties, puberty, the start of a meaningful relationship, stress in family relationships or moving house. These times of change can be especially difficult for looked after children as they are less able to cope with instability and uncertainty. Sticking with and pushing through stressful situations is a challenge and he will need help to identify that stress is affecting him. Sometimes, the triggers can be much less obvious and subtle, such as a touch, smell or even a feeling associated with previous trauma.

We discussed in Chapter One how babies and infants rely on the adults around them to help work out how they are feeling. When an infant feels upset he looks at his parent's face for an explanation of how he feels, a bit like a mirror being held up to reflect back an image of their internal world that says 'You are upset' Feelings become understandable and linked to events. But what happens when parents are not interested in holding back a mirror? Research has shown that children who had been neglected found it harder to discriminate different emotions in the faces of other people (2), which meant that understanding other people's emotions was much harder, and it was harder to connect with others in meaningful ways.

What about if a parent holds up a mirror that distorts and reflects back different feelings than her child, feelings that are angry or hostile images? How and what does a child learn about his feelings then, and how does he develop an ability to manage feelings? Imagine that when an infant feels upset, instead of seeing this feeling reflected in his parent's face he sees aggression. In other words, looking at his parent can be scary. When children experience this, they become emotionally aroused and distressed and might either turn away from their parents, or look at their parents but zone out, or look right through them. Once a child witnesses his parents' unhealthy ways of expressing their emotions, trusting his own feelings becomes difficult and they become harder to understand, which can make emotions feel scary and overwhelming. The knock-on effect of this is that children who are exposed to overwhelming experiences can feel unable to cope with their emotions, or lack the ability to understand them. There is a strong link between how much young children can use language to talk about their emotional life and the quality of their relationships with caregivers. Language delay is common in preschool children coming into care.

Earlier on we looked at how being able to understand emotions gives us greater control in how we behave. So then it follows that a child who has difficulty understanding emotions may find it extremely hard to manage his behaviour during periods of stress or intense emotion. His ability to understand his own mind, to link together how he thinks and feels and to be curious about who he is, is underdeveloped. No one has helped him with this before.

How can you understand misunderstandings together? A child would rather jump from one event to another without much reflection. He may have limited curiosity about himself, why he does things, the impact he has on others and how emotions help us connect.

How sensitive children see and 'do' relationships

What would it be like to grow up in an environment where you had to be alert and vigilant all of the time? It must be a bit like the difference between swimming in a shallow swimming pool and being in shark-infested waters. If you see a black shadow under the water, you would probably have two very different reactions: in the shark-infested water you would probably feel certain that the shadow is a shark, a threat to you, even if you cannot see under the water. Your brain would slip automatically into the 'fight-flight-freeze' response, a physiological response to perceived threat whereby the body releases a combination of a neurotransmitter called epinephrine and various hormones, which work together to create a boost of energy. Well the same goes for children in chronically traumatic environments. They become hypervigilant to threat and danger, although in their case the threat is their parents.

This exaggerated response to a perceived threat, which, to your child, has been an adaptive and helpful way of functioning in the past, is brought into your home. Just as you cannot see below the water to see what the danger really is, he cannot see beneath your actions and see what your intentions are when, for example you ask him to stop doing something. People have been hurtful and punitive before to your child and, just as you wouldn't question what the shadow is under the water, he won't question your motives either, certain that they are negative. His perception of you at times may become fixed and guided by previous situations in previous homes. This will be the case however kind and loving you are being, as this past experience of trauma is powerful and has become his 'script' for how adults will behave towards him.

> Bill, an 8-year-old boy in a foster home, was being told 'No you can't go out on your scooter without your helmet.' Billy immediately reacted, saying: 'I hate you, you can't make me wear it! I hate you, you are mean!' Billy thought his foster parent was being horrible and didn't like him. He stormed off upstairs.

We have discussed how children are sensitive to their parents' feelings. Well your child might have become hypersensitive, especially to signs of negative emotion. Research has showed that children who had been physically abused interpreted and understood emotional signals in facial expressions differently from children who had not been abused (2). They actually overrated anger and aggression in faces, seeing danger and threat where there was little evidence of these things. What would this be like for children?

120

It shows just one reason to be even more aware of how you are coming across. What might appear to be an irritated facial expression to one child is more likely to be experienced as angry to the child who has experienced early trauma, causing them to spin into a fight-or-flight response.

A child's ability to trust other adults is also compromised when he experiences ongoing abuse or neglect at the hands of his primary caregivers, or when his caregivers are unable or unwilling to protect him from ongoing abuse or neglect. Children learn fear and self-reliance instead of safety and trust. This makes it doubly hard for a child to work through misunderstandings as he may not trust why you are asking him to think through situations. A deep mistrust of adults skews how he will experience your parenting.

How these children see themselves

In Chapter Four we looked at the helpfulness of a small amount of shame in helping young children learn about acceptable and unacceptable limits (3). Experiencing shame motivates young children to not behave in a way that they predict will upset their parent. When being told off, the impact of shame is reduced when parents reconnect quickly with their children so they can still feel loved and valued. For example, a child has been told off for grabbing the pudding first before his playmate can help himself to his serving. The parent reprimands him and says 'It's polite to let your friend choose first.' Not wishing this feeling of shame to be a big deal, though, the parent then goes on to sit down at the table for tea and gives the child a reassuring hug. Unfortunately, some children are not given the opportunity to reconnect to a parent and instead can be left in a state of prolonged shame. Additionally children tend to blame themselves for any negative events that happen in their lives and perceive that direct messages from parents back this up, for example 'If only you didn't cry everything would be okay!' or 'If you were a good boy Daddy wouldn't send you to your room.' What would this be like, how would you make sense of these experiences? Unfortunately, children can internalise this experience of shame in turn affecting their psychological development: remember shame is an overall sense of being bad. A child is likely to conclude that he is unlovable, ineffective, helpless and worthy of rejection.

A child will then carry this negative perception of himself into his new home. So, getting told off, being disciplined or lectured all have the capacity to lead him into a state of shame. Children will avoid feeling this if possible, acting tough, getting angry, lying, denying, blaming others or refusing to talk about something that happened. Again, this makes understanding misunderstandings very difficult, as, for the child, an exploration of a situation and his behaviour feels a bit like getting him to admit what an awful person he really is.

What can you do to help your sensitive child?

How can you parent a child whose mind has been so affected by past experiences? What are the challenges, and how persistent can their difficulties be? Fortunately, there is good news: your child is not limited by his past traumas. He has strengths and toughness that can be built upon. Many children are able to recover and lead positive lives as adults. Also, through your care and Reflective Parenting, you are giving him the best possible chance of progressing to a satisfying and fulfilling life. You can offer a nourishing environment for him to grow and recover. Here are a number of specific things that you can do to help him recover.

The ideas here essentially are the ideas explored in the rest of this book, just modified and with various aspects enhanced. They are:

1. *Always keep in mind your, your child's and the family's emotional thermometer*
2. *Create a shame-free zone*
3. *Use an enhanced Parent APP*
4. *Create an environment of curiosity*
5. *Celebrate resilience*

Always remember your, your child's and the family's emotional thermometer

Chapters Two and Three discussed the importance of being aware of how you feel. This is so very important for children recovering from traumatic experiences, whose thermometer is sensitive and set on alert, and who are watching you and expecting negative things to happen. This may not be obvious at all in some situations, or may present itself with a sudden outburst or refusal to follow a direction. So being more aware of how you are coming across is vital, as when a child's emotions are highly aroused, this can overwhelm him and spin him into a fight-flight-freeze response.

Some additional ideas from those in Chapter Three to help you lower your emotional thermometer include:

- Remind yourself that you are not to blame for your child's problems.
- Create links with other parents in similar situations, whether this is through fostering networks or adoption support groups. You can hear about other people's struggles, but also share their joy and pleasure in their experiences.
- Be realistic – change does not happen overnight, or in a week or a month.
- Redefine your role. Sometimes we encourage adoptive parents to see themselves as co-therapists, who are not only offering a loving home, but who also have a task at hand – to help their child to recover and be able to make trusting, healthy relationships.

As well as your own emotional thermometer, remember your child's. Strong feelings and flight or fight responses can cause him to have even more fixed and skewed ideas about you. It's easy to reflect, sitting on a beach afterwards, that the black shadow in the sea was most likely a rock or seaweed. However, thinking like this while swimming is more difficult. When your child is angry and upset at you, it is extremely unlikely you can help him see things differently in that moment so this is not a great time to ask him to reflect on events. Instead, giving space, using humour, doing something wacky or using distraction may be more effective. Or in extreme cases sitting outside a door while a room is being trashed might actually be more helpful. Pick your timing carefully and accept that this is the way you need to handle your relationship. It's important not to lose sight of how extremely sensitive a child like this can be, and that this sensitivity will underlie everything he feels and does.

What do we mean by the family's thermometer? Well, this is thinking more generally about the *rhythm* of your house. How loud is it, how predictably do things happen? Do people shout down the stairs? Do random friends drop in without notice? Do you have set routines? Asking yourself questions like this about how your home functions and how things might impact on your child can really help you to consider what the best environment is for him. You might find that periods of quiet are actually harder for him, and make him feel more anxious and stressed, in which case thinking about how to help him with these particular times becomes more important. Again, if you keep your child's sensitivity in mind, it will be easier for you to see that the environment needs to adapt to him, certainly at first, and not the other way round.

Some of the best ideas when you are holding in mind the idea of lowering the emotional temperature in the home come from thinking about the every-day parenting of toddlers. Toddlers thrive on predictability, structure, the authoritative parenting styles we described in Chapter Five and a matter-of-fact approach to behaviour – just the things that your sensitive child needs to feel secure.

Create a shame-free zone

Shame is an experience we all want to avoid. However, if you have a gen-erally positive sense of yourself and you have felt accepted and valued by people in your life, you will be more able to withstand shame and get past the feeling. However, children who have experienced trauma in their lives find this feeling too much and because they cannot fall back on a positive view of themselves will avoid feeling shame at all costs. Negative behaviour can escalate, parents in turn can become more frustrated and disappointed, which then impacts more on the child and an escalating cycle of negative interactions begins.

With this difficulty and sensitivity in mind, Table 7.1 suggests what com-mon parenting practices you might choose to avoid and which you might choose to use.

The concept of 'Two Hands' (4) – managing behaviour on the one hand, and seeking to understand it on the other – discussed in Chapter Six is really important for the children described in this chapter. Daniel Hughes, a clini-cal psychologist based in the United States who has written a number of books on parenting (5), came up with this concept as a way to help children who struggle to learn from their behaviour, who need support and under-standing and the experience of parents trying to understand them. However, these children also need boundaries and to get used to the idea of parental care. Your child will be much more likely to accept a consequence if he sees that you understand why he has done something, and this is less likely to make him feel shame.

Table 7.1 Common parenting practices to avoid or choose

Avoid	Choose
Conveying personal disappointment in your child's behaviour 'I'm so disappointed in you. You know I don't like it when you do that!'	Using empathy and support 'This is tough for you I think. We will get through this together, I think you need my help to do that!'
Questions and language that might suggest blame 'Why did you do that?'	Language of gentle exploration 'That seemed hard for you, I wonder what was going on there?'
Punitive responses, such as Time Out – telling your child to sit somewhere, alone, for a determined number of minutes, withholding attention.	Supportive responses such as Time In – asking your child to sit somewhere, nearby, to express his feelings and cool down. During this time, validation of his feelings and often just connection is all that is needed.
Using illogical consequences 'You didn't go to bed on time. That means you can't go to the park tomorrow.'	Using natural or logical consequences 'Well, it's hard for you to settle at night. I think that means you need help to calm down a little. We are going to try to shorten your play time before bed and have some relaxing down time.'
Showing how invested you are in him changing his behaviour	Showing how it is in his best interest to think about his behaviour
Insisting on discussing something when he is aroused and/or demanding prolonged direct eye contact.	Finding ways to discuss things, rather than letting an issue slip through unresolved When situations have calmed down, talking through problems during car journeys when your child is looking out of the window can be helpful, or at bedtime, when you are looking at a book together.
After a misunderstanding, leaving him to dwell on it on his own	After a misunderstanding, reconnecting as soon as you can and as soon as this is likely to be successful
Not thinking ahead to situations where he is likely to fail A quiet restaurant for a lovely meal, which may seem ideal to you, could be stressful for him.	Scaffolding situations so that he can succeed and increasing supervision making it more likely he will succeed

Use an enhanced Parent APP

The main modification of the Parent APP for this group of children is to place an exaggerated emphasis on the 'P' for 'perspective taking' as this aspect becomes especially important. Try really hard to see things from your child's perspective, and remember that how he sees the world is often tainted by abusive experiences. If you are the parent of a young child who has suffered an early trauma, we know it must be hard on you to be viewed sometimes as someone who is unloving or untrustworthy, but bear in mind that it must be even harder for your child to overcome his feelings of mistrust. He needs empathy for how hard and unfair the world can feel through his eyes.

One meeting with Billy and Jan, a 15-year-old boy and his foster carer, involved us creating different coloured lenses to put over a pair of his glasses. The idea was to highlight how we can all see situations differently, we filter different parts of the same situation without realising it. The colour of the lens related to what kinds of earlier experiences we had. Billy made his red and he realised that if he wore his glasses with a red lens for long enough he would start to not notice that the world was red. He got used to it. He chose red as he felt it reflected the danger that he remembered at home, but also how he often saw people's intentions as hostile and abusive. This gave Jan a helpful language to use with Billy, asking for example if he had his red glasses on today or whether he could see that she was not letting him go out late because she cared about his education, not because she was mean.

In this example Jan was accepting her child as he was. His difficulties were a result of past abuse, but she knew that if she didn't take care, she might interact with him in a way that contributed to these difficulties. By finding a different way of communicating with him, she could separate out her actions from his past and help him to see her more from the inside – to understand what her real intentions were.

Your child needs to develop his sense of why he keeps behaving in ways that make his life difficult. However, when you help him in this exploration, this must be done with a genuine interest in his perspective. He might not actually have a clue about the *why*, so gaining an insight into his actions is very much work in progress, and work that you will have to start for him. Parenting a child who has had difficult early experiences can't just be about giving consequences to things. You must try to understand what is going on inside his mind.

We visited a children's residential home recently. The home was fully embracing taking the perspective of their children. Staff were repeatedly encouraged to see the world from the children's perspective, from thinking about who was on shift to who should wake up a child, and that ideally the child should know in advance about what would happen rather than feel like it was a random event in an uncertain life. Staff were prompted to think about what would be the experience for a child of having an unfamiliar voice outside a bedroom door. How might this experience set them up for the day?

Create an environment of curiosity

The Parent APP encourages parents to be attentive to and curious about their children. For children who have not experienced a parent who has been interested in their developing minds or whose parents misread their minds, this aspect of the Parent APP will be difficult. However, it is imperative for children's long-term development that they are able to reflect on themselves and others in a way that does not feel dangerous or confusing.

Do try to encourage your child to be curious about you, in a way that is positive. You can help him see your intentions more clearly. If for example you are handing him his lunch for school, why not say once in a while, 'I gave you that because I care for you!'

Try also to encourage your child to explore his own mind, why he does things or thinks in certain ways. Be mindful, though, that this is likely to bring a strong sense of shame, so pick your moments and be genuine in your attempts. This exploration might be around positive as well as negative feelings – 'Hey, how come you gave Fred that toy? Did you want him to play with you?'

Celebrate resilience

Children who have faced adversity and have difficulties in their lives as a result of this also have strengths and resilience. Sometimes this may not be obvious, but the difficulties that they display pale into insignificance in comparison with the difficulties that they have had to cope with in the past. They have survived these experiences.

It is really important to identify your child's qualities. What do you like about him? What are his strengths? Think of a quality you feel he has, for example kindness. Take note of every time you see him acting in a kind way, and make a positive comment about it. For example, 'That was really kind of you to give Johnny your toy!' As his everyday experiences are so tainted by how he sees himself and the world, by pointing out his good qualities, he can begin to take note of them himself. It can take a conscious effort to do this, to label positive qualities and successes, and even as therapists we can often forget to do this, but it can be invaluable. We talk more about this in Chapter Eight.

Continue to help your child build a more positive view of himself and gain more confidence in his strengths and abilities. What is he good at? What are his skills and how can they be challenged positively? Think about your use of praise. Over time, carefully used praise will help him respond to what you tell him, so if you don't regularly point out positive actions, your child might struggle to notice when he does something positive! What different messages would you like him to hear and start to believe? How can these messages be given effectively? Praise is only really useful when it is linked to something specific, rather than general like 'You are a good boy'. Why not praise a skill like problem-solving or a good communication skill? To really surprise him, why don't you write a special note and put it under his pillow for him to find, for example 'I thought the way you handled the situation with Dad was great yesterday, you really tried hard to see things from his point of view', or for a younger child 'I love you' might go down well.

Finally, it is important to celebrate your own resilience. Try looking back regularly on your progress and celebrate small achievements and goals. As well as being good for your self-esteem, this will also make you resilient when you come up against the next parenting obstacle. Attribute your successes to your own ability or parenting qualities. You could think: 'I am making a difference to his life, I have the ability to be a top parent.' Attributing even small successes to things you've actually done and choosing to see them as evidence of your ability or potential is simply what the world's successful people do.

Children with Asperger's

The second group of children who find it extremely challenging to think about what's going on in other people's minds, and whose own minds are hard to make sense of often for their parents, are children on the autistic spectrum.

There is something known as a spectrum for children with autism, ranging from children who are autistic with quite profound disabilities, including significant language and cognitive delay and behavioural problems, to children who have no language delay and are usually high functioning, with the exception of significant difficulties in important areas of social interaction, restricted interests and repetitive behaviours. Here we will focus on those children who are at the higher-functioning end of the spectrum, who we know as children with Asperger Syndrome. The diagnosis of Asperger Syndrome (AS), or Asperger Disorder as it is also known, was removed from the 2013 (fifth) edition of the Diagnostic and Statistical Manual of Mental Disorders (DSM-5) (6) – the recognised textbook for clinicians – and replaced by a diagnosis of autism spectrum disorder (ASD) on a severity scale. However, the term 'Asperger's' is still commonly used and many find it is a more helpful description than mild ASD, partly because of the distinction between children with and without the language delay. Asperger's is characterized by significant difficulties in social interaction and non-verbal communication, alongside restricted and repetitive patterns of behaviour and interests. It differs from other autism spectrum disorders in that people with this diagnosis do not have language or intellectual (cognitive) delay. Although not required for diagnosis, children with AS often display physical clumsiness and a peculiar use of language. Many of the parents we see in our clinic tell us that their child has an 'odd' or idiosyncratic way of speaking that marks them out as different from their friends.

How understanding others is difficult for children with AS

Children with AS are thought to find social interaction difficult because they struggle to be able to take another person's perspective. This can make the way they interact different and their peers can find them difficult to relate to because they might appear to want to do things always in their own way. In fact, behaving in an inflexible way is more about their feelings of confusion about how exactly to do things anyone else's way. We want to discuss how, in our view, this group of children and young people do have the capacity to take another person's perspective, and give and receive empathy. We appreciate that in fact, this view is quite contentious with some professionals and it is important not to ignore the fact that people with AS are not quite as good as the rest of us at understanding the meaning and intentions behind people's actions. Research evidence shows (7), however, that people with AS do have the networks in their brains for understanding meanings, but that these are just active to a *lesser* extent. Neuroscientists in the field of ASD are researching whether children and adults with ASD can in fact learn skills of perspective taking. Ranging from studies giving children oxytocin nasal sprays (sprays which release a naturally occurring hormone – oxytocin plays a critical role in sociability) to engaging in social skills training programs, to combinations of both, there is emerging evidence that the brains of people with AS may not be quite so fixed as had been thought. Some studies show that when oxytocin is used together with intensive interaction (which involves use and understanding of eye contact and facial expressions, taking turns in exchanges of behaviour, developing and furthering vocalisations) with a responsive parent, children with ASD become significantly better at taking another person's perspective. The bad news is that this effect doesn't last for long after the intervention, so in fact the brain hasn't permanently changed at all, just learned a new skill, which can't be sustained.

While there is ongoing debate and research as to the extent that this group of children have minds that are flexible, we have made interesting observations in our own clinic on work that we have carried out with young people, and this together with research on interventions with this group of children and young people (8) has led us to conclude that the idea of Reflective Parenting as a means to increasing the flexibility of these children's minds is an important and exciting one.

Let's consider the experience of children with AS and try to enter into their world.

Sensory sensitivity

As well as finding it hard to appreciate things from another person's point of view, we find that for children with AS, sensory sensitivity can be a major issue. That is, the feel, smell, sound and sight of things in their environment are experienced differently and more acutely than others. Let's look at an example of a 10-year-old boy, Jacob, with AS, and his mum Laura.

> *Jacob became highly agitated because he didn't want to wear the pair of trousers his mum suggested he put on for a family trip out. He got more and more distressed and angry, and eventually became tearful, running away from his family and hiding in his wardrobe upstairs. Laura eventually took the decision to go out as a family with him still wearing his pyjama bottoms as these were the only thing at the time he found acceptable and comfortable enough. She reasoned some people might stare, but most people probably wouldn't even notice that they were pyjama bottoms. At least her son would join the family on their trip out. After an hour or so wandering around, seeing her son happily chatting away to his brother over lunch, Laura approached him and asked tentatively, 'Everything alright now?' Jacob replied, 'Fine, sorry Mum. But you see, it might just feel a bit itchy to you, but to me, wearing those trousers is like being inside a termites' nest.'*

Several important things strike us about this scenario. At first, Jacob was showing his distress through his behaviour and couldn't express what the real problem was, aside from that he hated the trousers his mum wanted

him to wear. Notably, once he had calmed down (think back to our advice on striking when the iron is warm) he was able to say explicitly that what he felt was entirely his own experience – and one that might be very different to his mum's understanding – 'to me' being the important words. Once he was calm, he was also able to let his mum know that something she might perceive as maybe a bit itchy and uncomfortable, to him felt as uncomfortable as being inside a termites' nest. This description made it easier for Laura to relate to him, to get inside his experience, much more so than had he said, 'I just don't want to' or something similarly oppositional – which is what was usually shouted in the heat of the moment.

Using an enhanced Parent APP with intense emotions

Another important thing to note is the way that feelings seem to be so extreme when they are expressed by someone with AS. It is very common for parents to tell us that their child doesn't just get mildly annoyed, but is *furious* because a flickering light can feel like hot needles being stabbed into their eyes. It is important not to underestimate the very real discomfort they feel and instead note to ourselves that the experience is not exaggerated, but is really experienced much more intensely. If, with your child, you try to think 'A bit itchy to me, is an unbearable termites' nest to you,' then you are on the right track to being a bit more *mind-minded*. Using an enhanced version of the Parent APP with AS children, as with looked after children, will mean that you are focusing more than usual on trying to take their perspective. It might require a bit more work, but bear in mind there is an *accentuation* of experience, be it sensory, emotional or behavioural, and so taking your child's perspective on this becomes even more important, not only in helping them, but in bringing down the temperature of your own emotional response.

There are multiple examples of this that you may be familiar with as parents, such as noticing that mild irritations felt by you or your other child may be experienced and exhibited as volcanic fury by your AS child. Again, these feelings are real, and experienced with the intensity in which they are described. Finally, in the case of Jacob and his mum, notice that when Jacob was feeling more in control of his own emotions, he was able to see that he had had an impact on Laura's, and had enough insight into this to say 'sorry'. Many parents in clinical sessions have commented that their child will seem to express remorse after an outburst, but that they are never sure if this is really meant or not. We would encourage you not to doubt this, and to try to use this instead as a springboard for getting into a more mind-minded conversation about both how great it is that they must have noticed their behaviour was having an upsetting effect on you, and also how much you appreciated that they want to try to change the feeling you are left with for the better. This can be said in really simple, straightforward words. Keeping in mind again that you are using an enhanced Parent APP, then providing empathy also needs to be done at these critical points with an extra emphasis, as this will also help to bring the emotional temperature of the situation down, and make it more likely that your child can then go on to reflect a bit on his behaviour. It is also important to tell your child when you think you got it wrong about what he was really thinking and feeling, or why he behaved in a particular way. This helps to model your mind to your child and the difficulty everyone experiences – not just children with AS – in getting to the heart of what is really going on in someone else's mind.

Challenges to the AS child's parent

Before we get on to the very practical steps concerning how you can help your child with AS using a Reflective Parenting approach, it is important to look at the experience of the parents of this group of children. We are slightly wary of lumping these all together, as of course every child is dif-ferent, but there are some common experiences that we have heard from parents. We think it would be useful to share these, most notably because becoming aware of your own feelings, as we talked about earlier, is the first step towards becoming a reflective parent.

One of the first things we would like you to think about if you are a parent of a child with AS is that your child has a deficit. This is not a particularly nice word, or that comfortable an idea to come to terms with. But if you imagine that your child was, say, not able to walk easily, would you make him climb a set of stairs every day, or would you adapt your house and the things you did together, according to his disability? The reasons for keeping this in mind are that, first, understanding that your child has limitations that are not his fault can help you to control your own feelings and reaction to his behaviour. And secondly, keeping your child's deficit in mind can help you to understand your own feelings of loss, particularly around the loss of the so-called 'normal' things that you expect from your child. Lastly, thinking in this way helps to pitch conversations and structure the environment around these difficulties, in other words, keeping this deficit in mind helps you to think about changes you need to make to fit with your child's needs.

We are encouraging you to think like this mainly because it is important to recognize that in accepting your child as being different you will undoubtedly have to face some difficult feelings of loss (for the child you may have expected to have) as well as anger, sadness and other uncomfortable emotions. It can feel very difficult to accept that your child is not able perhaps to have the kind of to-and-fro reciprocal conversation you have with others, including perhaps your other child. You may feel frustrated and irritated when your child continues to talk at you about something, regardless of the many signals you've given off that you have something to say or to do yourself – a common trait in children with AS. Noticing, naming and accepting these feelings in yourself is important as they are very valid. It's at these moments that it's particularly important to reflect on what the actual limitations are that your child faces. So, it's a balance between accepting their limitations and adopting a stance that encourages more flexibility, that is gently nudges your child to think about other people's points of view. Accepting your child's limitations should not mean that you can't adopt an approach which seeks to develop the skills that he is grappling with, particularly the fundamental ability to understand himself and others.

Difficulties experienced by fathers of children with AS

This can be particularly difficult for fathers, who usually have fewer outlets than mothers for their feelings about their children. Being the parent of a particularly challenging child with AS can lead to feelings of alienation, and we know of one father who said that he felt so angry at seeing other dads enjoying 'normal' activities with their sons, such as football on a Saturday, that he avoided other parents, choosing to retreat into the safe world of his work instead. Another father described a difficult interaction with his son with Asperger's and then said that afterwards, as he sat on the train going to work, he had the strong image of his child 'floating away in space in a space suit, out of my reach'. It might help these fathers to talk with other dads of children with AS and to share experiences. The father we've described found that talking with another dad of an AS child, sharing their experiences and feelings of anger, helped to normalise the experience of parenting his child. He also found that trying to imagine what this feeling of being disconnected might feel like for his child helped him to feel more empathic towards him.

Feeling disconnected from your child

The feeling of disconnection between parents and children with AS is a common experience. Just as important as the impact of you as a parent on your child's ability to regulate his own emotions is the impact your child will be having on you and your own capacity to regulate *your* emotions in his presence. Parents can experience a profound lack of emotional connectedness with their AS child that feels qualitatively different from the experience of being with a child *without* AS. The sense that you are not being related *to* on an emotional level as a human being, with feelings, thoughts and emotions of your own, can be experienced as alienating and unsettling. With these strong parental feelings in mind, let's look at the example from a parent of a child with AS who came to our clinic.

> Janice is a young mum who has two daughters, Amy, aged 6, and 18-month-old Rosie. Janice recalls in her first assessment that in the relationship she has with Amy, she feels as if there is a 'black cloud hanging over us'. In taking an early history, we learned that Amy's dad died, and that there had been a less than ideal relationship with him before this, as he came in and out of Amy's life. Janice also said that she had suffered from post-natal depression. We started to think with the family about the origins of their difficult relationships, which started in the first few years of their life with their children. The history of Amy's early development, and the observation of Janice and Amy in a ten-minute play session, revealed a striking lack of emotional response from Amy, despite the number of times Janice initiated interaction with Amy and the number of invitations she offered to enjoy some close, warm time and physical contact with her. When we asked more about the relationship, Janice acknowledged that well before Amy had lost her dad, she had felt that it had always been a struggle to feel a really strong emotional bond with Amy. We asked about everyday interactions and shared pleasures, and Janice told us that when they watched television, whereas

Janice would get involved in the relationships of the characters and their lives, Amy only noted the superficial details, such as how they looked, and appeared to miss, or completely fail to understand any of the dynamics between the characters. Janice became upset when talking about the experience of being with her daughter and said, 'I feel guilty, but when I'm with Rosie, even though she's much younger, I just feel as if she's more with me if that makes any sense?'

This feeling of being with your child, but somehow still feeling alone, is an important one to note if you are working towards trying to be a more reflective parent to a child with AS. It is not as straightforward as simply mirroring how your child feels. For example, you may think they are feeling lonely because they've left a play situation, but they may very well not feel that lonely at all for much of the time, and may in fact feel much more comfortable when they are on their own. Working with Janice, we encouraged her first, by using the Parent APP, to tune into this state of mind both in herself, and in relation to how her daughter might feel, which helped her to shift from looking at what Amy *does* to looking at how Amy *feels and relates*. In this complicated dynamic there are different feelings to attend to. First, Janice needs to accept her own feelings of being emotionally disconnected from her daughter. Whereas she wants a shared moment of connection, her daughter Amy wants just to watch TV and isn't too concerned about this being a shared experience. The fact that Amy isn't concerned about this being a moment to share with her mum leaves Janice feeling even more isolated. However, if she can pay attention to her own feelings, and recognise that they are simply different from how Amy is feeling, it can help her to feel less isolated. After all, Amy may be enjoying having her mum present, but not able to express this to her. If Janice can make the shift to thinking about how Amy feels, this becomes an important one in helping Janice think about how the world might be perceived from Amy's point of view. Although this shift might be uncomfortable, because it is often difficult to think about our children's deficits, it might start to have an impact on how Janice understands and responds to her daughter. Ideally, this would eventually lead to Amy starting to pick up the skill of taking an interest in other people's perspectives and learning the social skills that come with this.

Strengths of the AS child

That said, there will also undoubtedly be differences about your child with AS that should be celebrated instead of only focusing on the deficit. For example, many children with AS have great imaginations, and will often rely on their imaginative world for comfort and stimulation when the challenges of interactions in the outside world become too much. Equally, their attention to detail and precision can be extremely useful in many situations. As long as you can understand your child's *need* for precision, by taking their perspective, then you will hopefully be able to get alongside your child and support them in using this strength to their advantage in life. Some children with AS are very good at being able to see both viewpoints in an argument, without becoming emotional about either perspective – this can be a strength in later life. And the ability to focus on an issue, without getting distracted from it, is a huge strength, particularly academically. There are many other strengths and differences from non-AS children that can be celebrated, and one of the consequences of being a reflective parent with your AS child is that you will start to pay attention and to validate their different perspective on life, which will not only enhance your child's self esteem, but will increase the feeling of connection between you.

How to help children with AS expand their awareness of themselves and others

Once you have been able to accept the limitations of your child and very importantly your feelings about these, the next step we'd like you to take is to start to help your child to learn how to appreciate other people's minds, and to feel more connected to you and others. After all, the target for most parents of children with AS, as well as just to feel more connected with their child, is to help their child to feel more comfortable in the world and in his relationships with others.

A common misperception is that kids with AS are generally poor both at recognising and naming emotions. Interestingly, AS kids are able to identify well the emotional state they are experiencing themselves – in fact if you are a parent of a child with AS you are no doubt very familiar with strong expressions of emotions from your son or daughter – but they are much less able to identify the emotional state in another person. One practical way to tackle this issue, if you are a parent of a child with AS, is to name emotions constantly in yourself, and also in the world around you. This can be done in the most mundane of moments, and doesn't have to be anything too complicated. For example, watching an episode of a soap, such as *The Simpsons* or *Tracy Beaker*, with your child offers lots of opportunities for commenting on the emotional states of others. For example, 'I think Bart's feeling embarrassed by Homer again because he walks around the house in his pants!' or 'It must feel really lonely at times for Tracy, living in a home without her parents.' These statements or reflections demand nothing of your child, other than to just note what you've said, and hopefully start to notice that there is more to Bart Simpson than a skateboard and spikey hair, and that he actually has a set of emotions, related to the people and things happening around him. The more you introduce this 'mind-minded' approach to everyday conversations in the family, the more familiar your AS child will be with commenting on what's happening on the inside as well as the outside of people. Through repetition and rehearsal over time, you can start to see real changes in how your child talks about people, which begins to include statements about people's states of mind as well as what they look like or behave like on the outside.

Mind-blind, or mind-short-sighted?

Baron-Cohen (9) coined the term 'mind-blindness' in the context of research he carried out called Theory of Mind (for further explanation see Introduction) in autistic children, and it is important to keep this concept in mind when thinking as a parent how you can be more mind-minded. Baron-Cohen and his colleagues described mind-blindness as a cognitive disorder, where an individual is unable to attribute mental states to themselves and others. In other words, the person is unable to think about their own thoughts and feelings or another person's. As we have talked about throughout this book, the understanding of your own mind and those of other people's is one of the key elements of Reflective Parenting. If you have a child who is not capable of seeing or understanding the beliefs and desires of others, you might wonder if being reflective can really help.

What would happen, though, if the environment the child lived in was constantly, rather than intermittently, providing perspective-taking training, or to put it another way, if there were to be a parenting environment created where the child's mind is at the centre and sitting right next to you, the parent, with your own thoughts about your child and the world? Within this kind of reflective environment it seems perfectly possible that a brain that struggles to be social could become more so. Take the following example of a 12-year-old child with AS and his parent, where the mum is trying to create this kind of environment.

Mum: *'Dan, did you remember to pack your stuff for Rugby later? You've got that after school remember? And there's a drum lesson at 3.20. Hang on, come here, are you wearing the same shirt you had on yesterday? I can see a stain down the front. Can you go upstairs and change that please before school?'*

Dan: *(holding his head tightly and making a noise) 'Arghh, too confusing. Can you just stop talking mum? I'm not going to Rugby. I don't like Rugby anymore. And I had drums yesterday. I can't change my shirt now, I'm going to be late. Arghh (holds his head again, covering his ears). You're making me really frustrated. Why are you shouting?'*

Mum: *'I'm sorry. That was too much information all in one go wasn't it? It's confusing for you when I ask you about more than one thing at a time. And I shouldn't ask you just as you're getting ready to leave the house.'*

Dan: *(taking his hands away from the side of his head): 'You were saying it in an angry voice.'*

Mum: *'Was I? Well, sorry I didn't mean to sound angry. I think I get a bit stressed in the morning when there are so many things to remember and I'm trying to get your brother to put his shoes on, and listen to him too. I should tell you these things the night before probably. We could have a chat about it before bed time. You know what? The shirt doesn't matter too, it might make you feel more confused and rushed if you change that now. Have a good day at school, love.'*

Some people argue that if a child has 'mind-blindness', as is thought to be the case with autism, then trying to help that child to think about himself and others may not be beneficial. So, in your interactions with your child with AS, are you trying to be more mind-minded with a child who is completely blind to your mind and his own? We would suggest here that it is not mind-blindedness as such, but instead **mind-short-sightedness**. With this more hopeful conceptualisation of the AS mind, we would like to set out how as a parent you can try to develop a more clear-sighted view of your child's mind, from both the parent's and child's perspectives. We are encouraged by our work with young people with AS who, through having an approach that focuses on the key elements of Reflective Parenting (attention, perspective taking and providing empathy), have been able to develop a greater capacity and skill in understanding that other people have thoughts and feelings appreciably different from their own. We should stress again that perspective taking and providing empathy in particular need to be emphasised so that the communication to your AS child is clear. There is growing evidence that teaching perspective-taking skills to people with AS using interventions such as video modelling of social skills and interactions that encourage these skills are effective (10).

One of the first things we noticed in our work with children and young people with AS is that during the assessments we did when they first came to see us, they were able to talk clearly about how they felt, and how they felt in relation to other people. As one 10-year-old said, prior to diagnosis, at a stage when he was feeling particularly unhappy, 'I know there's something different about me. I'm just not like everyone else. And I don't really "get" other people.' This kind of statement is not uncommon when assessing young people for traits of ASD or AS, and it is this kind of insight that belies a greater capacity for reflecting on feelings, both in themselves and in others, than we might have previously thought possible. It's the foundations for this type of perspective taking that we want to help you build on if you are parenting a child with AS and are feeling frustrated about how to help him develop better social relationships and insight into others.

Building up emotion understanding

So how can these networks in the brain for understanding the meaning and intentions of others be exercised so that an emotion-understanding 'muscle' is built over time, and other people's intentions can be better understood?

Tony Attwood (11), an expert in the field of AS and autism, comments that when a young person recognizes that he is different from other children, a constructive response to this realisation is to observe people in order to try to analyse their behaviour and motives, or to become an expert mimic of emotions in order to be accepted and included. If you spot your child or teenager with AS behaving in this way, it's a very good sign indeed. One way of encouraging this is to try to persuade your child to take up a drama class, or if he can't face this, to mimic somebody he has seen on TV or in a film, or read about in a book. All aspects of pretence are great for the development of the skills you are trying to introduce him to, because they are all about entering into the mind of an 'other'.

Strategies for tackling behaviour of the AS child

As a parent trying to communicate with your child in moments of high emotional arousal you might find yourself unable to think, and your focus is on how to manage and control behaviour, as opposed to understand, empathise and reflect back to your child. It will feel hard to apply the Parent APP in these particularly intense interactions. However, if you think back to the idea of striking when the iron is warm, you will hopefully be able to see that a good time to apply the Parent APP is when your child has managed to calm down a little. Although this is true for all children, if you again think that there is the need to use an enhanced Parent APP with an AS child, it is even more important to mark out those times when you are waiting for your child to calm down, and give him the feedback that you are doing this. For example, you might say, 'I know it is easier for you to think about what you want to do or say next when you are calm, and it all feels too confusing until you've done this, so I'm going to leave you alone until you feel a bit calmer and less confused, and then we can talk.' If you think back to the strategy of giving your child Time Alone, it is important that you introduce this to your child and help them practise it at a set time of day perhaps, before you can suggest to your child that they use it to help them calm down or to regulate their feelings a bit better.

Trying to be more aware of how things look from your AS child's perspective needs to be coupled with behavioural strategies that can be learned and rehearsed over time by your child until they become embedded in his skills, eventually enabling him to develop an unconscious understanding of the rules of social interaction. It's not actually as complicated as this sounds, and really amounts to helping your child to figure out when someone has good intentions and how to please people.

Behavioural methods such as showing your child safe ways to express and manage his anger, and rewards for not exploding with rage and keeping calm, are all helpful. You may find, though, that for your child there is a secondary gain in explosive anger, in that he may actually feel more in control at these times. As well as trying to manage his behaviour, try to *name* for your child what you think is happening, that is try to help him understand this need for control.

Your child might have the need for control when he is feeling insecure or experiencing a sense that he doesn't feel connected to others, so it can be helpful to act and speak in a way that makes your child feel more secure at these times. Of course, our instinct at times like these is just the opposite. Parents find themselves, often to their regret, shouting at their child when their child is exploding, and if our understanding is correct that it is at these moments that the AS child is probably feeling a lack of security, this will only compound the feeling. Referring back to the Parent APP, using an enhanced version of this means that you will have to not only first get your own feelings under control, but then have to work harder to see things from your AS child's point of view, in order to help him feel better connected to you and less isolated.

Again, thinking back to the concept of striking when the iron is warm, it is nearly always better to step back, allow your child to calm down and, with a focus on keeping calm as your specific goal both for him and yourself, think about his feeling of insecurity and reflect this back to him, with a clear statement about how it must be; for example tell him you can understand that it is very frightening and confusing to feel that you don't have control over things that happen.

Advantages of being reflective with your AS Child

Some might argue that we are trying to force children who are naturally more solitary to become something that makes them uncomfortable.

Children with AS may state a preference for being outside of a social group, without friends or close confidants. They may tell you, much to your concern, that they prefer to be alone. However, one of the reasons for promoting Reflective Parenting even more with this group of children is that there is a heightened risk that AS children will be exposed to the kind of problems other, more social children may be naturally protected from. For example, they may be more likely to be bullied, get lost when going somewhere new if they are a bit older, or feel depressed and anxious. While it is important to respect your child's need for time on their own, time with their routines, comforts and moments where they are free from the confusion of interacting with others, we also want you to encourage a more *relational* existence because there is good evidence that being connected to and interacting with others offers some sort of protection from the harsh realities of life.

It is a common concern of parents with children on the autism spectrum, and parents with a child who is fostered or adopted, that their child struggles to make and to maintain friendships. Using an enhanced version of the Parent APP, particularly when it comes to helping your child learn to see things through someone else's eyes, then is especially important when it comes to helping your child to develop and maintain friendships. As Higashida (12), a young person with autism, says, of course he wants friendships, he just doesn't know how to go about making friends. It's a common perception that children with ASD *want* to be on their own. As Higashida says, 'Why would anyone want that?'

In addition to helping AS children develop their relationships with others, Reflective Parenting also offers advantages to their educational placement. A recent study (13) found that where parents of children with ASD were able to see things from their child's point of view, and where the attachment between parent and child was secure, these predicted children's educational placement in inclusive programs 4.5 and 8.5 years later, over and above the prediction offered by children's IQ and their interactive competence.

Connection not correction

We talked about the importance of connection not correction earlier in the book, and this is possibly even more critical for both the parent of a child with AS and the actual child. Cast your mind back to the father who pictured his child floating in space in a space suit, far away from him and cut off from earth. This particular image came to this father on his way to work after a particularly difficult argument with his son that morning. His son had been extremely agitated about going swimming and not being able to find his goggles. He then escalated this to feeling that they were the 'wrong goggles' because they were too tight on his head, until eventually he was curled up in a ball in the corner of his bedroom screaming and banging his own head because he didn't want to go to school at all. He couldn't articulate what he felt other than anger at this point, and his dad shouted back at him that he would be late for school and to get out of the house with his swimming kit. This exacerbated his son's feelings further.

We might try to understand his feelings a little better if we turn to his father's experience on the journey to work, and his vivid image of his son floating away from him in his space suit. Our understanding of this might be that his father was accurately reflecting on his own feeling of being unable to reach out to his son when he is distressed, but also accurately tuning in to his son's feeling that he is alone in the world – feeling as if he is somehow detached. Connecting to this feeling at times when you might otherwise get angry can not only increase your empathy for your child, but crucially get him to do what is needed, or socially expected, at this particular time. Connecting in this way may be more successful than simple behavioural strategies and outright bribery. As we have said many times in the book, the impact on your child of your use of your attention, empathy and perspective taking is very powerful in changing the way your child behaves.

When your child is really angry, it can feel like he is being totally unreasonable and out of order, and you may feel as though your feelings and point of view are ignored. At these times it is easy to slip into methods of parenting that are centred around controlling your child's behaviour. Feelings of resentment can quickly build when the behaviour we see is so difficult to manage, which does not naturally lead us to feel empathic.

Emotional overload

Try to imagine your AS child as a can of fizzy drink. Every time you ask a question that is about emotions or relationships you are giving the can a little shake. The drink gets a bit fizzier every time you ask another question, make another statement or introduce a seemingly complicated emotion into your child's mind. Eventually, the can becomes too fizzy and explodes. You've given it too many shakes. Try putting the can down on a nice, flat table and just letting it sit still. It stays fizzy, but is much less likely to explode. A word often used by people with AS in conversations about emotions or relationships is 'confusing'. This is actually a very accurate reflection, and shows some capacity for thinking about other people's thoughts and feelings. Connecting with this confusion rather than trying to unravel it is probably the best place to start. After all, children with AS don't benefit from explanations while they feel confused.

Learning to be more aware of other people's minds

Sarah, a mum to a boy with AS was feeling sick and tired of coming in from work and being 'bombarded' by her son with AS, along with her two other children, with the details of things they had done with their days, with no regard for her own feelings or thoughts on her day. Sarah's son with AS, Harry, was particularly vociferous, in relaying every detail about his day. Harry's mum Sarah decided to get him to practise asking her about her day when she got inside the house (and had taken her coat off) after she came in from work. Sarah noted that at first Harry only asked her a question in order to be able to then tell her about his latest progress on his favourite computer game. After a while though, she noticed that he began to ask her a bit more detail about her day, and seemed interested in whom she had spoken to at work. He even started to contribute ideas about how she might handle certain situations at work.

It is an interesting question whether Harry's questions were a socially learned behaviour. Or did he learn that there was something inherently rewarding and interesting about having a social interaction simply for the sake of it? A reciprocal to-and-fro conversation, simply for the sake of enjoying the conversation and finding out about someone else's mind? It leads us to reflect on whether in fact all social skills in childhood are initially learned behaviours that become gradually embedded and incorporated into children's understanding of and curiosity about other people's mental states? What Harry's mum noticed over time was that he started to generalize this 'How was your day?' question to asking other people about their lives, thoughts and eventually feelings about things. In other words, he started to become curious about the workings and inside story of other people's minds.

REFLECTIVE PARENTING SUMMARY

SENSITIVE CHILDREN

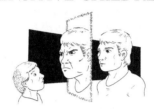

What do we mean . . .

Applying the principles of Reflective Parenting, and enhancing certain aspects, to help children who are particularly sensitive to the minds of other people / struggle to relate.

It helps you by . . .

Perhaps nowhere is it more important to be able to step back and realise that how your child sees his world is very different from yours. Remembering this will help you a great deal to remain calm and to bring the qualities of the Parent APP to your interactions with your child.

It helps your child by . . .

Children with difficulties in understanding other people and how they work need an enhanced Reflective Parenting stance in order that they can begin to learn to appreciate the thoughts, feelings and intentions of other people through parental guidance. Your sensitive child needs help, support, understanding and encouragement to be able to relate to other people and lead positive and fulfilling relationships.

It helps your relationship by . . .

When you are caring for a child who finds it difficult to understand and control their own emotions, and also understand other people's minds, adopting an enhanced Reflective Parenting stance will reduce your feelings of being isolated from one another and not understood. You and your child will gain a better connection and understanding of each other from your using a reflective approach with him.

Keep in mind . . .

1. Be aware, as much as possible, of your child's sensitivity and how he sees relationships differently – particularly during challenging times.

© 2016 Alistair Cooper and Sheila Redfern.

2. Hold your child's emotional thermometer in mind – it reacts differently from yours and other children's. It could take your child longer to cool down from an emotion that might be more intense than one you, or another child, experiences.

3. Make your intentions clear – don't assume your child understands why you do things. It is important to be explicit about what is going on in your mind and why.

4. Even if you find it hard to relate to his experience, make sure you validate your child's feelings – they are real and strongly felt. Use an enhanced APP, where the emphasis is on perspective taking.

5. Be as clear and open with your own state of mind as possible so that your child doesn't have to struggle trying to understand what you are thinking and feeling. It is harder for sensitive children to understand the intentions behind your actions.

6. Notice your child's strengths and times when your child is less sensitive to how others act.

7. Sensitive children may have an Inside Story that feels hard to understand. It takes time, patience and lots of empathy.

8

FAMILY, SIBLINGS AND FRIENDS

As children grow and develop, their social world becomes broader and other relationships become important. So when your baby becomes a toddler, you will find yourself becoming increasingly concerned with how he gets on with siblings or with friends when he starts nursery and then school. And the multiple relationships that your child starts to develop both inside and outside the home are dependent on his understanding of how relationships work in general, an understanding that has been built up over time from the countless interactions within his very early relationships with you and other important family members. These interactions create a model, or blueprint, held in his mind, and although your child is not aware of it, the blueprint shows how to relate to other people and what to expect from others when they relate to him. So how members of the family interact with each other around key events and situations is important and models to him what he can expect from people outside of the family. If he sees his family appreciating the thoughts and feelings of each other during good times and difficult times, he will learn over time that doing this is important for relating to others. Family life gives your child exposure to many other people's thoughts and minds so, in the context of his family, your child starts to see things from three, four or five different points of view, which provides a fruitful environment in which to learn about relationships generally. In this chapter, we will look at how you can be a reflective parent both in the family and through your guidance on your child's wider social world. We will look at how, as well as using the principles of the Parent APP yourself, you can encourage your child to use them too to have a positive impact on his relationships both inside and outside of the family. A reflecting parenting stance can directly influence your child's ability to socialise in his ever-expanding social world.

A Reflective Parenting stance applied to the whole family, as opposed to being geared exclusively towards your child, means trying to understand more than one person's point of view at the same time. It can be quite a challenge to hold in mind a number of perspectives and how they all might link together and affect each other. However, research shows that when families do this, communication and the ability to solve problems together will improve in the family. The outcomes for families where this approach is used in a clinical setting, using something called Mentalization Based Treatment for Families (or MBTF), show encouraging signs of improvement in family harmony when members of the family start to appreciate more the viewpoints of each other (1).

Naturally, over the course of his childhood, your child will have an increasing number of chances to practice the skills he has learnt from you. Just as your child's ability to understand others and take their needs and views into account develops over time, so does the widening of his social world – increasingly he is introduced into new and more varied social situations. And as his exposure to a more social world increases, he will become more and more affected by the experiences he has, and other people begin increasingly to influence your child. However, your support is essential still. By being reflective in your approach to him, he is able to continue to learn about social relationships and his role within them. Crucially, we come back to the point that how he learns to interact in the social world stems from his understanding of how relationships work – which he has learned from you.

The parental relationship

Parents may be in a relationship together, or have a parenting alliance, whereby they co-parent their child, even if they are not partners. If you are a single parent and have no contact with your child's other parent, this section of the chapter may or may not be of interest. It can be helpful, though, even if you are parenting alone, to think a bit about how the interactions between adults that are witnessed by children can impact on the children's understanding of you and of other people.

Using the Parent APP in your relationship with your partner means modelling to your child that it's important to pay attention to what your partner is saying, to try to see things from their perspective, and to provide empathy when it feels appropriate. After all, if you are working hard at trying to be more reflective in your parenting, but simultaneously using none of these ideas in your relationship with your partner or co-parent, this is going to be very confusing for your child. There is strong evidence to show that when parents are in conflict this has long-lasting damaging effects on children (2).

In adult relationships it is easy for us all to become entrenched in our own views of the world and a lot harder to be curious and attentive to the different perspective of our partners. This might be particularly true when we are trying to manage difficult behaviour in our children. It's hard to let go of the view that as parents we know best, and in many parental relationships there can be a dominant voice of the parent who believes that they know best of all. Where there is either a strong parental character, or a particularly vocal and expressive child or teenager, it is easy for this family member's perspective to dominate over all others, and for the other parent and child to feel that their opinions don't count for much. Being a reflective parent means being curious about *everyone's* perspective and not about giving a disproportionate amount of attention to one particular person's view.

We know that children observe their parents closely, and that their appraisals of how parents behave towards each other strongly determine how children expect their parents to behave towards them.

If then, in your relationship with your partner, you are showing interest, empathy for how they are feeling and an appreciation of what is going on in your partner's mind – and that they hold a different perspective to you – then your child is much more likely to expect that you will be similarly curious, empathic and *mind-minded* in your approach to parenting him.

Often we are so preoccupied with our own lives, making it hard to be empathic and mind-minded towards each other.

Let's look at the following scenario between Jon and Lisa and their two children, Charlie and Ella, and consider what is being modelled for the children:

> *Jon walks in the door from work at 6.30 p.m. His wife Lisa and their two children Charlie and Ella are sitting around the table just finishing up their dinner. Jon looks harassed and walks past them to the kitchen without a greeting, saying, 'You wouldn't believe the day I've had Lisa. Graham (his boss) called me in just as I was leaving and gave me a dressing down about an email I'd sent. He said that I'd gone over his head, and asked why I didn't consult with him first. He went on, and on, really having a go. But every time I've tried to consult with him before he's either too busy to bother, or doesn't seem to get what I'm on about anyway, so for once I thought I'd just get on with it myself. It was really embarrassing to be talked to like that in front of the others (in the office); he was pretty damn rude and aggressive.' Lisa says, 'Well, "hello". Aren't you going to say "hi" to the kids? There's no need to bring all that home with you. Charlie did his cross-country today, or did you forget about that? Aren't you blowing it all a bit out of proportion? You hate being criticised, but we all have to put up with stuff like that at work. Now, come and eat with us.'*

How do you think Jon feels? First, when he comes in the door from work, and then when he's heard Lisa's response to his attempt to unburden his feelings about the day? How would you feel in Jon's position? And how do you think Lisa feels? Finally, how do you think Charlie and Ella feel watching this interaction between their parents?

We would imagine that when Jon came home the first thing he wanted to do was to get something important off his chest that he felt strongly about. Although he expressed anger, we would guess that he was also quite upset; he said that it was 'embarrassing' to be reprimanded like that in front of his colleagues, so he felt this, too. Think about when you are feeling upset or hurt. What does it feel like to have someone deny how you are feeling, and tell you that you are wrong for expressing it (as implied by Lisa's response 'There's no need to bring all that home with you.')? We would imagine that what you might want, like Jon, is for someone first to listen (the 'A' for 'attention' in the Parent APP), and then to have some acknowledgement of how you are feeling. Having your partner being empathic and tuning in to your feelings would give you a chance to talk more about what's on your mind and what's really upsetting you. In the interaction between Jon and

Lisa, we can see that Jon's feelings about his boss were invalidated. He was also reprimanded twice; once by his boss for sending the email, and then by his wife, who told him that he was *'blowing it out of proportion'* and *'he hated being criticized.'* Similarly, from Lisa's point of view, she had been sitting with the children having dinner, and her mind was occupied with the things that they had been doing that day, particularly with Charlie's cross-country run. It is likely that she also wanted Jon to pay attention to what she was thinking and feeling, and was no doubt feeling hurt that Jon had walked past her into the kitchen without even a 'hello' to her or the children. We would imagine that might have partly explained why she was unable to show empathy for how Jon was feeling, and displayed irritation instead. Charlie and Ella might be experiencing a whole range of feelings, but what is being modelled by their parents is a failure on both their parts to appreciate what the other is thinking and feeling.

Let's rewind and rerun the scene, and this time imagine that the principles of the Parent APP are applied to the interaction between Jon and Lisa.

Jon walks in the door from work at 6.30pm. His wife Lisa and their two children Charlie and Ella are sitting around the table just finishing up their dinner. Jon looks harassed and goes over to the table, kisses Lisa on the forehead and says to the children, 'Hi, I'm so glad to be home to see you guys. I want to hear all about your day. I've just got to get something off my chest first with Mummy if that's okay?' 'You wouldn't believe the day I've had Lisa. Graham (his boss) called me in just as I was leaving and gave me a dressing down about an email I'd sent. He said I'd gone over his head, and why hadn't I consulted with him first. He went on, and on, really having a go. But every time I've tried to consult with him before he's either too busy to bother, or doesn't seem to get what I'm on about anyway, so for once I thought I'd just get on with it myself. It was really embarrassing to be talked to like that in front of the others (in the office); he was pretty damn rude and aggressive.' Lisa says, 'That's outrageous! You've done your own job, plus most of his since you've been in that place. Bad timing when you are under so much pressure already. And saying it in front of others, that's really unprofessional. Do you want to come and have dinner with us and talk later, or have a shower first and get your head together?' Jon imitates himself moaning about his job and his boss telling him off, which makes Charlie and Ella laugh, and says, 'We can talk later. So, what's happened in your day?'

What Jon manages to do in the rerun of this scenario is to be more aware of his own mind, plus be aware that there are other people, with other thoughts and needs, in the room when he walks in. Using humour, as Jon did here, is something we would greatly encourage you to do, both in your interactions with your child and your partner. Once you can laugh at a situation, it means you've taken a step back to observe what's happening and it can also be great for helping to take the heat out of a particularly stressful situation. When parents can laugh at themselves and at their mistakes in front of their children, they model a couple of important things. First, they are looking at themselves from the outside (from another perspective). Second, if you can laugh at yourself, by say imitating yourself when you are really annoyed or irritated, this is a good way of releasing a lot of tension and taking the heat out of a potentially difficult encounter. Crucially, your kids get to see that you can see things from several different perspectives and understand that your own is not necessarily the right one.

Conflict between parents

Almost any level of conflict between parents that takes place is bound to be upsetting for children. As far as children are concerned, the two people they rely on to make sense of their thoughts and feelings and the world around them are expected to be predictable and consistent. So what is the impact on children of parents falling out, and how can misunderstandings between the important adults in their lives be used to help children understand themselves and those around them, rather than confuse and frighten them?

In extreme cases, where the parental relationship is characterised by high levels of arguing and violence, the adults lack attunement with their child and instead pay more attention to their own feelings and the ongoing dispute with their partner. In homes where there is domestic violence, the parental relationship becomes quite toxic for the child. The parents usually fail to be mind-minded or empathic, and don't observe what's going on in the mind of their child.

Relatively recently, researchers have identified that it is not only relationships where there are extremes of violence, open hostility, or neglect that have a damaging effect on children, but there also appear to be damaging effects on children where parents are unable to resolve on-going conflict. When parents are emotionally withdrawn, estranged, or behave coldly towards each other, these difficulties can exert negative effects on children's development, including educational achievement, emotional arousal and regulation of behaviour, self-concept, social competence and long-term health (3, 4). Where these problems feature in the parental relationship, children can understandably become quite confused about what their parents are really feeling, both in themselves and towards each other. Moreover, parents can often mistakenly feel that it's better not to show their emotions in front of the children for fear of upsetting them. Unfortunately, what they often do instead is to ignore an important emotional conflict, or brood on a situation, but in a withdrawn way that leaves both partner and children confused about what the other parent is thinking and feeling. So, as parents, you have the difficult task of weighing up to what extent you share your thinking and feelings about your partner with your children. Too much sharing and children can become frightened and confused; too little communication and children have no idea how to read a situation or a parent's behaviour.

Of course, arguments and misunderstandings from time to time are a normal feature of the vast majority of parental relationships, and so trying to resolve these in a way that leaves the family unit intact, rather than ruptured, is incredibly important. When both parents are engaged in conflict – whether overt or silently hostile – their feelings are often running very high. It is hard for them to be aware of and reflect on their own or anybody else's state of mind – including their children's. This is a problem for your child, as his understanding of his own experiences is almost exclusively derived from you and your understanding of him. We have thought a lot so far about how a child needs to experience a Reflective parent who is able to reflect his feelings and intentions accurately – including negative feelings. If you think about when you are involved in an argument with your partner, whether it's a one-off or part of an ongoing conflict, particularly when it is an issue relating to the children, you are unlikely to be able to keep your child's thoughts and feelings in mind.

What if you were able to stop and notice that you were getting into an argument and begin to think about your child's experience when he sees and hears you arguing? First and foremost, you will have started to take into account the presence of your child and his feelings. In the heat of an adult argument it is easy to fail to notice that your child is even there. The way that you interact with your partner is acting as a template for how your child or children learn to understand about relationships, including resolution of conflict and feelings. If conflicts between you and your partner are poorly resolved, children, with this blueprint in place, may find it more difficult to resolve conflict in their friendships and relationships in later life, including with partners. Also, importantly, children find ambiguity extremely difficult to manage and it provokes a lot of anxiety, so leaving an argument unresolved can be very troubling for children. It is important to attempt to explain to your child something of your own feelings and to keep these distinct from how you feel about your child.

Let's look at the following example to try to understand how misunderstandings between parents can be made less threatening to a child from the outset, and even helpful to a child's understanding of thoughts, feelings and relationships in general.

> *Karen and Tom have been bickering around their children for much of the day. They went out with some friends of Karen's the night before, and Tom has commented that he finds Karen's friend Emma 'really full of herself' and not at all interested in how Tom's job is going, or for that matter, what he even does for a living. Both parents had a late night, and were woken up early by Molly, their youngest child (aged 2), and now they are sitting down to Sunday lunch. As the family sits around the table, Tom starts to tell Karen something about a presentation he has to give in the morning, but she appears not to take any notice, and is listening to what her middle child Sam has got to say about the homework he hasn't finished for French that he wants his mum to help him with. Tom suddenly bangs his knife and fork on the table and shouts at Karen, 'I might as well be talking to myself here, you're not in the least bit interested in my work are you?' Karen shouts back that she is interested, but there's a 'time and a place' and can't they just have a pleasant Sunday lunch together, and then adds resentfully, 'I'm sorry if I wasn't giving you enough attention. After all, I've only got three children to think about, and I've had about four hours sleep.' The parents bicker away in front of the children until suddenly Molly bursts into tears and drops her head on the table. Karen and Tom suddenly feel dreadful for the upset they have caused Molly, but are also feeling angry at each other.*

The first thing Karen and Tom might do differently would be to become more aware of the children during their argument, rather than wait until the argument is so bad that it makes Molly cry. When they see how upset Molly is, they could acknowledge how horrible it is to see people arguing. In this way they take on the perspective of their children, recognising the impact they are having on them, and move away from being preoccupied with their own feelings. One way of using this disagreement to help the children see how conflicts can arise and be resolved would be for Tom and Karen to explain to their children that parents, like children, sometimes fall out and get angry with each other, but that it is important to resolve this and understand what made each other angry in the first place. It wouldn't always be appropriate to give young children an explanation of the detail of why adults feel the way they do. In this example, Karen and Tom could think about modelling for their children that parents do fall out with each other, get angry, and find it hard to think about each other at these times, but that afterwards they can resolve things and be close to each other again. They could also show, perhaps after the argument, that they are interested in what the other parent had on their mind. This is naturally hard to do in the heat of the moment, and the temperature needs to cool down before any of us are very good at seeing things from another person's point of view.

If these kinds of arguments and misunderstandings can be explained and resolved in front of children, they are immediately both less threatening and valuable opportunities for learning about other people's minds. Again, humour can be a great tool here, too. One parent related how her partner's 'ranting' at other drivers when they went anywhere by car got turned into an idea for a game that could be played online. The dad in this scenario was forced to laugh at his own behaviour, and whenever the family caught him ranting in the car they would say 'Oh, oh! dad's gone online to play stock car crash racing again!' Being able to laugh at ourselves, and the often ridiculous side to arguments, models for our children that difficult feelings can be controlled, diffused and even lead to family regrouping.

Sibling relationships

One thing that is a given if you have more than one child is that you have to hold in your mind the needs of at least two children, as well as maybe a partner, a job, bills, meals and friends. The demands can feel relentless, and sometimes it can feel that there is a desperate need for a space of your own in your mind because there are so many demands being made of you. This can be especially true if you have younger children who seem to need constant stimulation and attention. With older children there is a different, but equally difficult dynamic involved in trying to keep the needs of more than one child in mind, particularly when they want to be more independent from you. It can be really hard to meet the demands of everyone, you can end up not only giving no time to yourself, but you might be unable to step back and see what is going on for your children.

Whatever the nature of a sibling relationship, it is often strongly ambivalent. It may not be a surprise to hear that research shows that interactions between siblings often contain both greater warmth and greater conflict than those found in relationships with parents or friends (5). Children are not born with the skills to work out differences, so they get into conflict at some point or other. As a result, these relationships hold far more opportunities to deal with conflict and to understand misunderstandings. Just as when you discipline your child, sibling difficulties can actually be useful opportunities to help your children work through disagreements, to turn

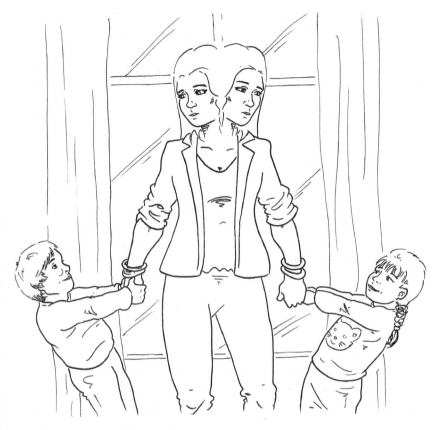

Trying to give equal attention to more than one child is a big challenge.

competitiveness into cooperation and resentment into appreciation. As a great deal of siblings' time is spent interacting with each other, with your support, they can gain much from each other.

Managing and supporting sibling relationships

On some days it can seem siblings argue about everything. They might argue about a toy being theirs, about whose turn it is to clear up, who watches what, who is the best player in the Premier League, who does better in school, etc. Some children seem to have personality clashes, or one or more children may have reactive temperaments that make compromise and adapting to change difficult. Alternatively, siblings might clash because a big age difference means they want different things or because they are close in

155

age and compete for the same things. Your children are sharing space and resources as well as sharing their parents.

What do you think siblings need from their parents and from their home environment to help them develop positive relationships? Try to imagine planting two seeds in the same pot. They are going to grow together, sharing the pot until they are strong enough to be planted separately in the garden. What do you think they need to be able to thrive together and not compete for the same resources? What conditions will help and how much might you need to help their growth? Just like seedlings, siblings need individual attention and nurturing, an environment in which to grow up together where they do not have to compete for resources and where direct attention is given to how they might be affecting each other.

Rest assured that if you have been following the ideas in the book so far you will already have been creating an environment where your children will start to get on better with each other. Not only will you have been enhancing the skills they need to relate to each other, but your children will also be feeling more appreciated and understood by you. Feeling appreciated makes it less likely to perceive a sibling as a direct threat. Giving loving guidance instead of punishment raises children who are happier and emotionally healthier, so they get along better with their siblings. Please also bear in mind, however, that it is normal for siblings to not get on all the time, and that this is not a result of bad parenting. In fact, learning to problem solve an argument can be one of the most useful skills that siblings can learn from their disagreements. Helping them work through disagreements and see the benefits of cooperation provide useful skills for life.

Attention

It can be really helpful to have an overall positive mindset when it comes to family relationships. Expect kind and cooperative relationships in the family, state these expectations and pay close attention when this is not happening and be curious about what has gone wrong.

> In Lisa's family, she and her partner put a lot of emphasis on building relationships in the family and wherever possible expected a culture of being supportive. Lisa, with this strong view, would be very interested when she felt these expectations were being broken. When she noticed her two children being spiteful and mean she saw this as an opportunity to explore what this was about.
>
> 'Hey kids, what are you fighting about? Do you think you can work out a solution all by yourselves without a grown up?'

Some interesting recent research on bullying between siblings shows that being bullied regularly by a sibling can increase a person's risk of depression when they are older (6). So it's important that parents pay attention to sibling relationships, and if they think a sibling is being bullied, intervene early to stop this continuing and to model healthy relationships.

There are other ways to encourage an atmosphere of cooperating other than expressing this directly in words. For example, siblings can be encouraged to pay more attention to one another's lives so they have a better appreciation of one another's personalities, likes and dislikes. Encourage them to recognize each other's achievements and offer each other congratulations for doing well at something. The positive effects of paying more attention to each other and appreciating each other's qualities are noticeable. Families can easily drift apart from each other when kids are ferried to and fro to a lot of separate activities, and a sibling group can lose the sense of being a unit and become instead a group of individuals. Why not play games or be active together? You could make room in the weekend for group activities. Having shared family traditions and rituals are important, too. This might be a special meal once a week or a regular Sunday trip, spending time with extended family, or creating your own way to celebrate traditional days – all these experiences create a bond and a shared identity that helps children feel closer. This needs to be balanced with giving each child some individual time, which in itself can lend perspective to thinking about another person's needs when you all come back together.

To really encourage your children to work together, why not every now and then set an incentive for them to cooperate with each other? For example, say:

> *'I love it when you two get on together. If you can manage not to bicker with each other during this drive I will let you both stay up a bit later tonight.'*

We all tell children when they are not interacting well – this seems to come easily. You could turn this on its head and pay attention to interactions that go well. You might want to give your children a special message when they resolve conflict well, or even a little reward very occasionally when you see them working things out together. You could go further and make an effort to point out whenever one sibling is having a positive effect on the other. 'Look, you made your brother so happy when you let him borrow your toy!' or 'Look how you were so funny and now he is smiling!'

> *Jon and his two children came home and found that Lisa, his wife, had left some chocolates on the table for them. Charlie picked them*

*up, took them to Ella and said 'Why don't you take one first Ella?'
Jon noticed this and said to Charlie, 'That is so thoughtful and
kind, Charlie' and ruffled his hair. A few minutes later he went back
to Charlie and Ella and said 'I feel touched at how kind Charlie was
back then. I'd like you both to have another chocolate!'*

Do you remember when we encouraged you in Chapter Four to try watching and waiting when it comes to paying attention? Perhaps you can try this, as sometimes staying out of the way and noticing can be helpful if you have a tendency to get too involved in your children's misunderstandings. Obviously there might be times you must intervene, for example if there's the possibility of physical injury or there is cruel taunting. But learning cooperation and problem-solving is an important skill in life, and siblings can learn this skill early on by working out problems together without your intervention. Watching also gives you time to see what is really happening in a disagreement, rather than assuming you know what has happened. Your children may need help to reach a resolution, but given a few seconds they might manage this between themselves. It also allows you to look at each child's viewpoint and ask yourself, for example, why are they arguing? Siblings are in close proximity to each other a lot of the time. They have to share resources such as space, toys and your attention, and arguments usually revolve around variations of one or other of these themes.

It's quite common for people to have experienced the feeling that another sibling received more parental attention and love. Perhaps this was relevant for you when you were thinking about your Parent Map, as this isn't uncommon for everyone at some point to remember feeling that their brother or sister was favoured by their parents, whether because their sibling was more intelligent, a boy or a girl, or sportier. As a child you probably did not blame your parents for this, but instead grew up to resent your brother or sister, making the likelihood of conflict greater. A simple way of avoiding this happening is to try to avoid comparing your kids to each other or to any other child. Love each one best. If he feels as loved as his sibling he won't feel jealous very often. That said, when comparisons are made between siblings with a friendly, good-humoured tone, children can often rise to the challenge of the competition with their sibling, and try to behave their best.

*'Why can't you put your pyjamas on like your sister? She's only 4
and she can do it.'*

How often does this sort of interaction happen in numerous homes across the world? It is so tempting to say this sort of thing, especially when it feels like for the last year you have been tearing your hair out in a constant battle to get your child to get changed without a fuss. Most parents say things like this at times; it's inevitable. What does it feel like, though, to receive such a comment? And how much harder would it be for the child when his 4-year-old sister comes up and says happily:

'Look Mummy, I've got my pyjamas on, he hasn't has he!'

With older children, you might choose to focus on the positive aspects of their relationship with each other as a sign of their growing maturity. For example, 12-year-old Maddy getting on well with her younger sister or brother could be framed as 'It's great that you don't get into squabbling with your younger brother and little sister any more. It's really nice for me and dad to hang out with you.'

Finally, children are more likely to fight when they get bored. At times, why not try to pay attention to when they are likely to start to get bored, intervene early and keep them occupied? It would be unrealistic to be able to do this all the time and would not give them a chance to learn to occupy themselves. However, you might find that when you are unable to give attention before they start to fight, you will have to give your attention anyway when they do fight but in a more stressful environment. An example of this is on a long car journey going on holiday, or a rainy day when the weather is too bad to go out anywhere with young children. A combination of giving attention to children in anticipation of these times, and setting aside time to play but balancing this with supporting children in having to create their own activities and use their imaginations are strategies that can prevent boredom from escalating into conflict.

Perspective taking

You can also encourage your children to use perspective taking to see things through another person's eyes. Evidence suggests that having a sibling can be an advantage when it comes to having knowledge and understanding of your own thoughts and feelings, and those of another person. In a study of young children's perspective-taking skills it was found that children with older siblings performed better on tasks where they were asked to take the perspective of another person (7). These children appeared to become more socially skilled through interacting with and learning from their older siblings. If you think about it, having a sibling with thoughts, feelings and desires that are different and separate from one's own offers an excellent opportunity for a younger child to reflect on the impact of his own thoughts and feelings on others, and vice versa.

Sibling misunderstandings are perfect opportunities to help instil the idea of taking another person's perspective in order to understand why people act in particular ways. Teaching children how to put themselves in someone else's shoes helps them to relate better to others and manage conflict more effectively. It promotes caring, respect and fairness. Research shows that children who have learned to value the views of others are more likely to include and appreciate children who are different from them or who are viewed negatively by others. Of course, all children can be taught the value of taking into account other's thoughts and feelings, but having siblings gives a great platform from which to highlight these things and provides a natural advantage. If you have just one child, you can have these discussions through friendships and other family relationships.

To help your child practice perspective taking, you could ask questions that encourage one child to put himself in his sister's or brother's shoes. Questions like 'How would you feel if . . . ?' can help your children learn skills for perspective taking. Asking questions in a supportive way helps children to think through situations and encourages them to take others' feelings and perspectives into account. Similarly, praising your child when he notices that his sibling might feel differently from him can do a lot to instil these perspective-taking skills, even if the comments are made in a moment of upset. For example, a child says,

> 'I hate Sam, he wants to play on his X-box, but I want to watch my programme.'

And a parent could respond by saying,

> 'Yes, Sam wants to do something different from you, it's hard when you can't both get what you want, you can have your turn in 20 minutes.'

Perspective taking can occur during conversations and family discussions – perhaps over dinner or in the car – that allow family members to talk safely and comfortably about problems or conflicts that they have with their brothers or sisters. Try to set expectations that family members listen to each other. You might find also it is easier to talk about other people's perspectives when it involves thinking about positive achievements rather than negative feelings. These family talks are good opportunities to practice the aspects of the Parent APP, which will help everyone feel that their opinions and views on things are equally as important as others'. If your children cut across each other during these discussions, this presents a further opportunity to encourage perspective taking. For example, you could acknowledge the child who has interrupted and say:

> *'I know what you are saying is important, too, but we are just lis-tening to Ella. She's also got something important to say and might feel upset if we don't listen to her. Let's listen to her first and then we can come and listen to you.'*

Provide empathy

All of the aforementioned tips will probably be less effective unless you spend time to validate properly and empathise with how annoying it can be to have a brother or sister sometimes. Remember how important it is to provide empathy if you wish to be a reflective parent? Without this final quality in your interactions, your children may feel that you do not really understand them and will be very likely to continue to feel resentful of their sibling. You need to make both children see that you get each child's per-spective and appreciate why it is hard for them to always get along well together, as only then can their resentment of each other decrease and your children can feel better about their relationships with each other.

> *Grace (aged 7) was playing in her room on her own and was engrossed with her arts and crafts materials. She had a great idea to make her Uncle a card because he had been poorly recently. Her younger cousin Freddie (aged 4) came charging into her room running over her materials, shouting and whooping. Grace's stuff was scattered around the floor, and she got angry and hit Freddie. Freddie screamed and ran out crying, telling Grace's mum that his cousin had hit him.*

In this example, Grace's mum had a number of different ways in which she could deal with this situation. She knew that Grace was going through a phase where she was struggling with her twin sister and so when her cousin was round her house she felt that he often got in her way. She also knew that it was not acceptable for Grace to hit her cousin. After comforting Freddie for a little bit she went up to speak to Grace, deciding to start by expressing what she thought might be Grace's perspective and calling her by her affec-tionate nickname to help Grace realise she was not about to get scolded.

> *'I'm guessing Freddie got in your stuff again Gracey?'*
> *'YES, he walked right through my stuff and mucked up my card.'*

'Oh no, after you had that great idea too! Is it ruined?'

'YES!!'

'I'm sorry Gracey, it can be really tough having a little cousin that doesn't take care and gets in the way. I know that it's hard for you Gracey.'

'It is Mummy, I hate it! Why does he do it?'

'Well, he is quite young I guess. I'm going to remind him again to not get in your way, and I might get him to help you clear a few things up. I think he just gets too excited sometimes and just forgets what he's doing.'

'Well he's so annoying.'

'I bet. I'd like to help you make your card if you want me to?'

'Yes I would.'

'Ok great. You probably don't feel like saying sorry right now, but it would make Freddie feel better, and you really must never hit anyone. I'm going to go and see if Freddie's ok now and I want you to stay here and tidy. Then I will come back and we can make that card together.'

Grace would be more likely to want to reconnect with her cousin if she felt understood by her mother. Timing can be crucial, as if your child does not feel you have taken his perspective into account first, he is unlikely to be willing to think about his sibling. Just telling him off or telling him that he cannot hit is likely to make him more resentful.

Friends

Lisa picked up 6-year-old Charlie and his friend from school and took them to the park for a run around before teatime. Sitting on the bench chatting with some other mums, her friend Kate asked, 'Where is Charlie's playdate then?' Lisa replied, 'Oh, that'll be the boy standing over in the opposite side of the playground – the one that Charlie's not talking to.' The other mum let out a knowing laugh – this was a typical playdate scenario.

Getting to grips with your own child's moods and behaviour is one thing, but trying to negotiate your child's relationships with others, and particularly when they are under your care for playdates, parties or sleepovers, can be a minefield of emotions. As well as the responsibility of looking after someone else's child, you will also no doubt be very concerned to see your own child behaving himself, getting on well with other children, and generally being what we think of as socially skilled.

Building friendships and negotiating these throughout childhood into adolescence and beyond is one of the main areas of concern for worried parents. This is completely understandable as our children's ability to get on with other children, and adults, is one of the markers for their general development, and also a marker for how we feel we are doing as parents. Parents often express great worries that their child doesn't have many friends, or is always getting into trouble and fights with friends, or finds themselves frequently upset or confused by their friendships. Reflective Parenting is not only a useful approach for helping your child to resolve some of these struggles and understand friendships, but it's also great at helping him to find it easier to make friends in the first place.

As your child grows older so does his social 'map', where his world expands and other relationships in it become more and more important. Just how does a typical child's world change? When your child is young, his world is you and his immediate family. However, from toddlerhood, where you notice and celebrate independence, through to 5 and 6 years of age, he becomes more assertive as he reaches out to others for friendship. Then, increasingly to adolescence, he will become much more aware of how popular he is and will increasingly spend time at friends' houses or get invited to more selective parties. His relationships with you and his immediate family, although still important, become less and less of a focus as his friends become more and more at the centre of his world.

The Parent APP is just one of the tools you can choose to use when thinking about how you might help your child to develop, and then nurture, his friendships.

Paying attention

When we talked about paying attention in relation to your child, we considered how this would have an immediate impact on your child's sense of being understood by you. The interest and curiosity that you show in what's going on inside your child will start to be reflected in the way that he behaves on the outside. This includes how he starts to take an interest and curiosity in what others around him are thinking and feeling. For example, in the playdate scenario, Lisa might start to express curiosity in what felt so hard about playdates for Charlie. You are a really important influence on helping your child become interested in other people, and as he gets older he will start to learn this from his teachers and other respected adults too. School-aged children will often comment that they like certain teachers because they are 'fair' and when they elaborate on this, it usually means the type of teachers who let each child take a turn and show interest and curiosity in what everyone in the class has to say at particular times.

Like a teacher then, helping your child to be interested and curious in what his friends have to say, and what they think about things, is a great way of teaching your child to be more reflective and cooperative, and will undoubtedly have the advantage of making him more popular amongst his friends. Imagine the following conversation, and think about what it feels like from Charlie's point of view:

Charlie: *'I got a brilliant Star Wars Lightsaber for Christmas Isaac!'*
Isaac: *'Did you? Were you excited when you got that? Wow! What's it like? Did you play with it in the holidays a lot? Can I play with it with you next time I come to your house? What colour is it? Does it light up?'*

In this brief exchange between two 6-year-olds, the curiosity that Isaac shows in his friend and his new toy is likely to make Charlie feel special and valued. Isaac, naturally, asks a lot about the toy as he is keen to play with it himself, but he is also curious to know whether Charlie was excited by getting it. The experience for Charlie of having his friend show curiosity in how he is feeling will be a factor in strengthening the bond they already have between them. Here is a conversation between two older children showing the same kind of attention and curiosity to each other:

Sam: *'So, what did you get up to in the holidays, Jamie?'*
Jamie: *'Not a lot, it was a bit boring after a while. We went away with the family, but there was no Wi-Fi at the place we were staying so you can imagine . . .'*
Sam: *'Blimey! What was that all about? What did you do then? Did you have to do loads of stuff with your family all the time?'*
Jamie: *(laughs) 'Yeah, lots of healthy walks and stuff, you know how they love all that. I missed seeing my friends, but still, it's boring being back in school too.'*

Sam shows his interest in both his friend's experience and how he felt about it, and this elicits a warm feeling in Jamie towards his friend and his school friends in general. In this exchange, the attention and curiosity of one friend in another also has the power to make them feel close to one another, and importantly to feel understood. One of our jobs as parents, then, is to help our children to show interest and curiosity in others; we have shown you how this can be practised at home with siblings, if they have them, and can then be extended to their wider social network. The overall aim is the same: to increase a feeling of connection and harmony between friends.

Perspective taking

Perspective taking is an important factor in children developing social skills. There is an established link between children who have poor perspective-taking skills and social anxiety. This isn't that surprising – imagine your child for example going to a party for the first time, where he knows some, but not all, of the children, and put yourself into his shoes for that moment when he first walks into the room where the other children are gathered. If your child has great difficulty in understanding what's going on in the minds of other people and really struggles to see himself in relation to others, he will easily be overwhelmed by situations where there are other children, and where there are games with rules and consequences. On the other hand, if you have been able to model to your child that it is important to think about different perspectives, and to accept that others may have an entirely different way of seeing the world, including different rules for games, then your child is more likely to enter into the party with a natural degree of trepidation, but with the social skills to be able to join in the games and play according to the 'rules' of the occasion.

One of the key factors in helping children to form a secure attachment to their parents is the parents' ability to reflect on what is going on in their own minds and their child's. We emphasise this throughout the book. Where children have had an early experience of feeling securely attached to their parents, they are better at being able to appreciate that other people hold different perspectives (8). This link goes even further to children who have these advanced perspective-taking skills being more 'popular' or well-liked by their peers. Moreover, the relationship between children's perspective-taking skills and their social skills appears to become more significant with age. So, for children over the age of 5, this relationship is even stronger, as children who have a good understanding of the way that other people think and feel, and who understand other people's intentions, do well in their interactions with potential friends in their peer group (9, 10).

Your job as a parent then, through using a Reflective Parenting approach, is to help your child to develop these perspective-taking skills, which are so vital to his developing social skills. By doing this you will not only be helping your child to have successful friendships, but you also help them to be able to negotiate some of the more tricky aspects of relationships with friends. So, in your everyday interactions with your child, the more you can show an interest in and curiosity about how things look from your child's point of view, and how things look just generally from other people's perspectives – walking in another person's shoes – then you will be helping your child with a whole range of skills, from learning to manage one's own emotions, through to managing relationships with friends. We hope we have shown you that this can be done during the most mundane of everyday interactions with your child, from watching TV together, having a chat about what went on in each other's days, and playing and reading together. Here is an example of how you might do this in relation to your child's friendships:

> Sam had one of his best friends, Ollie, round to his house to play in the garden and stay for tea. Sam's mum Karen sat outside with Ollie's mum chatting over a cup of tea while Sam and Ollie were bouncing on the trampoline. Ollie thought it would be fun to bounce in just his t-shirt and pants as it was a hot day, so he took off his shorts and went to get back onto the trampoline when Sam blocked his way. 'You're not coming on the trampoline Ollie, this is my trampoline, and there's only room for one person at a time to bounce on this. AND, the rule in this house is you're not allowed on the trampoline if you're in just your pants!' Ollie said to his mum, 'Mum, Freddie's not letting me play on his trampoline.' Sam shouted to his mum, 'It's MY trampoline, and MY house, and I don't want him on it. Not when he hasn't got his shorts on.' Karen, embarrassed by her son's outburst and apparent meanness towards his friend called to him, 'You will let Ollie on the trampoline RIGHT NOW. He's come to play with you, and you have to share.' Sam became more stubborn, and zipped up the enclosure to the trampoline, shutting Ollie out, who was starting to cry by now. Karen, becoming more exasperated and embarrassed by him, told him off further, saying, 'Right, well maybe Ollie won't want you back to his house if you're going to be so mean, and he won't let you play with his toys and trampoline.' At this, Sam got cross and angry and started to kick the sides of the trampoline enclosure. Meanwhile Ollie, shut on the outside of the trampoline, started crying and shouting at Sam to let him on.

What is going on for each child? And how might the elements of the Parent APP help Karen to resolve the difficulties between her son and his friend during this playdate? Her command to Sam to let his friend on, followed up by a criticism that he is being 'mean' and the subsequent threat that he won't get to go to his friend's house and play, are all exacerbating the situation, as Sam continues to dig his heels in, and Ollie gets more upset and feels left out. Uppermost in Karen's mind is no doubt the feeling that her son isn't being a very nice friend, and she is probably concerned about what her friend thinks of her son's behaviour. What she isn't able to do because of these intense feelings in herself is to think about what it might look and feel like from Sam's perspective, or what might have led up to his behaviour towards his friend. Let's go back and replay the scene, this time with some perspective taking thrown in:

> Sam had one of his best friends, Ollie, round to his house to play in the garden and stay for tea. Sam's mum Karen sat outside with Ollie's mum chatting over a cup of tea while Sam and Ollie were bouncing on the trampoline. Ollie thought it would be fun to bounce in just his t-shirt and pants as it was a hot day, so he took off his shorts and went to get back onto the trampoline when Sam blocked his way. 'You're not coming on the trampoline Ollie, this is my trampoline, and there's only room for one person at a time to bounce on this. AND, the rule in this house is you're not allowed on the trampoline if you're in just your pants!' Ollie said to his mum, 'Mum, Sam's not letting me play on his trampoline.' Sam shouted to his mum, 'It's MY trampoline, and MY house, and I don't want him on it. Not when he hasn't got his shorts on.' Sam's mum asks him, 'Is it bothering you that Ollie isn't dressed in his clothes?' Sam shouts, 'No! I just don't want to share my trampoline with him. It's mine!' Karen says, 'How about if you take turns going on, then you can each have it to yourselves for a bit?' Sam says, 'I'm going first though, it's MY trampoline.' Karen, trying to stay calm, says, 'Well, how about you show Ollie one of your star jumps, and then he can show you what he can do, while you come and sit with me? Do you want to check with Ollie if he's okay with that?' Sam excitedly says, 'Ollie, want to see my star jump then you can have a go?' Ollie's mum says, 'It's more fun if you can show each other your moves isn't it?' Within minutes Ollie and Sam are laughing at each other's tricks on the trampoline.

Providing empathy

Karen tried to see what was going on from his point of view and encouraged him to see that it would be more fun if he involved his friend. Had she gone the whole way and used the full Parent APP, she might also have been empathic towards Sam about his worry about his friend coming onto the trampoline without his shorts – however ridiculous this might feel to her, it was something clearly quite important to Sam. Of course, it is every parent's instinct to get their child to behave according to the social norms in this type of situation. We all want our children to share, be polite and considerate of other people's feelings. The problem is that how we go about trying to achieve this can involve making our children experience feelings of shame (telling Sam he's being mean) and threatening to take things away from them (Sam not being allowed to go to his friend's house). And all the time we are led by our own feelings of embarrassment, anger, irritation and desire to have our children do what we want and expect them to do. Making a small shift from this focus to first being attentive and curious and thinking about what's really going on inside the mind of our child, though, can help to de-escalate the situation much quicker and lead to greater cooperation. Also, by showing Sam that she is trying to see things from his point of view, Karen also modelled to him that this is an important part of relationships in general, making it more likely that Sam will want to see how things look through his friend Ollie's eyes in the future. When children like Sam learn to apply the same rules of curiosity, perspective taking and empathy towards friends, they in turn are becoming more socially skilled and well liked.

Empathy can be used in two ways. In the previous example, Karen was able to get Sam to be kinder to his friend Ollie by empathising with how he felt about his friend sharing his trampoline, and not being, as he saw it, properly dressed. Another way of using empathy to help your child develop and nurture his friendships is to get him to openly express feelings to his friends. Of course, with young children you will need to model this for them by saying things like, 'Oh, Ollie must have felt pretty left out when you closed the zip on the trampoline.' With an older child, you can encourage him to express his feelings by modelling this in your interactions with him, your partner if you have one, and his siblings in the home. You will soon see if you demonstrate how to express feelings, your child learns to do this spontaneously for himself and this becomes an important part of his developing social skills. In the example with Jacob and Jamie, Jacob's ability to empathise with the boredom of a family holiday when he would rather be with his friends, brought them closer together through a shared understanding. This feeling of being understood is of course one of the cornerstones of all relationships, and friendships are no exception.

REFLECTIVE PARENTING SUMMARY

FAMILY, SIBLINGS AND FRIENDS

What it is . . .

A Reflective Parenting stance when you are with family, siblings and friends is a way of reflecting about the many different relationships in your life, including your child's wider circle of family and friends.

It helps you by . . .

Being a reflective parent helps you to become more aware of the different thoughts, feelings and intentions of more than one child and more than one member of the family. It helps you to see that everyone in the family and in your child's wider circle has a different perspective, and allows you to reflect on these different views of the world.

It helps your child by . . .

Reflective Parenting in the family helps your child to learn to be curious and interested in the thoughts, feelings and intentions of his friends and siblings. Through this curiosity, it also helps your child to learn about other perspectives, and this helps him to manage his relationships with friends. Using the Parent APP in your adult relationship means that you will model attention, curiosity and empathic skills to your child.

It helps your relationship by . . .

Being more reflective in your parenting helps you to communicate better as a family and appreciate each other's points of view. Giving each of your children equal attention in turns will help siblings to feel equally valued and bring them closer to you, reducing competitiveness between them.

Keep in mind . . .

1. Your interactions and behaviour with your partner are closely observed by your children, and are how they will expect you to behave towards them.

2. Listen to your children with your full attention one at a time – encourage turn taking, but show each of them that you are interested in hearing what each has to say/seeing what each wants to show you. You could practice something known as 'parking' whereby you let one child know you are interested in what they have to say, but let them wait while you pay attention to the other child, then make sure you come back to the first child.

3. Helping your children to see things from other people's perspectives will help them to be socially skilled and get on more easily with friends and family.

4. Notice and pay attention especially to times when siblings are getting on well, but also help them to problem-solve differences. Working out a solution will train them in taking each other's perspective more.

5. Remember that in family life it's not going to be possible for everyone's thoughts and feelings to be taken into account at the same time. Practice being aware of, but learning to manage and hold on to, your own feelings – trying to understand several minds at once is really hard work.

6. Being reflective about what you think is going on in your child's mind will help him to learn to be curious about other people, and this will help support his friendships and relationships.

9

MENTALIZING DURING GOOD TIMES

When you start to think about what your child is doing, and on your relationship with him, it is easy to focus on what isn't going so well, on the negative behaviours and on the difficult times, because these are the things you want to change. Now we'd like to shift your focus towards thinking about the good times that happen between you and your child, when you feel close and warm, and when to also highlight the times when he is thinking about what's going on in other people's minds (mentalizing). Reflective Parenting is so much about creating a relationship with your child that is positive and supportive, and which by its very nature reduces negative behaviour patterns in your family – those patterns that occur when a lack of thinking about our own and others' thoughts and feelings leads to ever-increasing misunderstandings. Reflective Parenting is equally as important when you are enjoying good times with your child. When you adopt a reflective stance during enjoyable times with your child, he will notice your interest and curiosity about what he is doing. This will not only enhance his experience but will also increase the likelihood of these interactions happening again. Also Reflective Parenting can be really helpful when you notice times when your child is using those same reflective qualities in his own relationships, for example when he is showing an interest in how things look from another person's point of view and connecting with this. Sometimes, you might see the benefits of Reflective Parenting almost immediately when you notice your child appreciates that he is being thought about from the inside, particularly in his relationship with you. There are many long-term benefits of Reflective Parenting though that you might not see until your child gets a bit older and starts to become reflective in his relationships outside of you. You might notice your older child be reflective about some of the feelings that it seemed it was so hard for him to manage when he was younger, and this will be a nice bit of evidence that your Reflective Parenting has paid off.

Training ourselves to look for the times that things are going well doesn't come naturally always. Sometimes, we can find ourselves following up positive comments with a negative or critical one. For example, one parent, on being told by her 7-year-old son that he had made his bed said, 'That's wonderful Jack. Now why can't you do that every day?' It's all too easy to focus on what is not going so well, without even realising that you are doing it.

Being reflective during good times

You might walk into the sitting room, see your children playing together and as you sit down on the sofa say to them, 'Great to see you two playing together so nicely.' When you are trying to be reflective in your parenting, all times can be meaningful and offer important training opportunities. Each family inter-action helps you to think about how you have approached a situation and to recognise what is going on inside your mind, and allows you to help your child to understand why he is feeling a certain way. Of course, it would be unnatural to be doing this all the time in every moment of family life. However, try to make a conscious effort to think about what led to a positive feeling or a positive sequence of behaviour. What was this moment like for you and for your child? Was there anything you did to encourage the positive behaviour?

Seeing your children play can be a perfect time to help develop their reflective abilities.

At these times, try asking your child the question: 'What does it feel like when you play with your brother/sister like that?' and 'What do you like about doing . . . ?'

At the same time, you can try asking yourself the question: 'What do I feel about . . . ?' and 'What is my emotional reaction to . . . ?' during these good times.

Often we miss these opportunities within our adult relationships, too, failing to tell our partners or friends when they do something that we really like or that makes us happy and pointing out their mistakes instead. Yet we all know how good it feels when we are told that we've done something really well, or that we look great when we've dressed up to go out. On a superficial level, these compliments make us feel good, but they also go deeper, building up our self-esteem and our understanding of how others see us. It's exactly the same for your child. We may sometimes feel it's too embarrassing or awkward to say when we are really happy or pleased with someone, to *name* when something is good, and yet it really is worth getting into the habit of doing this, as it has a powerful positive impact on your child.

Matt came out of the kitchen and saw his children Grace and Lilly talking about their days, taking turns and listening to each other. He sat on the sofa and thought 'Great, I can get two minutes rest!'

How do Grace and Lilly know that what they are doing is helpful and positive? What is the impact when you consistently notice when your child misbehaves but take his good behaviour for granted? Of course, it is absolutely fine to take time out for a rest, but it's worth marking good behaviour and positive interactions before you do so. Behavioural techniques that you may be very familiar with, such as praising appropriate behaviour and ignoring disruptive behaviours, can be used here, by adding statements that mark what you see going on inside your child. For example, if we think of Grace and Lilly talking about their day and listening to each other, Matt might say, 'It's great how you two really listen to each other. It feels nice to have someone interested in your day, doesn't it girls? It's lovely to hear you chatting and getting on.' Or Matt could ask one of the children how they felt when they were asked about their day.

When you make these kinds of observations to your children about both what they are doing and how you think this might make them feel inside, as well as telling them how you feel about their behaviour, you are modelling for them how to notice good times in relationships and take an interest in another person's perspective. In everyday situations, it's good to get into the habit of asking questions and having conversations where you note and think about positive interactions. For example, in a conversation about a classroom activity you might ask your child about an interaction between him and his teacher, 'Why do you think she picked you first?' Or when you take your child round to a friend's house for a party you might ask, 'What do you think Jamie will feel like when he sees you arrive with his present?'

How can I make the best of good times?

Just as when you deal with challenging behaviour, to make the best of good times it is important to separate out things in your mind and ensure first that you're not being distracted by other strong emotions. This will enable you to have a good experience with your child, and you can be explicit about how you feel – let him know that you are enjoying being with him and doing what you are doing together. This may feel a bit odd or unnatural at first – it's something that most of us aren't really used to doing, but once you do start to get into a habit of doing this, you will quickly notice how your child appreciates it, and how much it encourages him to think about what certain situations feel like for him too. For example, at bedtime, you might comment on how lovely it feels when you read together and kiss each other goodnight, or express how happy you feel when your child hugs you and you hug him back. Or you might tell your child how good it makes you feel when you watch him play, or what a great time you had when you went to the football match together. The list is endless, but be reassured that you can't really give your child too much positive feedback. Children really love it when parents talk in a complimentary way about them, particularly because these conversations encourage a strong, affectionate bond and show commitment of your interest in and appreciation of how he thinks and feels when you make these comments. Even after difficult moments you can say, 'I still really love you, even though we had a difficult time earlier.'

Good times in the family

Family life can be hectic and chaotic at times, but within this chaos there can also be a lot of fun. As well as noticing when things are going well with your child, it's as important to notice and comment on when your whole family is having a good time, and particularly when family members are mentalizing well about each other.

> *Karen sits down to a family meal and notices that her three children are asking each other about their day at school. Her eldest child Maddy says to her brother Sam, 'So, what did you do in food tech today? Are you making Thai food the same as us?' Sam replies, 'No, we're making pasties. Thai sounds a bit more interesting. Did you have a laugh doing that with Ilsa and Sharni?' Maddie laughs and tells a story of them putting too many chillies in the food, which makes Sam, his mum and their younger sister Maddie fall about laughing. Karen comments, 'That was really lovely of you Maddie to ask about Sam's day like that. It's nice when you take an interest in each other isn't it? I love having meals like this with you three.'*

Not knowing and being curious

It's really important when you are reflecting on good times with your child that you make it clear that you don't know exactly what's going on inside your child's mind, but rather suggest how you think they might be feeling, and allow them to take the lead. You might express this by saying something like, 'Let me check if I've got it right . . . you want to play with the cars today because you found it too boring when you were drawing last time?' In this way you express that you don't really know for sure what your child is thinking, and you give your child the opportunity to tell you what is *really* going on in his mind, as well as showing him that you are really curious about whatever it is he is thinking/feeling at that given moment.

You can also practise this on your partner in front of your children so that you model for them the same idea – that none of us can know what's going on in anyone else's head at any given time, but that we are going to have a stab at guessing, and certainly show that we are curious to find out. So, for example you might say something like this to your partner in front of the rest of the family, *'I can't imagine what that was like for you (when your brother left you out of his birthday celebrations). Are you really bothered by that or is it not a big deal?'* In this statement you show that you don't know what is going on in your partner's mind, but that you are interested to learn, and this has a powerful effect on how your partner will feel.

With older children, showing them that you are curious about what's going on in their minds, whilst also validating their positive emotions might look something like this:

Karen notices that Maddy has been sitting at the table for over an hour after school, working on her French homework, and sits next to her and says:

'I can't imagine what it's like to have the amount of homework you kids get at the moment. I really felt for you last night when you had so much French homework. You spent ages on it; I was really impressed by how much effort and concentration you put into it. I bet you will do well on the test thanks to all that hard work . . . '

When your child is getting great pleasure out of something and is showing you how he feels about this, try validating this feeling, using an expression and tone that matches his experience. For example, when you see your child bouncing on a pile of cushions, and he looks at you and grins and laughs, a validating response would be, 'That looks so much fun, you're really enjoying bouncing on those cushions, aren't you?' Or for an older child who comes back from a trip to the shopping mall with his friends in a good mood, adopt a warm and friendly expression and tone to tell him, 'Great to see you've had such a good time with your friends. You seem really happy, love.'

Being reflective during play

Why is play so important to your relationship with your child? All children love to play, and play is fundamental to how they learn and develop skills in the early years. One of the most obvious areas where you can experience good times with your child is when you are engaging in play together. However, playing together does not always work out exactly how you would both like it to go, as illustrated in the following example:

'Mummy! Will you play cars with me?'

Six-year-old Charlie arrives at the bottom of the stairs carrying a large box with around 30 toy cars in it and looks up expectantly at his mum. Lisa was about to start preparing the evening meal and do a bit of tidying up around the house. She had done a half day in the office that morning and left at 2pm to pick up Charlie from school.

'Maybe in a minute Charlie, I've got to do a few jobs first. You get them out and start playing. I'll be there in a minute.'

Charlie tips the cars from his box all over the floor and in a huff says, 'You never want to play with me Mummy!' then stomps off in search of his dad's iPad so he can play a game on there on his own.

If this scenario sounds familiar to you, don't worry, you are not alone. Many parents find it hard to make the time to play with their children, for lots of different reasons. In Lisa's case, she felt she had other things that needed doing – she had to get some food prepared for the family and was feeling that the house was a bit of a tip. She was possibly also still holding on to some feelings from her morning at work, and so her mind was already a little preoccupied. From Charlie's perspective, being told 'in a minute' was a phrase that he'd obviously heard many times, and which he had come to learn often meant that playing together wouldn't happen. So, somewhat dejected, he reached for the iPad, which he could play with on his own.

There are some other possible emotions that might have been playing out here, too. As adults, we sometimes find it really hard to get interested in the type of play our children want us to join them in. Many parents find it hard to admit to themselves, never mind others, that pushing cars around the carpet for up to an hour or more is something they find really boring. The important thing then, is to find a way that play can be both engaging for you, the adult, and also feel interesting for your child; in this way you will create a better connection between the two of you, and play will become something that is mutually enjoyable and that also helps in your child's development. Play doesn't have to be a particular toy or game. It's surprising how much fun a younger child can have helping you load the washing machine or cook the dinner, if you inject humour, playfulness and some energy into these everyday chores. Older children can also be involved in cooking and gardening for short bursts of time. However rarer, child-initiated and child-led play can be a real treat for a child and an opportunity for special connection. One way Lisa could have responded to Charlie would be 'How about we play cars for ten minutes and then you can help me cook the dinner super fast?' This shows that you value both activities, and both of your priorities matter.

Respecting a child's autonomy during play

When you play with your child it is important to let go a little of the normal parenting need for control. A recent study (1) found that when mothers were highly controlling of their children's play, those children were less likely to want to engage with them. When you are playing with your child, if you can respect your child's need for autonomy you are also creating a positive relationship with them as your child will view you more positively, and in later childhood and into adolescence will be more likely to respect and respond to your view, but also will respond better to your setting ground rules and boundaries, which still need to be in place.

Importance of pretend play for children's development

Interesting research into the psychology behind children's play has identified an important link connecting the ability to engage in pretend play to the extent to which a child develops an understanding of other people's feelings and beliefs (2). Studies showed that the more parents talked to their children about the feelings they had during interactions, the more likely the children were to get involved in pretend play and vice versa, so children's involvement in pretend play also led them to be able to understand other people's perspectives and feelings about things. This research suggests that by talking about the way you imagine your child is feeling when you are playing together leads to a broadening of their imaginative play, which will undoubtedly be more enjoyable for the two of you.

Just as watching a television programme with your child might provide an opportunity to talk about other people's perspectives, so imaginative play opens up the possibility of talking about others' thoughts and feelings. For example, when you and your 3-year-old play with her dolls together, you can talk about what the dolls might be thinking and feeling, as well as what they are doing; you could think of a game where the dolls are all, say, pretending to be magicians who have come to your child's bedroom to turn it into a magical kingdom. Your child will not only get an enormous amount of pleasure out of seeing you get involved in her world of imagination, but also you will be helping her to learn something about how she understands people, which will assist her in her social life now and in the future. With an older child, a game of darts, or pretending to do karaoke in front of the TV, might lead you into pretending you are both famous celebrities competing against each other for fun. You could adopt the mannerisms and accents of these people in a playful way, if your older child doesn't find that too embarrassing.

How play is both fun and beneficial to your child

When you think about your own childhood, can you recall times when you and your parents played together, whether hide-and-seek, a board game or some other game you all enjoyed? Or perhaps your parents didn't get very involved in your play, instead leaving you to your own devices? If you have the advantage of remembering playing with your own parents, you will also no doubt recall that these occasions helped you to feel close to the people you loved. Whether playing in the sand on a family holiday, or playing trains with your dad or mum, these shared moments are the kind of childhood memories that stand out in our minds as adults. Play also allows us to make fun of ourselves and, often, when we make jokes about ourselves and our behaviour, we diffuse tensions and enhance positive feelings towards each other.

There are so many other benefits of play, one of the crucial ones being its role in children's development. Play acts as a catalyst for learning, as through play children make sense of their experiences and express their ideas and emotions. Play also gives children the opportunity to develop and practise skills such as self-control, turn-taking, following rules and developing their memory skills. Rehearsing and exploring adult roles (e.g. cooking, fixing cars) helps children move towards independence and is also an opportunity for them to explore how being someone else might feel. And when children engage in interactive play it also helps them to build relationships. The many different types of play – whether outdoor play involving lots of physical activity, indoor construction play, pretend play or creative play – help children to develop a variety of skills, from the ability to climb, balance, run and jump, or hold a pen, to cognitive problem-solving skills. And, of course, regular outdoor play, as well as having physical and mental health benefits for young children (releases endorphins, enhances positive feelings), also encourages parents to be more active, with the effect that the whole family is likely to develop healthy habits that promote physical fitness. Perhaps best of all, when parents and children play together, relationships are enhanced and family bonds are strengthened. Another big advantage of play is that it offers the opportunity to rehearse and rethink something that might be anxiety provoking or upsetting for your child. For example, playing school together might help your child to explore his feelings of stress or any problems that might be arising for him at school.

The benefits of play then are well known, but it seems that the opportunities for joint play have diminished over time as children are more likely to be involved in scheduled and structured activities, or plugged into digital devices. Indeed, with your older child, you may have the reverse experience of being with a toddler, and find yourself wanting to play with your child more than they want to play with you, as they sit engrossed in a solitary game on a device. Although it can feel like a losing battle trying to involve your older child in interactive play, there are ways you can get both younger and older children involved. For younger children, it's more about ensuring you do certain things with them, whereas for older children it might be scheduling a family half hour, watching a favourite programme together, having a meal out together or playing a game that spans the ages and is fun for everyone. You might have to set a time limit around the amount of time or times of day (avoiding meal times, or last thing at night perhaps) that your child is on a device.

As it can be quite hard to engage children at times, the easiest way to make the experience enjoyable is to take cues from what interests your child and follow his lead. Playing together will help you and your child to build a strong connection that he will rely on as he grows, and quite possibly will provide your child with memories that will last a lifetime. One dad noted that it felt difficult to 'snap into play' at weekends when he had had a busy week at work or been with adult friends. He reflected that what helped him to play in an enjoyable way with his children was to feel in a positive and calm frame of mind, to have time to play, to feel prepared and to be able to manage his own emotions. In fact, what he was articulating are all the elements that we've talked about throughout the book, and importantly, how being aware of your own emotions first puts you in the right frame of mind for entering into the world of your child, and makes you able to pay more attention to him, see things through his eyes a bit more and finally to empathise with his experience.

So, how can you make play work for both you and your child? If you think back to the Parent APP, making sure that you are in a calm enough frame of mind will ensure that you can pay attention to what's going on in your child's world. This isn't always easy, of course. For example, imagine you are walking your child to school and he's telling you that he's been made the 'eco' monitor in his class and he wants to count spiders' webs together on the way to school. Just five minutes previously, though, you had read a text from your mum on your phone that has made you feel really irritated. How likely are you to feel like playing a 'count the spiders' web' game on the way to school? Play can often feel easiest when it's something that you are prepared for in advance – it can be hard to snap into it, even though you know it would make your child happy. However, if you can recognise how you are feeling and manage to put this feeling to one side for even five minutes, your child will benefit from you entering into his world, and the walk to school will be much more enjoyable than the subsequent sulk or difficult behaviour that is likely to result if you ignore his request.

Tips for how to play successfully with your child

- Schedule play in advance – tell your child, for example, that you will play together after dinner, at 6pm. Check if there is a clear time when it can happen.
- If you try to do what comes naturally to you, playing together won't feel like a chore.

- Play to your own strengths, so if you are good at arts and crafts but not noisy play, don't feel pressured to play in a way that doesn't fit your style, but try your best to join in.
- Try letting your child take the lead and tell him, 'You can be in charge of our play for a while.' This takes the pressure off you and can give your child an important sense of control and responsibility and also a sense of how you trust and respect him.
- Follow through on your promises – if you've said something will happen, make sure it does, even if it's just for a modest amount of time.
- Stay in the moment and think about what might be going on in your child's mind. For example, if you are sitting with your child playing a game together, you could consciously try to shut out all other things going on around you and all other thoughts, and focus just on the moment of enjoyment between you and your child, and all the details of the game. Or, for example, if you're making a sandcastle on the beach, put your mind to the play, shutting out all external influences.
- Your child will take note of your expression and general demeanour, and when you are both involved in a mutually enjoyable bit of play, his excitement at your enthusiasm will make you feel good as a parent and valued by your child.
- If you really do find it hard to enter into your child's world of play, bear in mind that it takes practice. Try starting with straightforward activities, such as reading together, getting out a few toys that your child really likes or simply doing something outside that you both enjoy, such as kicking a football around.
- Start with ten minutes of play, then just as you might in the gym, build up the time you spend playing together so you increase your stamina for play.
- Don't try to fit in play time when you're mentally preoccupied. In other words, manage your own emotions before commencing play with your child, and explain to him that you need to 'cool off' from whatever is taking your attention before you can play.

There are also ways that you can avoid play pitfalls:

- Uninterrupted playtime with your full attention, even if it's only for ten minutes each day, will be more beneficial than ignoring your child most of the time and trying to engage intermittently for several hours. So, set yourself a realistic goal of how much time you have to play together, but then when you've set this, stick to the commitment and put all other things to one side.

- Children can at times appear to disengage from you. However, there are times when your child will be happily playing alone or with other children. At these times it's important to resist interrupting or taking over. It's important to check in with your child that he's okay with doing this.
- If your parents didn't play with you much when you were growing up, you may find that playing with your own child doesn't come naturally to you, and it is actually quite hard to engage in play, a bit like trying to do a 10km run when you've never trained. Just as going to the gym and practicing is important for your fitness for the run, so practicing playing will help you to find playing easier over time. You could start by introducing play into daily routines, perhaps play peek-a-boo when you're changing your toddler's nappy, play a guessing game when you're making breakfast for your preschooler, make a game of being mechanics with your primary-school-aged child when you're putting oil in the car and cleaning it, and make words out of license plates on car journeys with your older child.
- Sometimes children will disengage from play. Tuning into your child's interests, concerns and needs when he's playing is all about taking his perspective and seeing things through his eyes. When he experiences you doing this, whatever he's playing at the time will feel intrinsically more interesting to him, because he's got your full attention, and he will feel that you see the game in the way that he does.
- Games can often involve losing, feeling that things aren't fair or getting frustrated when toys don't work in the way your child wants them to. Provide empathy at this point, and make a point of naming how bad this feels; equally empathise with how great it feels for your child when he has got all his teddies dressed up for a teddy bear party, or with his excitement about playing a pretend game with his friends.

Trying to do too much

One of the curses of modern parenting is feeling as though you always have to be entertaining your children, filling their evenings with extracurricular activities and weekends with trips, playdates, sport, music, drama and so on. As much as these activities are important to some extent for your children, so is learning to play and use their imagination; actually, doing nothing is also quite good for them, too.

When you are with your child, does it seem like your child's mind wanders and he just zones out sometimes? We tend to get a bit too agitated about this, worried that our children aren't listening to us, have poor concentration or aren't doing anything constructive with their time. In fact, not only is this behaviour normal, but scientists now believe it is also necessary.

The brain has two 'attention' systems. One system is for focused tasks, while the second system is for 'mind-wandering', otherwise known as daydreaming. It is the second system that leads to creativity and also enhances your child's problem-solving ability. Too much activity can interfere with this. So it's important to make sure there is room in your child's day for doing nothing at all but letting his mind wander – you don't have to be doing things for or with your child all the time. The amount of devices that children and young people have can mean that it is a real difficulty to let your child have this experience of just letting his mind wander and do nothing. Just like a toddler needs to learn self-soothing skills, a child needs to experience some down time, even boredom, in order to learn to manage this state and to self-motivate.

Picking up on your child being reflective

Your parenting helps to shape your child and teaches him how to be reflective in his own relationships. He is learning from you how to use the qualities of the Parent APP for himself – how paying attention, taking alternative perspectives and being empathic to his and others' thoughts and feelings helps him get on with others, as he is more able to understand others' actions from the *inside* – to understand the underlying reasons and motivations for their actions.

So how do you know your child is being reflective about himself and about others, and what is the evidence that your Reflective Parenting is rubbing off on him? These are golden moments and clues that he is mentalizing and building up his ability to understand himself and others. So, when you do notice your child behaving or talking in a reflective way, how can you encourage and reinforce this ability in him and help him see how helpful this quality can be?

Noticing your child being reflective

The same qualities that are so important in your relationship with your child – attention, perspective taking and providing empathy – can help you to think through what you might notice your child doing when he is being reflective about his own mind and those of others around him.

A – Attention and curiosity

One of the first things you might notice when your child is being reflective is that he is paying attention to how he feels, and is able to link his feelings to things that happen to him. In the following example, Sam is talking to his mum about a situation involving his dad and is getting very agitated and upset.

> *Sam had been trying to tell his dad something about what happened with his friends at the park when they were playing football after school. However, his dad focused on the fact that he had dumped his football kit and boots in the corridor and told him to clear them away. Sam goes to speak to his mum Karen about how this made him feel:*
>
> *Sam says to his mum: 'He is so stupid. He always does things to hurt me, he doesn't care about me. Not one bit, I HATE HIM.'*
>
> *Karen listens to him and looks sympathetic to the fact that he feels hurt by his dad not asking about the game, but waits without saying anything back to him.*
>
> *Suddenly, Sam hesitates, only for a second, and says: 'I dunno, it feels really confusing. I just feel so mixed up how I feel about him.'*

What's important here is that Sam is indicating that, just for a moment, he is able to step back and pay attention to the fact that he is experiencing a complex set of emotions. Sam was able to pause and name just how confusing feelings can be about someone you are close to – that you can love a person and simultaneously find them infuriating and hurtful. This awareness might allow him to reduce the intensity of his feelings and realise that it is difficult for him to make sense of his father's actions.

In another example, Grace and her mum, Rachel, are recovering from the aftermath of a very difficult bedtime routine. Grace had become oppositional and defiant towards Rachel, reacting strongly to being asked to put on her pyjamas and brush her teeth. Rachel had had a difficult and long day looking after her parents, and found herself becoming increasingly irritable. She knew that she was bringing negative feelings into her interactions with Grace and that this was probably making the situation worse. Grace eventually became uncontrollably upset and angry at Rachel, pushing and hitting her. Finally, Rachel managed to get Grace to settle in bed; sitting alongside her after a cuddle she asks:

> *'Are you feeling alright now?'*
> *'Yes . . . bit better.'*
> *'Well, that was all a bit hard wasn't it? I got stressed out there.' Putting her arm around Grace again, Rachel asks, 'Are you alright then? What was hard for you?'*
> *'I was really angry with you.'*
> *'Ahh, you were. I was as well.'*
> *'I was really angry when you said you were turning off the television.'*

What's interesting in this scenario is that, with the warmth in the cuddle from her mum, first Grace is able to label an earlier feeling – that of the anger she felt when her mum wanted to turn off the television. She also seems to be genuinely interested in how she was feeling, expressed by the way she talks to her mum about what had happened. And she seems to be curious about her mum's point of view. These are all clues that Grace is trying to understand herself, especially her emotional world and why her feelings may have influenced her behaviour.

In both of the previous examples, children of different ages are paying attention to their own state of mind and voicing how they feel. It is Sam and Grace's curiosity of how their minds are working and why they feel a certain way that is important, not so much whether they are right or wrong in the conclusions they reach. This interest of your child in his own emotional state and how this links into situations is an important first clue of his emerging ability to be reflective. It might be as simple as one day your child saying 'I'm really upset', and he may not have much insight beyond this simple statement at first, but this shows that he is realising that emotions are important.

You might notice times when your child is genuinely curious about other people too. For example, your child may ask a direct question about why someone acted in a particular way, or he might volunteer a suggestion that indicates that he is thinking about other people and why they do things, as we can see in this scenario.

> Charlie came home from school and talked about what had happened with Max, a new boy who had just moved to Charlie's school and started in his class. Earlier in the day Max had been very bossy to Charlie and his friends, insisting that they play his game by his rules! Charlie said to his mum Lisa:
> 'Mum, Max is just so bossy, I didn't want to play his game at all, but I did.'
> Lisa asks, 'Really, why did you play if you didn't want to?'
> 'Max is new in school, I didn't want to upset him. Why is he so bossy? I think he is being bossy because he wants to make friends.'
> 'Maybe Charlie, why do you think that would make him bossy?'
> 'Maybe he just wants to make friends and is worried he won't. That makes him more bossy.'

So Charlie is displaying curiosity about Max and has already thought about why he is being bossy. He is open to discovery about what might be influencing Max's behaviour in a way that goes beyond simply 'He is just a bossy boy'. Charlie is curious about seeing Max more from the *inside.*

P – Perspective taking

You might also start to notice your child taking different perspectives on why he acted in particular ways or felt particular things. Returning to the first example with Grace and her mum, where they were talking about their difficult moment together, Rachel decided to carry on this conversation and said:

> 'Maybe me saying I was going to turn off the television made you angry, but, thinking about it, you seemed quite angry before I turned off the television.'
> 'Umm, I don't know why I got so angry then.'
> 'Let's try to figure it out shall we? It's a Friday, so I guess this is the end of a busy week for you? Perhaps you're tired? Or maybe something happened at school and you still feel a little upset about it?'
> 'I am tired.'
> 'Are you?'
> 'Sometimes I think I get more angry when I am tired, I think that's it Mum!'
> 'Yes maybe, I know I'm more grumpy when I am tired.'

Breaking down this scenario, there are lots of really helpful things happening. In her interactions with her mum, Grace is experiencing that learning about feelings is helpful and important and it feels okay to do this with her mum. At the same time her mum is showing that she's interested in how her daughter feels and why she feels this way, but she isn't trying to *tell* her how she feels, or why, but helpfully suggests a few options. While it's important to let your children see you being curious, being a 'mind-reader' can be very annoying for children (and adults) as this can feel as though others are telling them what they think, and often this doesn't match how they really feel inside. In Grace's case we can see that she is gradually changing her mind about why she got angrier than normal during an everyday routine – that she is developing a helpful ability to shift perspectives about her own thoughts and feelings. It's worth reflecting on this ability in your own life, thinking about the times when you are able to recognise that you may have overreacted in a situation with a friend or partner. It can be invaluable, but difficult, to notice times when your emotional 'temperature' became too high and consequently affected your behaviour. Over time, as Grace becomes more aware of how her thoughts and feelings have affected her behaviour, this will help her relationships. For example, she will find it easier in her present and future relationships to make amends after misunderstandings and ensure that her relationships continue through difficult periods, so that she can build relationships that are stable and less likely to break up. For example, if Grace were to find herself disagreeing with a friend at school, she might be more likely to reflect afterwards on how she reacted to what her friend was saying, and go back to her friend and make amends.

Reflective Parenting will also start to have an impact on your child's ability to see the perspectives of other people and noticing this is as important as noticing his self-reflections. When you read books to your child, this is a great opportunity to begin to ask him about the characters in the stories and why they have acted in certain ways, so that he learns to see things from someone else's point of view and avoid jumping to conclusions about other people's actions. Simple perspective taking can happen quite early on in your child's development.

> *Ella is listening to a bedtime story about a princess and her father, the King. In the story the King forbids his daughter from dancing and going to parties with her friends. Ella's mother stops and asks,*
> *'I wonder why the King wouldn't let his daughter go to dances with her friends.'*
> *Ella replies, 'He doesn't like dancing!'*

While it is doubtful that this is the reason why a king would not let his daughter dance, this is however quite a typical response from a 4-year-old, and indicates that she is able to think about the king and take his perspective. In another example, Lisa had asked her husband Jon to buy wrapping paper on the way home from work, as it was her mother's birthday. Her mother was coming over early the next day and Lisa needed to wrap her present. Jon walked through the door without the paper. Lisa asked:

> *'What happened to the paper?'*
> *'Oh no! I completely forgot about that!'*
> *'I can't believe it Jon' said Lisa, 'Just one thing I ask you to get and you don't get it! Do you not care about my mother?'*
> *Jon walked up the stairs in frustration. Charlie was listening to this interaction and, sensing that his mother was stressed, said:*
> *'I think Dad had a really busy day again Mum. He always forgets things when he has a busy day.'*

In this example, Charlie is both showing some awareness of his mother's feelings as well as offering an alternative explanation to why his dad forgot to bring the wrapping paper home. When you notice this ability in your child it shows your child's growing awareness of how people see things in different ways.

P – Providing empathy

Imagine you have had a tough day, you felt very criticized by a close friend and you are feeling low. Do you feel you deserve comfort and support, either from other people or from yourself? Are you likely to get a blanket, a cup of cocoa, curl up on the sofa with a favourite film and feel sorry for yourself? Your ability to experience difficult feelings and tolerate them is learned mainly from your earlier childhood experiences with your parents. This self-supporting approach can be such a healthy way of approaching emotions – for these often everyday events to be less painful, you need to have low levels of self-criticism and an ability to soothe yourself. Just as you have learned the ability to soothe yourself, your Reflective Parenting communicates to your child that his feelings are important and manageable, that he deserves your empathy and support. You may then start to notice that your child is able to behave in a way that indicates that he has empathy and compassion for himself, which is a sign of mentalizing. This is a sign that your child is able to look at himself and his emotions from the outside. Let's look at the following example. Lilly has come with her sister Grace to stay with her father after school and explained that her friends refused to play with her. She told her father that this made her very sad. At bedtime Lilly is lying in bed and Matt says:

> 'Well . . . I think you might have had a difficult day Lilly!'
> 'Yes Daddy. Can I have another big cuddle?'
> 'Of course you can Lilly. You need one probably!'
> Matt gave her a big cuddle and said:
> 'Tomorrow is a different day, I love you!'
> He saw Lilly deep under her blanket, snuggling up to her favourite teddy.

This ability to comfort yourself or let other people comfort you can really help deal with the adversities of life. With this ability to fall back on, we are more able to take ownership of our own thoughts, feelings and actions and have compassion for ourselves. And for your child, he will be more able to tolerate difficult feelings, and not feel bad or guilty when relationships go wrong and instead be more able to take steps to make amends.

You might also notice that your child is able to be empathic towards others. For example, Charlie is speaking to Lisa about his 7th birthday party, who he wants to invite and what kinds of games he would like to play. His sister Ella is also in the room. Charlie suddenly says:

> 'I'll be getting so many presents, won't I Mummy?'
> 'Yes you will because there are lots of people coming.'

'But what about Ella . . . Can't you get her a dolly too? She would get upset otherwise.'
'That's really thoughtful of you to think about how your sister might feel left out.'

Impressively, here Charlie has managed to shift his attention from his own interest and excitement to consider his conversation from his sister's perspective. Not only this, but also he has been able to connect with how he imagines her to be feeling. Charlie is bringing the quality of empathy into his relationship with his sister – the same quality your child shows when he gives you a cuddle a few minutes after you have said you have a headache, even though he is upset you aren't playing with him, or when he saves you a sweet for when you come home from work.

Maddy was having a few friends over for a sleepover for her birthday party and was running around the house, shouting with excitement about them all coming over, and what they were going to eat for snacks late at night, which movie they were going to watch, etc. when she saw Sam looking down and biting his bottom lip. Maddy said, 'Sam, I hope you don't feel left out 'cos we're staying up late? Do you want to hang out with us earlier on and then you could come ice-skating tomorrow with us? I don't want you to feel left out.' Tom, their father, told Maddy, 'That's kind, thinking of your brother's feelings when you're excited about your sleepover.'

Helping your child develop reflective capacities

Once you start to notice times when your child is interested in what is going on in his mind and other people's minds, what should you do? Although parents can't be expected to be therapists, there are some really useful strategies to help you respond well when you notice your child being reflective. How you respond depends very much on the situation, the age of your child and the importance of the situation. Bear in mind, if you are interested and curious about your child's perspective, these strategies, or prompts, should come quite naturally:

A. Comment on what you notice
B. Expand and be curious
C. Explain what you liked or why it might be important

Comment on what you notice

By commenting when you notice your child being reflective, you highlight his behaviour, helping him to notice what he is doing and that you see it as important and helpful. There are plenty of ways you could do this:

> 'I saw you really think about how you feel there. And it was great that you told me how you felt, instead of shouting.'
> 'Hey you really thought about that didn't you?'
> 'When you did that, I was very impressed by how you tried to get your head around the situation and work it out.'
> 'I was really interested when you asked me what I thought about that. You kind of paused and thought about me. I think you wanted to find out didn't you?'
> 'You seem to be getting a lot better at calming yourself down first and thinking about what you want to say rather than just exploding.'

Expand and be curious

You can take your interactions a bit further, continuing to use the qualities of the Parent APP. If you sense your child is happy to discuss a situation a little more, try asking a bit more about why he felt a certain way to try to see things from his perspective: what does the situation look like from his point of view, and what new insights might he or you have? Showing that you are curious, using an expressive, interested voice, can really help your child to open up more so that you can explore situations together:

> 'Oh, what made you think like that?'
> 'Did things look different once you'd realised that?'
> 'How do you feel now?'

Explain what you liked or why it might be important

For instance, it might be helpful to explain what you liked about him thinking in a certain way. You can explain why the way in which he dealt with a situation seemed important to you, and how this different way of thinking about things – that is his ability to think about others – *might* help come up with different kinds of solutions when he finds himself in a troubling situation. Returning to Charlie talking about the new child in his class, Max, Lisa is impressed that her son was thinking about Max and what might have been going on inside his mind, why he was being bossy. She said:

> 'I really like the way you thought about that. I didn't think of it like that! So I guess if you are right he might get less bossy when he settles in a bit.'
> 'Yes maybe.'
> 'That's really interesting Charlie, thinking stuff like that.'
> 'Why?'
> 'Well you seem to get it that that's how Max feels. He might be trying to be the centre of attention because he feels worried. I really like that. You also carried on playing with him, I guess you were trying to help him fit in and feel better?'
> 'Yes' said Charlie.
> 'Imagine if you just got angry because he was being bossy. Would you have stopped playing?' asked Lisa.
> 'I would have walked off like Reece did. Max might have got more worried then!'
> His mother replied, 'He might get more bossy then! But you carried on playing with him; he might actually turn out to be a really good friend. You just need to wait and see.'
> 'He got less bossy at the end of the day. He asked me what my favourite game was, too.'

So reflective parents, such as Lisa, search actively for examples of good reflective abilities in their children, positively frame them and make them more likely to happen. This brings meaning to these interactions. In another example, Charlie tells Lisa that he would like to go bowling for his party.

> 'That's a good idea love, do you think your friends know how to bowl?'
> Charlie replies, 'I'm not sure, maybe they don't all. But if they don't know how to play, they could just watch.'
> 'Do you think they would still have a good time if they just sat around watching?'
> Charlie seems to consider this a bit and says, 'I think, hmm, I really want to go bowling. No, I know. I want a football party, everyone in my class knows how to play football. Some people might not like football, but everyone knows how to play it. Hmmm, I don't know they might not like football.'

Lisa replies, 'It's good you're thinking about your friends Charlie. So, what would be the best solution?'
'Football Party!'

Here, the important point is not the solution that Charlie arrives at, but the reflective capacity he shows when thinking the situation through. This is what his mum notices and rewards with her comment that he is thinking about his friends.

Being reflective within your relationships means thinking about and reflecting on what you do and what you assume other people do. However, it is a skill to be able to do this well, one that you are helping your child develop. By noticing and highlighting these emerging abilities in your child, you are encouraging him to bring these skills into his interactions and enabling him to have more harmonious and stable relationships with you, your family, his friends and teachers.

REFLECTIVE PARENTING SUMMARY

MENTALIZING DURING GOOD TIMES

What it is . . .

Mentalizing during good times means thinking about the thoughts, feelings and intentions of others in your family and encouraging children to develop their own reflective skills through modelling Reflective Parenting to them, particularly when you are enjoying time together and experiencing positive behaviours in your child.

It helps you by . . .

Applying a Reflective Parenting stance and thinking about the mind of others in your family when things are going well will help you to have more enjoyable and harmonious times in your family and in your interactions with your partner and child. Having other members of the family notice something about you that you might be thinking or feeling that they like helps to build your self-esteem.

It helps your child by . . .

In positive interactions with your child where you express curiosity and interest in him, he will be more likely to increase his positive behaviours and interactions with others. Modelling a Reflective Parenting stance at these times helps him to feel close to you and enhances his or self-esteem as the focus is on his ability to think about himself and others clearly.

It helps your relationship by . . .

Taking a Reflective Parenting stance with your child during periods of play and good times means that you and your child will get to appreciate the experience of being validated and held in mind and it will increase the likelihood of you wanting to enjoy these times together again. Seeing your child's world through his eyes will allow you to enter into his world of play and enjoyment with greater interest and enthusiasm, bringing you closer together.

Keep in mind . . .

1. Highlight when things are going well, particularly in interactions, and say this out loud to your child.
2. Show curiosity about what made things work well/feel good.
3. Model stepping into someone else's shoes and seeing things through their eyes and note aloud to your child how that feels, in a positive way.
4. Help your child or children to problem solve by asking how they might imagine what someone else thinks or feels about something – with the focus on something positive.
5. The more you see things through your child's eyes, and are curious about what is going on inside his mind, the more enjoyable and rewarding your times together will be as he responds to your attention and curiosity.
6. Try to always reward (with your interest and enthusiasm) times when your child is thinking through how things might look and feel for other people. It is not so important whether these are negative or positive feelings.
7. Start with setting aside time to play together – even ten minutes a day will feel great to your child – and find something you can both enjoy.
8. Playing doesn't come naturally to everyone. It can take practice.
9. Notice when your child is being reflective about himself and others – this is evidence that your Reflective Parenting is rubbing off on him
10. Encourage your child to be reflective and reinforce this ability as it will help him build up his understanding of himself and others.

Conclusion

Hopefully we have convinced you that being a reflective parent has a great many benefits. By turning the focus of parenting onto your relationship with your child and asking you to reflect on what you hold dear and important, you will now be in a better position to create more harmonious relationships within your family. Crucially, when your child feels valued and understood, the potential for unwanted behaviour decreases too, so not only can you help him feel great, but he will also behave a bit better too.

If you have come this far in reading a book that encourages you to think about the way you parent and why, then you have already made a great start on the road to becoming a more reflective parent. The subtitle of our book suggests we are offering you a guide to understanding what goes on in your child's mind, but in fact what we have really tried to do is get you to come up with your own guide, which comes from how you make sense of how you think and feel in relation to your child. Being reflective in your parenting isn't easy, and it simply isn't possible for any of us to do all the time. But do notice the impact on you, on your child, and on your relationship when you do manage to take this stance, and hopefully that will spur you on further. You will start to see this in how your child relates to other people and, how his friends see him, and a great outcome would be if you started to see signs of your child becoming a reflective parent himself one day with his own children, your grandchildren. We hope that this book stays with you in your mind when you are with your children throughout the years to come.

10

REFLECTING ON THE BOOK

We can never be sure what is going on in our children's minds, or anyone's for that matter, so it feels really important to check things out with each other from time to time. When we got to the end of this book, we thought that equally, it would be important to check if the ideas about Reflective Parenting that we have set out made sense to you parents. The following conversation between us reflects our discussion about the ideas we have tried to communicate, and also how we use Reflective Parenting in our own work and with our own families.

S – Can people's level of Reflective Parenting vary? Do you think it is possible to be a reflective parent all of the time?

A – I keep rehearsing and trying to keep these ideas in mind. I think it's definitely about training yourself to build up these skills over time. I think I probably use it *after* a situation. I think I use the principle to reconnect with my kids after a difficult moment. But I hold the general ideas in mind. The term that really helps me, which I picked up from reading Daniel Hughes, is 'connection rather than correction': trying to re-establish a connection with my child when we've had a bit of a rocky encounter. What do you think? Is it hard for you to be reflective all of the time?

S – Of course, it's not something anyone can do all of the time. Probably even the most reflective parents are only doing it around 30 per cent of the time, and that's fine. I've found it really helpful to try to separate out what I'm feeling from what my children are feeling. So being really aware of my own feeling as being distinct from theirs. So, if I find myself being snappy, I try to stop myself in the moment and think 'Am I shouting because of something that they've done, or because of how I'm feeling?' And then I've found that being really open about that in the moment has helped to de-escalate the conflict. So, I've just caught myself and said something like:

> *'Mum's been really snappy because I've had such a horrible day. My knee is really hurting today so I've been in a grumpy mood, it's nothing to do with you',*

The two of us reflecting on the book.

I've found that's been quite helpful in immediately stopping feeling angry at my kids. They haven't felt so falsely accused probably. Of course, there are plenty of times when I don't do that too.

A – So, being aware of your mood and how you're coming across plays a big part in how reflective you can be at any given time.

S – Yes, I've found that separating out my own and my children's feelings has been quite helpful. Paying attention I think is incredibly powerful. So this morning, even though it's a busy morning before school, I made time to sit down with my youngest (6-year-old) boy and said 'let's have a little chat while you're having your toast' and we just chatted about anything, and I made a bit of extra time. I didn't do a few other things I might normally have done before the school run, loading the dishwasher and stuff like that – I left those things. Then, as I was going upstairs to get his football kit, he shouted out to me 'can I have some more toast and another little chat?' I thought that was really nice. It was only 2 minutes and he'd really appreciated it and it made the school run go really well. We both benefited from injecting just a short amount of attention-giving into a really busy morning.

A – Yeah. That's interesting. I find that I probably don't use the APP all of the time, and just every now and then I come back to it. I don't use it explicitly all of the time but there are some points when I definitely do go back to it. Maybe that's a helpful point – we're not talking about using this model every second of the day with your child.

S – That's right, so if a parent asked us 'When should I be really conscious of these ideas and when should I be using it?' What do you think we should tell them?

A – I think it's mainly really helpful around discipline and strong emotions. So, when a child is doing something that you don't like, that you don't agree with, and you want him to behave differently. Or when he is doing something repetitively that might get him into some sort of trouble. Or when he has a strong feeling about someone or something that's happened. The APP is quite useful then to really help deal with these tricky moments. I think that's the thing that's helped me most with my parenting – seeing that most children misbehave – is how to reconnect with them and help them develop an awareness of their inside stories.

S – Hmm, you want them to behave well too presumably?

A – Yes, but I want to develop awareness as well as promote good behaviour – I think better behaviour follows once children are more aware of how they're feeling. I think if you have a good connection, your child feels understood by you. And you're at least some of the time feeling connected to him. Children like that – to feel connected, and they're more likely to behave better, which goes back to your point about paying attention before the school run. Like you, though, it's not something that I always spontaneously do, and I might have to remind myself to use this approach until eventually it becomes more spontaneous.

S – Thinking about the APP, I've found that what works well on its own is providing empathy, when I find I haven't really got an answer for some of the problems my kids have. So say things they feel aren't fair. For example, my youngest wanted to go for a sleepover and it got cancelled because the little boy was unwell. So, he was really angry that his friend wasn't well enough to have him for a sleepover. And he couldn't really get into feeling sorry for his friend too much, which I sort of could understand, because he was just feeling sorry for himself. And he started throwing things around the bedroom, and trashing my bedroom a bit really. And I was feeling a bit cross that he was doing that, because I'd just tidied up. But what worked again, really straight away, was me just saying:

> 'That's really rubbish for you that you can't go.' He was saying 'it's not fair, not fair', and I said, 'it ISN'T fair, it's horrible. You were really looking forward to it, and now you feel really fed up that you can't go. And I wish I could change it, but I can't and that's how it is. But its rubbish for you, and it doesn't feel fair.'

And he stopped chucking things around. So it did stop the behaviour, and improved the connection between us. Whereas if I'd have shouted at him to stop trashing my bedroom, which I kind of felt like doing at the beginning, he would have got more upset, I would have felt bad, and I think he would have felt told off for feeling upset, because he was upset more than angry, but it came out as anger. So I suppose that's the other thing that's helpful about the APP, is trying to think about what your child is really feeling, because what you might *see* and what he is feeling can be quite unconnected – I saw anger and aggression towards me and my things – when what he was feeling was really sad. I had to remind myself and make a conscious effort to try an empathic approach, and I think it's important that people reading this book realise it doesn't come naturally necessarily.

So it can be helpful to connect with that. I suppose you're right, it's helpful to use the APP when you need to discipline, to address a strong emotion, but you don't always need to use it in your everyday interactions. So, it's interesting isn't it, because we have a chapter on good times. Maybe it would be easy to miss out on using it during those good times? For most of us learning new parenting skills, the starting point is probably during difficult times as it can be so helpful then, then once you get used to the APP it can be great to use during good times, when it can be really enhancing and have wonderful long-term effects.

A – Isn't it important to set boundaries too though around children's behaviour? I was thinking that some parents may read this and think that there are other methods that are much better, and quicker, at getting their children to behave better. You know, things like Time Out, taking privileges away and so on.

S – Well, that depends on what you want to focus on doesn't it? Your focus might be immediate behavioural change, or for some people the focus could be the relationship and having a better connection. For an immediate change in your child's behaviour then sometimes other strategies do work quickly, but they might not last and the connection between you and your child can be affected. It feels important to think about the long term for your child's behaviour and emotional development, and not just to focus on changing the behaviour immediately, although of course sometimes just empathising can change the behaviour straight away. It also has the advantage of keeping the warmth between you both, and bringing you closer; I guess it's that part of the puzzle to figuring out what's going on in a child's mind that we want parents to keep in mind, however frustrated they are by their child's behaviour. Perhaps we ought to think a bit more about what is going well in the relationship too, and how parents can miss these opportunities for connecting and being reflective?

A – I think it's well worth not missing that, as we can easily just focus on when things aren't going well, can't we? Do you think for some people, though, that there are so many other things going on for them in the rest of their lives that it's hard to think about their child's inner world?

S – Yes, I was wondering next about a parent who might say, 'I've got a massive overdraft, my house is in disrepair, I'm at risk of losing my job, I've been worried about money for a long long time, plus my marriage isn't so great right now.' I was worried a bit about how this parent might think 'how do I let go of all that stuff and turn my attention to what's going on with my child, in my child's mind?'

A – Pretty tough, yes, very, very tough. But I guess the principles would be even more important for that parent. However hard that may be.

S – What might they be able to use do you think to help them?

A – I think they might find it helpful to go back over Chapters Two and Three, which talk about how important it is to separate out your own concerns from that of your family's. This is not easy stuff, especially if things are really difficult, like you just described. I guess we're not asking people to let go of all their other worries. I mean that's impossible, isn't it, to let it all go? But it's great that they are bringing up these preoccupations in the first place. I guess they are being aware of how it influences them – using their Parent Map.

S – What do you think you might do if you were in that situation and needed to stop your own preoccupations affecting your relationship with your child so much?

A – I think I would need to be realistic and be aware there would be times when I would be bringing my own stress into my relationship with him. At these times I really find it hard to think about what my child's inside story might be. I just focus on the fact that he's behaving badly, so I would have a really simple story about why he's doing that, like 'he's just pushing the boundaries'. I guess I would try to set aside times with my child when I really try to focus on just being in the moment with him, and seeing the world from his perspective as well, even if it's just for a few minutes. That would bring about a better connection, a better behaviour and a more enjoyable time, and even if that was just for short moments, that would be of benefit to me and him. Also I would tell my kids this is something that's on my mind and it's not something that you've done.

S – I think I might try to do something outside of the whole situation for myself – to try to deal with those preoccupations elsewhere. So I might try to recruit supports, go and talk to friends more. Or if I was on my own wait until the children are in bed and phone somebody, because that would be difficult if I didn't have a partner to talk to about those things or I didn't have a supportive partner. Dealing with my preoccupations somewhere else would probably give me a sense of release so that my worries wouldn't filter into the relationship with my children. So, can you relate to that feeling of being so preoccupied with something in your own head that you can't connect with your family?

A – Yes, I really like all of these strategies – getting outside support is really important, and so is approaching your family with a new perspective, which can be hard, but managing to set stresses aside and just spend time watching and being with your family can be so beneficial.

S – If I'm preoccupied with something that's a real worry and then they're behaving really badly, I would probably snap really quickly.

A – Hmm, so what would you do then?

S – So, then I'm less likely to think 'oh, this is MY state of mind'. I'm more likely to get angry with my children and think 'why are you bothering me now?' or 'that's really irritating, you're making a demand on me'. I'm more likely to have a lack of insight at that time. I might just not handle it well in that situation, but come back to it later when I'm calmer. Parenting is really hard isn't it? And we all make mistakes but reflecting on those feelings is important . . . reflecting on our own behaviour not just our kids.

A – What about the concept of validation? Shall we recap on that, it's pretty important too isn't it?

S – Well I was thinking that it's important for parents and children to feel validated – acknowledged and heard, they can make any changes in how they are behaving, really. But it's not just validation, is it? Children and parents need to feel that they are being empathized with for how they feel. So I suppose, for example if I was feeling that someone had just pushed me aside on the tube train and grabbed my seat and then I told that story to my husband and he ignored that and asked me if I'd bought any milk, I would feel invalidated and probably feel more upset and preoccupied with the injustice of that situation than if say he had said, 'Oh yeah that happened to me the other day, it's horrible on the tube, isn't it? Are you okay?', and then he might say 'did you get any milk?' still but I'd be able to answer that question more easily. I might feel that it would be okay to have someone ask something *of* me after I felt validated. Whereas if I felt invalidated and then someone made a demand of me, I would be probably be more likely to feel sorry for myself, with a 'no one is listening to me' kind of feeling.

A – So, how does that apply to our readers? They might feel totally overwhelmed and that we are adding to their stress by asking them to just drop all that and think about their children.

S – Yes, they might feel that it's all very well telling them to be reflective but actually things are quite hard for them. But I suppose we're not saying that, are we? When we talk early on about paying attention to your own feelings we are saying that *has* to come first. You can't do any of these things with your children until you are aware both of how you feel and why, and feel validated in that. If you don't feel validated in your feelings, it's going to be hard to give your children any of this Reflective Parenting they need.

A- There's also being able to forgive yourself for having difficult interactions with your kids every day, or feeling like this is all useless and I can't do it, it's all too difficult. Instead, it's really helpful to hold in mind that although you can't do it right now, tomorrow might be different. When you wake up you might have a really nice moment with your child that you really want to make the most of.

S – So, one thing I was thinking about was whether people might wonder if we're saying that it's okay for children to be naughty as long as you know why they're doing it. I've been wondering if people might feel that we are advising them to drop their boundaries, and be softer with difficult behaviours. But we're not saying that, are we?

A – No.

S – So what are we saying then?

A – Well, we're saying that children are naughty, that's part of their development. But a good way to manage behaviour – to reduce bad behaviour and to think about behaviour – is to understand what that behaviour is about. What you chose to do about that once you've worked that out, we don't really go into this much. I'm not aware of any evidence that looks at the behavioural strategies that parents who are more reflective use compared to others. You know, do reflective parents use Time Out or not? Perhaps if they do, they are likely to use Time Out in a particular way. They might be really willing and eager to reconnect with their child afterwards. So I think the strategies aren't quite so important as how you apply them, and how you help a child to think about things. So, if children are stealing, how do you stop them? It depends more on thinking about why they are stealing, what's going on, and to help them think about that. You might want to think about what that's about? Certainly we wouldn't be communicating (in this book) to children that it's alright to steal. If for example I found my child stealing, then I wouldn't condone it. There are limits, aren't there? I would try to make clear with my child that just because I'm having this conversation with you about what led up to your action, this doesn't mean I'm okay with you stealing and that you're not in trouble. I'd want you to know though that I'm trying to understand it, and to help you feel close to me while we're talking about it, but you'd probably still be annoyed when I tell you you've got to pay it back out of your pocket money.

S – We are not suggesting parents never disapprove of behaviour, but that they can try to help their child manage the feeling that led to the action in the first place.

A – Hmm, I think what's hard is to try to separate out not disapproving of how a child is feeling from what he is doing when he is feeling that way. There's a difference. It's important to accept what a child is feeling, even if you don't accept why he is feeling that way. He has got a feeling that's valid for him at that moment. What we're trying to do is get a child to understand that feeling and to find a way to experience that feeling without doing something that's going to get him in trouble. Or that's going to hurt someone else or something. So it is really helpful when his emotional experience is accepted by the parent.

S – You'd have to have those two things in mind. That there's a limit to certain behaviours that are and aren't okay, but that you are open to understanding what went on behind the behaviour – the inside story. Can we be clear with people about when they might try using the Parent APP then?

A – Yes, sure. Well the good thing about the APP is that it helps you get behind the way your child is behaving. Also you can use it in the moment, or actually sometimes it's better after the moment. Rather than insisting that your child listen to you, while you are both getting annoyed and irritated, instead try waiting 5 minutes, and then think about why your child wasn't listening to you in the first place, and once you do this – stand back and think about what your child might have been thinking – you can often manage to have a different conversation.

S – Some people might say, 'I haven't got the time to do that.' I haven't got time to stand back and think about what my child's doing. Busy job, few kids, etc. What would you say to them?

A – Yes, it can feel hard to find time, and we haven't got a quick fix unfortunately for difficulties that happen between parents and kids. It is important to find a bit of time if you really want to change patterns of behaviour and aspects of the relationship you have with your child that you're not happy with.

S – How much time do you think they need?

A – It doesn't take long to think about someone's perspective. We're saying about half a minute maybe. To approach your child with interest and being interested in what's going on in his mind just for a few minutes is really helpful to him and to your relationship with each other.

S – It's incredible how quickly that can take effect, isn't it?

A – Yes, and you might learn something about why your child's not listening and you might respond differently to your child. It might make your life a bit easier when there is a change in how he is behaving.

S – Yeah, that's helpful. I wonder if people might also read this and think 'Reflective Parenting sounds like it might take a long time to work? Aren't other things quicker?' They might feel if they shout at their children then they will do what they're told a lot quicker?

A – Yes, Reflective Parenting doesn't always change behaviours straight away, although it can – remember what you were saying about the morning rush and your son being much happier when you were interested in him amongst all the mayhem? But yes, what about parents who find it hard to not shout at their children? What would we say to them?

S – Well, I think I'd say it's quite normal and that everybody from time to time shouts when they get angry.

A – Do you think it's alright to shout?

S – I don't think it works. I don't think it's very nice for the child. It's not very nice for the parent either, so I don't think anyone really enjoys shouting. But if I think about what it's like to be shouted at – that's where I think perspective taking is helpful – if I thought about what it would feel like if someone shouted in my face – and how horrible that would be – that I would feel frightened, or ashamed or scared. Then I imagine me as a 5-ft-7-in person towering over a small child and shouting in his face, at which point I think I'd be able to connect much better with the feeling that it's actually probably quite terrifying. And it might achieve what you want . . .

A – Yeah, I was going to say, it might work.

S – Of course, there are obvious occasions when you shout, for example when you can see that an accident is about to happen, but it works because I imagine a child would be frozen at that point. If I shouted in a 4-year-old's face to GET OFF THE SOFA, I'd probably get what I wanted *in that moment*, but then what I would be teaching him that you can get people to do what you want if you scare them into it. Then, I might find that he is a bit edgy and jumpy and anxious, not knowing when he will be shouted at again.

A – So, yes, if it's not a good strategy, how can a parent manage to stop shouting?

S – Well, there are a few things you could do. One strategy would be to first separate out your feelings from what's going on inside your child. The second would be to think about what's making you shout, why you feel so angry. Then you might go back to your Parent Map and think about whether there are things on there that make you shout a lot as a parent – say past history of being shouted at yourself, stressful things in your life right now, etc. Once you have figured out how these things affect you as a parent, then you can start to make some changes in your approach, and hopefully stop shouting as much. Why might a parent shout?

A – Because a child is misbehaving.

S – How does shouting help? Does it make a parent feel better?

A – I'm not sure, but it is really hard to stop it!

S – Perhaps, as well as trying some perspective taking, imagining how it would feel like for the child might help. Getting inside his mind. And also maybe accept that sometimes you will shout, because you can't always be in control of your feelings. So, forgive yourself and think, actually, as long as you're not doing that all of the time, it's not too terrible if it happens just occasionally. People do shout. Siblings shout at each other, don't they?

A – I'm thinking more about what you said about the Parent Map and how that might come in handy.

S – What are you thinking, Ali?

A – I guess we might suggest to a parent you're shouting because you're getting really emotional. Most people shout because they're angry or aroused in some way. So it might be important for that parent to really reflect on themselves and think about times when they are more likely to shout, and times they are less likely to shout, and to really try to think about that. So, is it first thing in the morning when you're feeling totally rushed and the children are just taking ages to get ready for school? It would be worth then thinking about how you can order your morning, so you don't get so irritable and start shouting.

S – Yes, definitely being prepared probably helps with not shouting. I'm also thinking about parents who use hitting, and how this needs to be thought about seriously. I think anything where you are losing control of your feelings to the point you are frightening your children is something important to address. And I guess if you imagine what a child sees, if he sees you losing it and being out of control, then how can he learn to manage his own feelings if he sees that you can't manage your own?

S – Back to this question though about whether other things work quicker, I'm still wondering about parents who might ask, 'What is the proof that Reflective Parenting helps children and their families?'

A- Well, there is research evidence where parents are reflective, their children can manage their emotions better and have better relationships with people. Professionally, I've found that using this approach has helped improve relationships between parents and kids. Personally, it makes it so much easier to manage difficult times and for me to feel I understand my children and how they're feeling and behaving. I think seeing the benefits to the child and how he understands his emotional world is a longer-term effect. But in terms of some situations, it can also have immediate benefits.

S – Can you think of a good example?

A – You know, a child is shouting and saying 'you're so mean, you're so mean, and you don't let me do anything!' Rather than punish your child for using words that you don't approve of, just reflect back and give some empathy and say, 'I'm really sorry, that's really hard and I know it does feel really unfair' as that can have a dramatic effect on your child who feels really understood, and who sees that you care about how he feels. Your anger can dissipate and the situation just stops without you having to punish your child at all. Whereas if you use Time Out in a punitive way, because you feel he is being rude and you also feel angry, this can make your child feel resentful and angry; it might diminish the behaviour, but it can actually increase negative behaviour and disconnection. I wouldn't necessarily say Reflective Parenting takes longer, but certainly the main additional benefit of course is that you get a better connection between you and your child, and he feels understood.

S – There are probably many more questions that people will have after they've read the book, aren't there? I think overall, we would just want people to give it a try and to know that it takes time and practice, but if they try modelling being reflective in front of their children they will start to see some real benefits. I've noticed that with my own kids, after a long time trying this approach out, they are gradually starting to make reflective, mind-minded comments about others in the family, and some of this has taken years and is on-going work. For the families we've worked with too, it's good to see that over time, helping parents and children to be more interested and curious about other people and what's going on in their minds has long-term benefits for children's behaviour and their relationships with other people.

REFERENCES

Foreword

Cote, S.M., Vaillancourt, T., LeBlanc, J.C., Nagin, D.S., & Tremblay, R.E. (2006). The development of physical aggression from toddlerhood to pre-adolescence: A nationwide longitudinal study of Canadian children. *Journal of Abnormal Child Psychology, 34*(1), 71–85. doi: 10.1007/s10802-005-9001-z

Introduction

1. Fonagy, P., Steele, H., & Steele, M. (1991). Maternal representations of attachment during pregnancy predict the organisation of infant-mother attachment at one year of age. *Child Development, 62,* 891–905.
2. Fonagy, P., Steele, H., Steele, M., Leigh, T., Kennedy, R., Mattoon, G., & Target, M. (1995). Attachment, the reflective self, and borderline states: The predictive specificity of the Adult Attachment Interview and pathological emotional development. In S. Goldberg, R. Muir, & J. Kerr (Eds.), *Attachment Theory: Social, Developmental, and Clinical Perspectives* (pp. 233–278). New York: Analytic Press.
3. Fonagy, P., Gergely, G., Jurist, E.L., & Target, M. (2002). *Affect Regulation, Mentalization, and the Development of Self.* New York: Other Press.
4. Bowlby, J. (1958). The nature of the child's tie to his mother. *International Journal of Psycho-Analysis, 39,* 350–373.
5. Ainsworth, M.D.S., &Witting, B.A. (1969). Attachment and exploratory behaviour of one-year-olds in a strange situation. In B.M. Foss (Ed.), *Determinants of Infant Behaviour* (Vol. 4., pp. 111–136). London: Metheuen.
6. Fonagy, P. (1989). On tolerating mental states: Theory of Mind in Borderline Patients. *Bulletin of the Anna Freud Centre, 12,* 91–115.
7. Meins, E., & Fernyhough, C. (1999). Linguistic acquisitional style and mentalising development: The role of maternal mind-mindedness. *Cognitive Development, 14,* 363–380.
8. Preemack, D., & Woodruff, G. (1978). Does the chimpanzee have a theory of mind? *Behaviour and Brain Sciences, 1*(4), 515–526.

9. Fonagy, P., Redfern, S., & Charman, T. (1997). The relationship between belief-desire reasoning and a projective measure of attachment security (SAT). *British Journal of Developmental Psychology, 15*, 51–61.
10. Biemans, H. (1990). Video home training: Theory method and organisation of SPIN. In J. Kool (Ed.), *International Seminar for Innovative Institutions*. Ryswijk: Ministry of Welfare, Health and Culture.
11. Trevarthen, C. (2010). What is it like to be a person who knows nothing? Defining the active intersubjective mind of a newborn human being. *Infant and Child Development, 20*(1), 119–135.

Chapter One – The origins of Reflective Parenting

1. Fonagy, P., Steele, M., Steele, H., Moran, G., & Higgitt, A. (1991). The capacity for understanding mental states: The reflective self in parent and child and its significance for security of attachment. *Infant Mental Health Journal, 12*, 201–218.
2. Gerhardt, S. (2004). *Why Love Matters: How Affection Shapes a Baby's Brain.* Hove: Brunner-Routledge.
3. Schore, A.N. (2001). Effects of a secure attachment relationship on right brain development, affect regulation, and infant mental health. *Infant Mental Health Journal, 22*(1–2), 7–66.
4. Schore, A. (1994). *Affect Regulation and the Origin of the Self.* Hillsdale, NJ: Lawrence Erlbaum Associates Inc.
5. Thomas, D.G., Whitaker, E., Crow, C.D., Little, V., Love, L., Lykins, M.S., & Letterman, M. (1997). Event-related potential variability as a measure of information storage in infant development. *Developmental Neuropsychology, 13*, 205–232.
6. Fonagy, P., Target, M., Steele, H., & Steele, M. (1994). The Emmanuel Miller Memorial Lecture 1992. The theory and practice of resilience. *Journal of Child Psychology and Psychiatry, 35*, 231–257.
7. Meins, E., and Fernyhough, C. (1999). Linguistic acquisitional style and mentalising development: The role of maternal mind-mindedness. *Cognitive Development, 14*, 363–380.
8. Trevarthen, C. (2010). What is it like to be a person who knows nothing? Defining the active intersubjective mind of a newborn human being. *Infant and Child Development, 20*(1), 119–135.
9. Nagy, E. (2010). The newborn infant: a missing stage in developmental psychology. *Infant and Child Development, 20*(1), 3–19.
10. Csibra, G., & Gergely, G. (2009). Natural pedagogy. *Trends in Cognitive Sciences, 13*, 148–153.
11. Grienenberger, J., Slade, A., & Kelly, K. (2005). Maternal reflective functioning, mother-infant affective communication, and infant attachment: Exploring the link between mental states and observed caregiving behavior in the intergenerational transmission of attachment. *Attachment and Human Development, 7*(3), 299–311.

Chapter Two – The parent map

1. Kohn, A. (2005). *Unconditional Parenting: Moving from Rewards and Punishments to Love and Reason.* New York: Atria / Simon & Schuster.
2. Emde, R.N. (1983). The pre representational self and its affective core. *Psychoanalytic Study of the Child, 38,* 165–192.
3. Brown, G.W., & Harris, T.O. (1978). *The Social Origins of Depression: A Study of Psychiatric Disorder in Women.* London: Tavistock.

Chapter Three – Managing your feelings

1. Kennedy, H., Landor, M., & Todd, L. (2011). *Video Interaction Guidance – A Relationship-Based Intervention to Promote Attunement, Empathy and Wellbeing.* London: Jessica Kingsley Publishers.

Chapter Four – The 'Parent APP'

1. Fonagy, P., Redfern, S., & Charman, T. (1997). The relationship between belief-desire reasoning and a projective measure of attachment security (SAT). *British Journal of Developmental Psychology, 15,* 51–61.

Chapter Five – Helping children with their feelings

No references.

Chapter Six – Discipline: Understanding misunderstandings

1. Doyle, A.B., & Moretti, M.M. (2000). Attachment to parents and adjustment in adolescence: Literature review and policy implications. CAT number 032ss. H5219-9-CYH7/001/SS. Ottawa: Health Canada, Child and Family Division.
2. Doyle, A.B., Moretti, M.M., Brendgen, M., Bukowski, W. (2002). Parent child relationships and adjustment in adolescence: Findings from the HSBC and NLSCY Cycle 2 Studies. CAT number 032ss. H5219–00CYHS. Ottawa: Health Canada, Child and Family Division.
3. Moretti, M.M., & Holland, R. (2003). Navigating the journey of adolescence: Parental attachment and the self from a systemic perspective. In S. Johnson & V. Whiffen (Eds.), *Clinical Applications of Attachment Theory* (pp. 41–56). New York: Guildford.
4. Alessandri, S.M., Lewis, M. (1993). Parental evaluation and its relation to shame and pride in young children. *Sex Roles, 29,* 335–343.
5. Alessandri S.M., & Lewis, M. (1996). Differences in pride and shame in maltreated and nonmaltreated preschoolers. *Child Development, 67,* 1857–1869.

6. Hughes, D. (2006). *Building the Bonds of Attachment* (DVD). Produced by Sandra Webb & Lunchroom Production.
7. Fletcher, A., Steinberg, L., & Sellers, E. (1999). Adolescents' wellbeing as a function of perceived inter-parent inconsistency. *Journal of Marriage and the Family, 61*, 300–310.

Chapter Seven – Helping sensitive children work through misunderstandings

1. Steele, M.J., Kaniuk, J., Henderson, K., Hillman, S., & Asquith, K. (2008). Forecasting outcomes in previously maltreated children: The use of the AAI in a longitudinal adoption study. In H. Steele and M. Steele (Eds.), *Clinical Applications of the Adult Attachment Interview* (pp. 427–451). New York: The Guilford Press.
2. Pollak, S.D., Chiccetti, D., Hornung, K., & Reed, A. (2000). Recognizing emotion in faces: Developmental effects of child abuse and neglect. *Developmental Psychology, 36*, 679–688.
3. Schore, A. (1994). *Affect Regulation and The Origin of the Self*. Hillsdale, NJ: Lawrence Erlbaum Associates Inc.
4. Hughes, D. (2006). *Building the Bonds of Attachment* (DVD). Produced by Sandra Webb & Lunchroom Production.
5. Hughes, D., & Rothschild, B. (2013). *8 Keys to Building Your Best Relationships (8 Keys to Mental Health)*. New York: W. W. Norton & Company.
6. American Psychiatric Association. (2013). *Diagnostic and Statistical Manual of Mental Disorders*. Arlington: American Psychiatric Publishing.
7. Frith, U., and Frith, C. (2009). The social brain: Allowing humans to boldly go where no other species has been. *Philosophical Transactions*, November.
8. Feldman, E.K., & Matos, R. (2014). Training paraprofessionals to facilitate social interactions between children with autism and their typically developing peers. *Journal of Positive Behaviour Interventions, 15*(3), 169–179.
9. Baron-Cohen, S. (1995). *Mindblindness: An Essay on Autism and Theory of Mind*. Cambridge, MA: MIT Press.
10. Charlop-Christy, M.H., & Daneshvar, S. (2014). Using video modelling to teach perspective taking to children with Autism. *Journal of Positive Behaviour Interventions, 16*(4), 12–21.
11. Attwood, T. (2007). *The Complete Guide to Asperger's Syndrome*. London: Jessica Kingsley Publishers.
12. Higashida, N. (2013). *The Reason I Jump: One Boy's Voice from the Silence of Autism*. London: Hodder & Stoughton Ltd.
13. Smadar, D., Oppenheim, D., Koren-Karie, N., & Yirmiya, N. (2014). Early attachment and maternal insightfulness predict educational placement of children with autism. *Research in Autism Spectrum Disorders, 8*(8), August.

Chapter Eight – Family, siblings and friends

1. Keavney, E., Midgley, N., Asen, E., Bevington, D., Fearon, P., Fonagy, P., Jennings-Hobbs, R., & Wood, S. (2012). Minding the Family Mind – The development and initial evaluation of mentalization-based treatment for families. In N. Midgley & I. Vrouva (Eds.), *Minding The Child – Mentalization Based Interventions with Children, Young People and their Families.* London: Routledge.
2. Rutter, M. (1981). *Maternal Deprivation Reassessed,* 2nd edition. Harmondsworth: Penguin.
3. Amato, P. (2001). Children of divorce in the 1990s: An update of the Amato and Keith (1991) meta-analysis. *Journal of Family Psychology, 15*(3), 355–370.
4. Davies, P.T., & Cummings, E.M. (2006). Interpersonal discord, family process, and developmental psychopathology. In D. Cicchetti & D.J. Cohen (Eds.), *Developmental Psychopathology: Vol. 3: Risk, Disorder, and Adaptation* (2nd ed., pp. 86–128). New York: Wiley & Sons.
5. Dunn, J., Creps, C., & Brown, J. (1996). Children's family relationships between two and five: Developmental changes and individual differences. *Social Development, 5,* 230–250.
6. Bowes, L., Wolke, D., Joinson, C., Lereya, S.T., & Lewis, G. (2014). Sibling bullying and risk of depression, anxiety, and self-harm: A prospective cohort study. *Pediatrics, 134*(4), 1032–1039.
7. Perner, J., Ruffman, T., & Leekam, S.R. (1994). Theory of Mind is contagious: You catch it from your sibs. *Child Development, 65*(4), 1228–1238.
8. Fonagy, P., Redfern, S., & Charman, T. (1997). The relationship between belief-desire reasoning and a projective measure of attachment security (SAT). *British Journal of Developmental Psychology, 15,* 51–61.
9. Slaughter, V., Dennis, M.J., & Pritchard, M., (2010). Theory of mind and peer acceptance in preschool children. *British Journal of Developmental Psychology, 20*(4), 545–564.
10. Redfern, S. (2011). Social cognition in childhood: The relationships between attachment-related representations, theory of mind and peer popularity. Institute of Psychiatry, King's College London. Doctoral Thesis.

Chapter Nine – Mentalizing during good times

1. Ispa, J. (2015). Unpublished research from the Early Head Start Research and Evaluation Project – to be published in *Social Development* (2015).
2. Youngblade, L.M., & Dunn, J. (1995). Individual differences in young children's pretend play with mother and sibling: Links to relationships and understanding of other people's feelings and beliefs. *Child Development, 66*(5), 1472–1492.

INDEX

abused children 120–1
adolescence: conflict 100; friendships 163
adoptive parents 115–18
aggression 118, 120
Ainsworth, Mary 8
alcohol 47
anger: Asperger's children 140, 142; authoritarian parenting 111–13; distractions 91–2; empathy and 79, 88; facial expressions 120–1; parental conflict 151–4; as response to stress 200; shouting 203–4
antisocial behaviour 109
anxiety: perspective taking and 78; social anxiety 165; and state of mind 47–8
apologising 95–6
arguments *see* conflict
Asperger Syndrome (AS) 115, 128–43: emotion understanding 139; emotional overload 142–3; expanding awareness 136–7; feeling disconnected from child 134–5; mind-blindness 137–9; Parent APP and 131–2, 139–40; parental experiences 132–5; sensory sensitivity 130–2; and sociability 129–30; strategies for tackling behaviour 139–40; strengths of child 135–6
attachment ix, 4: Asperger's children 141; attachment theory 3, 8–9, 11; and mentalization 9; past experience and 24, 25; and perspective taking 165; and popularity 78

attention 196: authoritarian parenting 112; brain systems 183; distractions 91–3; friendships 163–4; noticing your child being reflective 183–5; Parent App 69–74; sibling relationships 156–9
attention-seeking behaviour 22, 71–2
attunement 11–12, 17–18
Attwood, Tony 139
authoritarian parenting 71, 108, 110, 111–13
authoritative parenting 108–11, 112
autism spectrum disorder (ASD) 128–9: in babies 15; mind-blindness 137–9; theory of mind 11; *see also* Asperger Syndrome

babies: attachment theory 8; brain development 15, 85; communication 20; facial expressions 20; interaction with others 13–14, 19–23; learning to manage feelings 15–18, 119; newborn babies 19–20; relationship skills 18–21; temperament 14; theory of mind 11
Baron-Cohen, S. 137
behaviour: age-appropriate 62–3; Asperger Syndrome 129, 139–40; assumptions about 62–3; influence of emotions 85; meaning and intention 6; misbehaviour 98–114, 201–2; noticing good behaviour 172–4; perspective taking 74–8; reflective functioning 10; sensitive children 118–19; setting boundaries 99, 102, 104, 198; and shame 100–1; snap

empathy 197–8; and Asperger Syndrome 132; authoritative parenting 109, 112; friendships 167–8; helping children cope with their feelings 86–8; noticing your child being reflective 188–9; Parent App 78–82; parental relationship 148; in play 182; sensitive children 125, 126; sibling relationships 161–2; theory of mind 11
epinephrine 120
eye contact 21, 61, 70, 130

facial expressions: Asperger Syndrome and 130; babies 20; managing your feelings 60; marked-mirroring 17–18, 87; sensitive children and 120–1
family life 146–7; Mentalization Based Treatment for Families 147; mentalizing during good times 175; parental relationship 147–54; sibling relationships 154–62
fathers: parents of Asperger's children 133–4; see also parental relationship
feedback, positive 174
feelings see emotions and feelings
'fight-flight-freeze' response 120, 121
Fonagy, Peter 5, 9
forgiveness 64–5
foster parents 116–18
friendships 141, 162–8

good times, mentalizing during 171–94

health 47
Higashida, N. 141
hormones: and baby's development 14–15; 'fight-flight-freeze' response 120; and sociability 129–30; stress hormones 118; touch and 94
hugging 94–5
Hughes, Daniel 104, 124, 195
humour: helping children cope with their feelings 90; parental relationship 151, 154; in play 179

illness 47
imagination: Asperger Syndrome and 135–6; pretend play 178
infants see babies

insecurity: Asperger's children 140; authoritarian parenting 113
interactive play 179–80

jealousy, sibling relationships 158

Kennedy, Hilary 11
kindness 127

language: Asperger Syndrome 129; and expressing emotions 119; mind-mindedness 10; sensitive children 125
lateness, anxiety about 42–3
laughter see humour
life events 48
limits, authoritative parenting 109

manipulative behaviour 63
marked-mirroring 17–18, 87
maternal mind-mindedness 10
Meins, Elizabeth 10
mental health, and state of mind 47–8
mental states see mind
mentalization 3, 9; brain development in babies 15; during good times 171–94; Mentalization Based Treatment for Families (MBTF) 147; and misunderstandings 99
mind: mind-blindness 137–9; mind-short-sightedness 138–9; 'mind-wandering' 183; Parent App 67–83; Parent Map 32; reflective functioning 10; Theory of Mind (ToM) 10–11, 137; see also mentalization
mind-mindedness 3, 10, 25–6; and Asperger's children 132, 136–7; authoritative parenting 109, 112; and babies 16–17; helping children cope with their feelings 89
mirroring: and Asperger Syndrome 135; empathy 87; marked-mirroring 17–18, 87; mentalization 9; sensitive children 119
misbehaviour, discipline 98–114
misunderstandings: in adolescence 100; apologising for 95; authoritative parenting 109; effects of 86–7, 103–4; parental conflict 151–4; sensitive

116–17; conflicts 101–4; emotions and 33; empathy 78–82; feelings of connection 100–2, 104; friendships 162–8; influence of past experiences 23–5, 36–9, 43–4, 64–5; parental relationship 147–54; relationship skills in babies 18–21; sensitive children 115, 120–1, 141; and shame 100–1; sibling relationships 154–62; social relationships 146; and state of mind 39–40; theory of mind 11
religious beliefs 40
resilience, sensitive children 127–8
respect, authoritative parenting 109–10
role-play, importance of 179
rules, authoritative parenting 109

school: Asperger's children 141; imaginative play 179; paying attention 163–4
security: attachment theory 8–9; insecurity 113, 140; reflective parenting 24–5
self-acceptance 64–5
self-awareness: sensitive children 119; *see also* Parent Map
self-esteem 107, 128, 173
sensitive children 115–45; Asperger Syndrome 128–43; curiosity 127; emotional thermometer 123–4; how they see themselves 121–2; Parent APP 126–7; relationships 120–1; resilience 127–8; shame-free zone 124–5; traumatised children 115–28
sensory sensitivity, Asperger Syndrome 130–2
shame: authoritarian parenting 112; dealing with feelings of 107; impact on behaviour 100–1; sensitive children 121–2, 124–5, 127
shouting 203–4
sibling relationships 154–62; attention 156–9; empathy 161–2; managing and supporting 155–6; mentalizing during good times 172–4; perspective taking 159–61
sleep deprivation 46–7
social skills 146; anxiety about 165; Asperger's children 129–30, 141,

143; perspective taking and 78, 165; and sibling relationships 159; 'social brain' 15; theory of mind 11
stealing 201
Steele, Howard 5
Steele, Miriam 5
stress 199–200; anger as response to 200; and baby's development 15; effects on brain 118; life events 48; sensitive children 118–19; stepping back from feelings 57–8; triggers for strong emotions 44–5
support 63–4, 125, 199–200

tantrums 59, 70–1
Target, Mary 5
Tavistock Clinic, London 8
teachers, paying attention 163–4
teenagers *see* adolescence
temperament: baby's 14; sibling relationships 155
Theory of Mind (ToM) 10–11, 137
thermometer, emotional *see* emotional thermometer
Time Alone 92–4, 140
Time In 125
Time Out 92–3, 125, 199, 202, 206
tiredness 46–7
toddlers 124
touch, helping children cope with their feelings 94–5
traumatised children *see* sensitive children
Trevarthen, Colwyn 11, 19
triggers, strong emotions 41–5
trust, sensitive children 121
Two Hands approach 104–8, 111, 124

validation 80, 82, 86, 88–9, 200–1
Video Home Training (VHT) 11
Video Interaction Guidance (VIG) 11–12, 60–1, 69
violence, parental conflict 151
voice, tone of 59

watching children 71–2
Woodruff, Guy 10

zoning out 118, 182–3